Geldof in Africa

Bob Geldof is a musician. He was the lead singer of The Boomtown
Rats and has recorded four solo albums. In 2005, he received
the Outstanding Contribution to Music award at the Brits.
He is involved in television, radio and technology companies.

In 1984, Geldof initiated Band Aid, a record for the victims
of famine in Africa. The following year he organised the Live Aid
concert while establishing and chairing the trust which would
administer the $180,000,000 raised by the venture.

In 2004 he was appointed to Prime Minister Tony Blair's
Commission for Africa, and in 2005 initiated the Live 8 concerts
to successfully implement the Commission's proposals through
the G8 Summit.

His work in Africa continues.

For further information contact:
www.bobgeldof.info
www.commissionforafrica.org
www.data.org
www.makepovertyhistory.org
www.live8live.com

Praise for *Geldof in Africa*

'An entrancing book – reflective, insightful and angry where appropriate' *Time Out*

'Brilliantly written… as splendidly raw, ramshackle and powerful as its author' *heat*

'A genuine talent for capturing personality, landscape and colour… wit and undeniable passion' *Big Issue*

'It's shocking. I didn't expect, or want, to have to say this – but it's shocking because it's brilliant. He has managed to reach into the soul of what he calls the Luminous Continent, and it has taken possession of him. Geldof doesn't shy away from the sense of despondency. His photo-vignettes or micro-essays are often spluttering with fury. And incredulous horror. Just as often, Bob is very, very funny.' Sam Kiley, *Evening Standard*

'Extremely well written and often remarkable' *Sunday Times*

'Mesmerising and illuminating… a kaleidoscopic and at times poetic odyssey' *Radio Times*

'*Geldof in Africa* deserves enthusiastic reviews, if only because Geldof has – with typical defiance – flatly refused to dish up bland pap… insisting on intelligent discussion of real political issues' *Sunday Telegraph*

'A poetic, articulate tribute from a man whose actions speak as loudly as his words' *Daily Mail*

'One of the most eloquent and intelligent things to appear for a long time' *Daily Telegraph*

'Impassioned and ever in awe to this continent for which he continues to do so much' *Metro*

'Vintage Sir Bob' *News of the World*

'Geldof is a superb guide to this most generalised about, and least understood continent, negotiating a fine balance between his well-informed passion and his instinctively sardonic humour. Articulate and funny… excellent' *Guardian*

'An intelligent and insightful writer' *Evening Standard*

'Beautifully written, passionately eloquent and unexpectedly poetic… a skilful reporter explaining the magic of a continent' *Daily Telegraph*

'Remarkably intelligent … impossible not to be entranced' *Observer*

'Brings the politics and geography of the many different Africas to life with great insight' *Daily Mirror*

'Mesmerising, an intense, personal journey. Eloquent… and vividly poetic… simply enchanting' *Daily Star*

'Excellent. Frank and outspoken, the Geldof perspective is always a valuable one' *Observer*

'Eloquent and intelligent … studded with historical illumination, stunning photography and impassioned insights' *Daily Telegraph*

'Engaging and entertaining … passionate and filled with wonder, admiration and excitement, as he strides across the sun-drenched landscape like some rangy cowboy' *Evening Standard*

'Beautiful and elegiac … a beguiling mix of high-ground morality, mystical anthropology, pressure politics and a love letter. This is the agitprop version of Michael Palin. His hard-edged energy is a welcome antidote to the soft, sybaritic voyeurism of most television travel.' A.A. Gill, *Sunday Times*

'Something special… intelligent and lyrical' *Sunday Telegraph*

'Fascinatingly candid and gritty … an uncompromising commitment not only to Africa and Africans, but also to the truth' *Travel Africa*

'Geldof gets Africa' *Evening Standard*

'A remarkable book. Like a bootboy Michael Palin… an idiosyncratic insight into an immense continent. Full of anecdotes and telling asides, and with stunning photography, this magical book lights up the colours of Africa' *Irish Independent*

With grateful thanks to
John Maguire, Paul Vallely, Pete Briquette and Pat Savage
The production team for 'Geldof in Africa' – Rebecca, Claudia,
Frank, Amanda, Darren – and all the production crews
Lucy, Ollie, Zita and Jamie at Data
Susan Sandon
Richard Collins
Rowena Skelton-Wallace
David Eldridge and the guys at Two Associates
Neil Bradford
Anna Simpson
Nikon UK

Geldof in Africa
Bob Geldof

Additional Photographs **John Maguire**
Additional Text **Paul Vallely**

Published in the United Kingdom by Arrow Books in 2006

3 5 7 9 10 8 6 4

Copyright © Bob Geldof, 2005
Additional Photographs © John Maguire

Published by arrangement with the BBC
BBC logo © BBC 1996
The BBC logo is a registered trademark of the British Broadcasting Corporation
and is used under licence.
Series Producer and Director: John Maguire
Executive Producer: Phil Craig
A Ten Alps/Brook Lapping production for BBC Television

First published in the United Kingdom in 2005 by Century

Arrow Books
The Random House Group Limited, 20 Vauxhall Bridge Road, London, SW1V 2SA

Random House Australia (Pty) Limited
20 Alfred Street, Milsons Point, Sydney, New South Wales 2061, Australia

Random House New Zealand Limited
18 Poland Road, Glenfield, Auckland 10, New Zealand

Random House (Pty) Limited
Isle of Houghton, Corner of Boundary Road & Carse O'Gowrie, Houghton 2198, South Africa

Random House Group Limited Reg. No. 954009

www.randomhouse.co.uk

A CIP catalogue record for this book is available from the British Library

Papers used by Random House are natural, recyclable products made from
wood grown in sustainable forests. The manufacturing processes conform to the
environmental regulations of the country of origin

ISBN 9780099497967 (from Jan 2007)
ISBN 0 09 949796 4

Designed by Two Associates
Printed and bound in Great Britain by Bookmarque Ltd, Croydon, Surrey

For Jeanne, Feefs, Peach, Pix and Tig

One day I will take you there

Gold/Slave Coast
Sahara Desert
The Great Rift Valley

★Tunis
TUNISIA
MOROCCO
ALGERIA
LIBYA
WESTERN
SAHARA
Tropic of Cancer
MAURITANIA
MALI
★ Nouakchott
NIGER
CHAD
Timbuktu
Niger
SENEGAL
Mopti
Niamey
THE GAMBIA
Bamako Djenne BURKINA
N'Djamena
GUINEA BISSAU
Ouagadougou FASO
GUINEA
(BENIN)
NIGERIA
GHANA
★ Abuja
SIERRA LEONE
COTE
TOGO
D'IVOIRE
Lomé Ouidah
CENTRAL AFRICA
LIBERIA
Yamoussoukro
REPUBLIC
Accra
Porto
CAMEROON
Bangui
Novo
Gulf of Guinea
Yaoundé
Congo
EQUATORIAL GUNEA
Equator
Libreville
REP. OF
THE
GABON
CONGO
DEM.
REP
OF THE
CONGO
Brazzaville
Kinshasa
South
CABINDA
(Angola)
Atlantic
Luanda
Ocean
ANGOLA
NAMIBIA
Windhoek
★
Tropic of Capricorn
SOUTH
AFRICA

Foreword

This started as a book of a television series. TV reduces everything. It's not great for 'feeling' or giving a sense of place. You wander into shot, spoiling a perfectly decent scene, and all too often end up reducing a complex idea to a two-line inanity. But, weirdly, sometimes it works out okay. I'm crap at it, though the pictures are good and give you a sense of the utter wonder of Africa, that most sensuous of continents. Great director, lousy presenter. It doesn't matter anyway because I love it there.

I took some pictures while I was there. Here are a few. I also kept notes and thoughts and bits 'n' bobs which I've extended here. The whole of the last year has for me been focused on Africa. I did the series which visited thirteen African countries. I was part of the Prime Minister's Commission for Africa (which you should read if this or the series interest you) and I conducted African seminars for the Commission in the major capitals of the world. You think I'd be sick of it by now. I'm not. Because I believe we're finally on the brink of helping to change the situation of extreme poverty for the better. And I want to help do that.

Here are the things I saw. Or felt. Or things that popped into my head that may make sense or may not. They ramble around like a TV show – which is the way it should be. Snapshots of the mind. I hope they will give you a sense of the experience and the place.

If you ever get the chance, go there. It feels like ... going home.

Bob, June 2005

November 1985

Everything was final. Everything dark.

Without squinting you could see the dim but huge and perfect sphere of the sun through the clouds of soil, turned to dust and risen 30,000 feet into the hot and dry sky.

It was like watching the cold English sun through a dusty window on some late October afternoon. But this sun burned. It burned everything. It burned so hot it was burning the continent beneath my feet.

For all of my life I had wanted to stand in that place which for us represents the end of the earth.

Well, I stood, mute with shock and gazing like Cortez with wild surmise not on some vast new ocean but at a sea of sand that moved and tumbled, as rough as any sea I've known. It whined across empty streets. It kicked dust devils into the already brown and heavy sky. It whipped itself furiously into hot gales around the crumbling clay houses and shrieked its way through the ropes and tents of Timbuktu.

I was standing not only at the end of the earth but at what seemed to me to be an end of the world.

The desert is an all-devouring rapacious thing. It is alive and, like a wild uncontrolled animal, while it is on the move it is not possible to approach it with anything but fear. It invades you. It rips your clothes, sandblasts your face, glues your mouth. It clogs your nose, it cakes and mats your eyes, it plugs your ears, it cuts your skin, it dries you out, it kills your land, it burns you. It destroys all until it buries you alive.

I stumbled through Africa. I staggered through the shattering insouciance of the capital cities. I see-sawed between the passive and sometimes criminally stupid rationale of the government administrators and the often patronising whining of the 'old hand' aid agency headquarters and on into the grinding despair and grief of the affected areas. We shuttled between war zone and desert, famine and refugees, pomp and degradation, reason and chaos, sublimity and absurdity.

We would retreat at the end of each country in total confusion but with blessed relief to the small plane that had carried us in computerised luxury to this version of the apocalypse. There we would sit in our world attempting to make sense of what we had just seen and gratefully left behind: the scale of the horror, the utter devastation, whole civilisations cleared, languages erased, buildings buried, mass exodus, war, brutality and an incomprehensible stupidity and cruelty. But it was too big.

Reacting to Africa and its whole mad evil, my mind would toss out absurdities to compensate for the horror overload: jokes and football songs and phone calls home at 35,000 feet.

But nothing we could invent would be as absurd for me as reality.

I understood that these countries were doing me great honour by the ceremonial welcome they gave me. But I'd never viewed a guard of honour before, nor had any wish to. I felt ridiculous and a fake. I felt uncomfortable when groups of children would sing songs about me and at me. Not anticipating this kind of thing and never having had to deal with it before, I simply pretended I was someone I saw on the news – which I was, anyway. So I became confused still further. I understand that they were saying thank you through me to millions of people, but as the disparity between the ceremony and protocol and the real reason for being there became ever clearer I grew terse and impatient. But they were being kind and I was trying not to be rude.

Still it became an exercise of will to continue. An unremitting catalogue of misery, a marathon of figures to be assimilated, reports read, proposals listened to, meetings, meetings. My mind swam with the jargon: 'rehabilitation', 'long-term development', 'displaced persons', 'stimulate the rural economy', 'depress the local market'.

But indignation was only a short drive away. Down in the camps whole nations lay huddled, wasted and ill. What everyone in those meetings was talking about was nothing less than the African holocaust. What they were describing was the death and hunger, the humiliation and hurt of millions upon millions of people who need not suffer it. What the figures meant was the sum total of our disregard for each other. What they added up to was the cost of all this dying to us all.

In Chad alone there are over three hundred separate languages, totally distinct from one another. Some of them have gone already. I never heard them but I miss them. In these ways the lights of human genius wink out.

This journey was not some jaunt into a personal heart of darkness nor was it a dilettante's voyeuristic dip into the pitiless pain and degradation of others. It was a trip to refocus my outrage.

In the boredom of administration, explanation and justification you begin to lose sight of the purpose and reason for your anger. Questioning and rationalisation begin to replace impulse and action. Then it is essential to recharge the batteries of grief.

The learning process was beneficial, the visible achievement satisfying, the contacts and meetings worthwhile ... but who cares?

I'm not thinking about those things tonight. I'm thinking of what I saw. What I saw was humanity laid bare, degraded and shamed by its own malignant hand.

Bob, November 1985

The Little Black Baby Box

The Little Black Baby Box always looked a bit chipped around its cardboard edges. Same picture. Three- or four-year-old Little Black Baby staring out, healthy enough, from the left-hand side of the six-by three-inch box. Slot slashed in the middle on the top, grubby with dirty finger marks. We were expected to drop bits of pocket money into it. I can't remember doing that. I can't remember anyone else doing it for that matter.

It was never to do with starvation or poverty per se. Occasionally the messaging would become the *poor* Little Black Babies, but this was usually added during Retreat Week and was an attempt, I suppose in retrospect, to leaven the load from the dire admonishments preached against the perils of masturbation.

The trouble was that, in general, the first breasts any of us ever saw would have been a young black African girl's. Why else would we have hoarded the remorselessly dull stacks of *National Geographic* magazines in the school library? Why else would we ever have gone to the dentist if not to steal the ageing piles of distinctive yellow-covered magazines with the wholly unconvincing cover photographs of grouper fish? Everyone knew that inside was a tumbling hoard of naked breasts. Beautiful girls leaping unclothed into waterfalls and rivers, water gleaming and sliding off their magnificent bits an' bobs, and strolling, gorgeously nude, through dappled, vine-dense forest glades, sunlight bouncing off their shining pertness and maybe, best of all, carrying things on their heads so that their perfect breasts were thrust proudly forward, agonisingly, longingly, piercingly spearing the tumultuously forming sexual synaptic membranes of our frontal lobes . . . And it was all legit!

How come? Did no one notice African women were gorgeous and had no clothes on? What was going on? We even got extra grades in geography for our keenness in additional study material! It was all considered very mind-expanding. It certainly was that. But didn't they see it wasn't just our minds that were expanding?

As the anti-wanking sermons droned on ad nauseam we would be asked to consider the sanctity of the individual, the potential of every sperm, the beauty of humanity, and that God held equally sacred each one of us, up to and down to the most elevated of our world and the savage pagan in the jungle. Of course, we were considering. Boy, were we considering. At that very moment, at that immediate, instant suggestion, we were considering like crazy. The savage beauty, the sacredness, the sperm, the jungle. Heavy boyish sighs and stifled man-moans would resonate around the kitsch school chapel to the evident consternation of the visiting sermoniser. 'What is that noise? Stop that noise! The next boy who makes that noise will see the dean after church.' We couldn't wait to get to the library for the daily post-church run on well-thumbed, sticky *Nat. Geogs.*

Or was it something darker?

Were these beautiful people, these sublime women, not really seen as being like us? Were they allowed to be naked because at some level they were still not considered people? They were still savages. Pagan savages who, once they understood God's intent, would immediately want to wear clothes, and in that very act of donning bras and skirt would have instantly joined the ranks of humanity, and tragically never be seen naked again?

Were they considered almost animals and objects of curiosity to be photographed as an equally objective and empirically beautiful beast like, say, a rhinoceros? That, almost by definition, they could not be viewed as men or women by any reasonable individual but as primitive exotics to be marvelled over in dentists' waiting rooms as one might marvel over a candy-coloured grouper fish?

Clearly, if this was the case then no sane, normal person would feel anything other than an objective intellectual interest and curiosity towards these primitives. To sexually admire or experience desire towards such creatures would be a human impossibility. An outrageous perversity. Even to consider such a suggestion would be ridiculous and akin to suggesting that one desired and lusted after the admittedly horny-looking hippopotamus on the facing page.

Well, God bless small boys then. They didn't care about that awful underlying assumption. They just saw gorgeous, beautiful, healthy girls that they yearned for. People who were human to the nth degree. Who longed for their own females to be as open and apparently free as those whose lives they imagined in the *Nat. Geog.* I was one of those small boys full of longing. Unbelievably, I was one of the lucky ones who got to see and experience the glamorous places we thought we could only ever dream about.

For the returned priests who longed for the beauty of these places and people they had seen in Africa – and, I suspect, for the feelings of worth they had derived from their jobs there – the LBBB was the valid distractive means with which to reminisce in some provincial classroom over the cadenced drone of Latin nouns, equations or Gaelic. For the bored classroom it was the moment when, if you chose correctly, you could interject wild, mad, adventurous ideas of Africa you'd picked up from the *Nat. Geog.*, Tarzan, Biggles and the rest of them.

The priest would be only too willing to go along with this pathetically obvious ruse, desperate to escape his own futility and boredom. The descriptions of place. The exact sensuality and otherness of Africa. All would be wondrously described and gradually the shifting and yawning would cease as we learned of tribes and dress and warmth and other religions (always 'pagan'). These were never dismissed but were talked about as if they were simply an error that needed correcting, but something which it proved stubbornly difficult to talk the local people out of and which, it would be explained, could be temporarily assimilated into the teachings of the one, holy Catholic and apostolic church.

What the priest meant was that he had had to go along with their beliefs and put a spin on it. It was he, a thick-accented young boy from the bogs who had been taught by these exotics that we now learned of. His eyes would shine as he explained, without realising it, how they had opened his world to the hugeness of his own God's plan. How their 'paganism' had expanded his primitive faith. And he marvelled and we marvelled and we'd dropped a stick of chewing gum into the Little Black Baby Box on the way out the door.

But the thing is, because the Box was everywhere and because it said Help the Missions or The Holy Ghost Fathers or the St Vincent de Paul Missions or whatever, because of its ubiquity it had disappeared. Hidden but in plain sight, obscured by familiarity like the beauty of a long-married wife.

But where it had disappeared into was our subconsciousness, I suppose. And because it was 'positioned' not as charity, but as positive obligation, it seemed okay. They were poor, we were poor: we ought to help. Of course the underlying message was that they were black and therefore 'pagan', and therefore required God's true word brought to them. But glaring poverty was all about us in Dublin in those days, so it was never really suggested that they were poor because they were black or that there was any indignity in that condition. That simply wouldn't have made sense to us and especially not to those country-boy priests who often came from a destitute countryside that still resembled a nineteenth-century print from the pages of our history books.

Bizarrely, unlike the naked people in *National Geographic*, the underlying assumption of the Black Baby Box was more, well, respectful, I suppose. Possibly because they were babies and therefore innocent it would have been assumed that it wasn't their fault they were naked. They just grew up to be pagan primitives! It was all terribly confused at the heart of the missionary rationale. The heart of the muddle.

It seemed that, unlike the adults, these babies were individuals – God's children, same as us, free will and all that, and, well, frankly they needed to be saved. Simple as that. It's a helluva job but someone's got to do it. It's a man's life in the Holy Ghost Fathers an' no mistake. It was never actually put like that, but that was what was meant or implied. And I do believe that this was an unconscious or unknowing or unaware notion and certainly would have been considered 'reasonable' for its time.

Yes, our 'darker brethren' were desperate to be rescued from the burning fires of their wrongheaded and frankly cockamamie idol worship. Not saved from their own nakedness or, worse, their incompetences and ineptitudes which is our modern version of the same. They just needed to be shown the light. The light then was our religious and moral-value systems; today it's our political and moral ones. Ultimately, perhaps I would prefer the naive Catholic version if I had to choose either stupidity. Or the least dangerous.

Over the years the Black Baby Box gradually stopped being about 'the missions' which were in effect religious proto-Oxfams and Save the Childrens. They became focused less on the spiritual and more on the financial, temporal and corporeal. The missions had morphed into aid agencies and projects which were often no less missionary, pious or blind in their zeal. I have met extraordinary men and women, priests and nuns, throughout my time in Africa. Strong, strong people whose lives have been dedicated to helping the poor, ill and hungry. You can rarely tell they are religious; they don't wear the clothes or other stuff or use their titles any more. Brother Gus and Father Jack. Sister Jemba. Father Tom from Limerick, forty years with the Turkana people on the Sudanese/Kenyan border and thousands of others all over the continent. They, the religious and secular, are extraordinary people who thought their lives best lived in imitation of their God's example or in accordance with their personal morality.

But back then, in the days of Biggles and Tarzan and tales of young, frightened Irish boys in tropically inappropriate woollen priestly garb, being told excitedly of a continent of amazing and infinitely strange exotic individuals who lived an unbelievably school-free life under the sun surrounded by some of the most beautiful girls we'd ever seen drove our parched, eager imaginations into a sort of manic hyperdrive.

God bless the *National Geographic.*

How else do you explain what happened to me?

Father Farrell's Malaria

As Fr Farrell grew sicker, he grew scrawny. He was thin anyway, but the malaria made him a stick insect. His neck protruded from the now too big dog collar like a turkey in a polo-neck jumper. In his long, black soutane, silent but trembling with fever, he looked like one of El Greco's attenuated monks.

I have no memory of whether he was a good French teacher or not. I suppose not, for my knowledge of that language remains as elusive as the cure for his illness. But in a grimly cruel *Lord of the Flies* way, his fevers and aches and sudden clutchings of the head when the chronic pains seized him gave him the same fascination we small boys could have from pouring boiling water on to ants' nests or pinning through their crunchy abdomens still live moths on to dart boards. We watched him with a sad, prurient, detached curiosity, thrashing impotently against his own pain.

At these moments his face would drain and the conjugation of the irregular verb would trail off into an agonised silence. Sometimes, if we were very lucky, he would emit an involuntary whimper. We were transfixed with morbid fascination at the sight of the vulnerable adult. The gods made mortal come crashing to the earth. We could help it no more than he, but one of us at least would find our hysteria impossible to suppress and through their hand-clamped mouth would emerge a qualified snigger, the guilty party

21

immediately attempting to essay the hilarity into a pantomime cough of deep seriousness.

But he knew. Of course he knew. Shaking, he would leave the class, hand trailing along the corridor wall for support; then, finding the teachers' room, Fr Farrell would, in junky-like fever, shoot himself up with blessed quinine.

One day when he'd left the classroom, white with pain, the flaps of fleshless skin that were now his neck hanging over the sides of the starched white collar, we waited the customary two minutes of feigned studiousness before erupting into the normal anarchy and I left for the toilet. In the hall the glass-paned door of the teachers' room was ajar and through it I glimpsed the pain-drained priest, frozen in stillness, his sleeves rolled up, the needle just above his arm. He looked up and saw me, his face a picture of utter misery. His eyes were small, black pins of pain. We stared at each other. He nodded at me and then pushed the syringe into his bony arm.

'It's the aul missions,' Fr Coughlin told me one afternoon in our house, staring unsteadily into one of my eyes. He was drunk as usual, and painting one of his execrable whisky oils of the Connemara boglands. 'Oh, they'll getchya all right. You mark my words, me boyo,' he said, slapping me across the back of the head for no apparent reason, after warning me against having 'a vocation'. I thought he'd said 'vacation' and was understandably bemused by this sudden interest in my holiday plans and the unsolicited advice against taking said break in the middle of the jungle.

Coughlin was almost envious of Farrell. From what we understood Coughlin had failed as a missionary and upon his recall had retrained as an exorcist, Gaelic teacher and drunk, all three being viable career options in the Ireland of the 1960s. My father and I supposed the rigours of Africa and devil expulsion explained the whisky.

Fr Farrell had done well enough 'out there'. He had quickly understood that, rather than resist it, if you went with the grain of the local culture the people who lived there might not think you that odd in believing God had come to earth as an Arab carpenter, annoyed the authorities and had sprung forth, three days after his death by execution, right as rain, good as new, hung around a bit, stepped on to a cloud and shot up into space and off to Paradise.

Some of them may even have recognised this as a kind of version of their own God story and not thought anything too weird about it. And maybe after a few attempts to explain why people should wear clothes in equatorial temperatures, Fr Farrell, too, would have ceased to notice nakedness and himself begun wearing less often the sweat-drenched woollen soutane over the heavy woollen trousers.

Gradually, if you hadn't succumbed to the many dreadful illnesses, the locals in their graciousness would accept you and in turn you would begin to appreciate them; you could see that what they needed was not necessarily a new or different version of God. That you had, in fact, perhaps fallen among one of the most spiritually aware societies you had ever encountered in your hitherto admittedly narrow life with its thin seminarian theologies.

In this way the missions could make you more holy. Your spiritual life expanded as you learned from them. Whatever Graham Greene-type doubts arose in your own faith, it was exposure to other lives, other ideas of what it is to be holy, that brought you back ultimately to your own culturally appropriate metaphor of the infinite. Your doubts evaporated among these people and you saw God as he also could be. Naked, kind, fierce, loving, in everything and everywhere. Existing not as metaphor or act of faith but as a tangible presence, as a necessary part of life. And then a mosquito bit you.

The boys called Fr Farrell 'Fergie' and he was more or less already mad at the time I wasn't learning French from him. He would gaze wistfully out of the long sash windows towards the school cricket pitch, his one obsession. It was a lonely furrow he had chosen to plough and perhaps in some understandable way it eased his pain.

No one in Ireland was interested in cricket. The few in the school that he'd begged, pleaded, cajoled and bribed with guaranteed French exam results to play were embarrassed by the frankly faggoty overtones we attributed to the fey cricket whites. It was all a bit 'English'. Whereas the quintessentially English game of rugby was the school's pride and was clearly comfortably manly.

On those interminable afternoons of hopelessness characterised by the rote drone of French conjugation and declension, long, tall Fergie would drift into a sort of cricket-induced reverie. He would discreetly scrutinise the state of the pitch from behind his blue-covered textbook. After school hours we would watch the gangly, stooped figure hauling at the heavy iron roller as he flattened his pitch to regulatory perfection. Backwards and forwards, up and down, up and down.

Sometimes during class hours a boy would mistakenly wander across the perfect grass. The priest became apoplectic. The long sash window would screech upwards, banging at the top of its rise, and the thin figure, hand on ledge, would vault from the opening in a blurred flurry of black soutane, clutching his priest-skirts and flying across the ground towards the startled boy, screaming at him to get off the holy turf. Once, thrillingly, he wrestled the wretched miscreant to the ground and pummelled him. He was led away by two other priests. The boy said he would sue. The dean beat him.

The last time I saw Fergie was at the final of his ill-attended Cricket League. I was walking down the school drive. He was umpiring. Various cricket-type shouts came from the field. The hallowed crack of ball on bat, leather on willow was as haphazard as usual. Suddenly I saw Fergie cry out, clutch his forehead and stagger back. He was suddenly jerked forward from the waist and vomited hugely on to his beautiful pitch and then, finally, he began to shake. He was led away. The game sort of dribbled out then. There was no result. There was no cup that year.

The Luminous Continent

The first thing you notice is the light. Light everywhere. Brightness everywhere.

The pupils recoil. They retract in fractions of time to pinholes through which the brain peers cautiously. The eyes become slits against the shocking glare of white. Light blobs trickle and skip behind your lids. You squint like a Nepalese sherpa on the slopes of Everest. You fumble on your forehead for the expensively useless sunglasses against this monstrous display of solar immodesty. The light hurts. It is a painful, sizzling glare and you cannot lift your head towards its source. You are pushed from behind and you walk down the steps of the plane. Hello Africa.

This is not the Dark Continent as so often described by writers from the gloomy northern skies of Europe. Not the Dark Continent at all. This is the Luminous Continent drenched in sun, pounded by its heat and shimmering in its blinding glare.

For the visitor it is a balm. The bones dry out. Wellbeing floods tight bodies as they swiftly warm. Coats and jumpers and jackets have become immediately ridiculous. The world feels renewed. Colour rediscovered. Shape without its shadows assumes an almost shocking clarity and dimensionality. You find yourself more ready to laugh. You feel healthier and you think, 'Ah, yes, of course it makes sense that man came out of here. How stupid we were to leave.' It's a good thought. A true thought. And a hopelessly romantic one.

For the sun is indifferent to us. Assume its good intent if you like; it will as much coddle you as it would crush you. It doesn't care. For all its ability to allow us to see the world it is blind itself. For all its generosity in feeding plant life it will as soon burn it. It can be the friendly harbinger of renewal, fertility and growth but in Africa it also kills in wanton numbers.

The sun does not rise here. To describe it thus implies a slow, gradual awakening. It does not ascend gracefully in a heavenly arc. It ambushes the night. Suddenly, leaping out from behind its own shadow, free of its self-imprisoning cloak of darkness, a ready-made ball of solid, triumphantly glaring light. It is a huge glaring Cyclops. An immediate challenge to anything under its dominion. It will kill if given a chance. It will deny life, drying anything to dust. The air does not warm then ease its way to a tepid heat. The sun slaps the night aside and is immediately hot. Is suddenly there. Present and material. It lends the air weight, transforming it from its thin invisibility of night to a heavy material substance. Something to be battled against and through. Where every indrawn breath scalds and all exposed flesh burns.

There is no seemly shading of demure pinks to oranges to yellows then white. None of the politesse of adjustment. No appreciation of the subtleties of temperature. No soft waking to the day, the cool of dawn, the gentle stirring of the land, the shading of the clouds before the clarity of noon. None of the quiet trembling of siesta heat, followed by the kindly decline into the soothing contemplation of the evening.

No. It catapults directly, fully formed, from the deep settled velvet dark of the African nightblack. Like some hideous quotidian jack-in-the-box it leaps leering into the sky, glaring manically and daring anything to stir.

The sun detests its great enemy – shade. Shade – the sole, great challenger to its sovereign reign. It will do anything to destroy it. It will suck the ground dry of water, dew or damp to deny the tree. It will pound relentlessly on the nomads' tented roof. It will stalk the verandahed pavements and eliminate the shadow of anyone foolhardy enough to challenge it and venture forth.

But still trees grow. And still people move. But they do so very slowly. The grace and elegance of human movement in Africa is not accidental. It is environmental. It is learned. The overriding consideration is to conserve energy. Every action must be considered and weighed against the draining torpor of the day.

Consider an African walking. You will rarely see one do anything as provocative as run. There is an effortless, upright elegance. A huge poise against the endless whiteness of the sky. There is nothing superfluous in the action. No sudden rushes. No flurries. Rather, a slow, rhythmic steadiness of unhurried ease wholly different from the flustered, busy, jerky, spasmodic rush common to the European.

The women, like models or ballerinas, gracefully upright, balance perfectly between sky and earth, their hips propelling them forward in a lullaby sway. On their heads improbable weights of stuff. Sewing machines, car parts, electric kettles, animals, huge bundles of wood or protruding carrots that make them resemble beautiful black Statues of Liberty.

And in the pasturelands of the Masai or the deserts of the Tuareg, the salt-flat depressions of the Afar or the highlands of the Amhara, in a landscape of nothing a solitary figure utterly still in this vast empty space standing on a single leg for ever. Motionless and still under the impotent sun and magnificent in his place. There is no need to hurry or move and there is no benefit in doing so.

No, this is not the Dark Continent. But many of us can only see Africa from the dark side of our mind. The impenetrable place, the unknowable minds. The hoards of walking skeletons, too weak to swat the flies that cover them in the stinking squalor of the relief camps. Or the disease-stricken people fleeing yet another nameless war between countries, clans, tribes or warlords. And, yes, all of that is true too much of the time, but in refusing to see the many other Africas we bring our own darknesses to bear. The same darkness Conrad or Stanley brought upriver when they wrote about this shimmering place as Darkest Africa. Still others fill the romantic space in their imagination with an Africa of 'unspoilt' child-like primitives and wild, beautiful creatures. But the reality is that this continent is all of that and has everything else. Rainforest, jungle, savannah, Mediterranean and coastal climates, with more fish and animals and birds, more peoples, cultures and languages than anywhere else on the planet. It is quite simply the most beautiful place in our world.

No, not the Dark Continent. This is the Luminous Continent.

The Chairman's Hat

It wasn't actually called house arrest but we couldn't leave the hotel. The chairman might be ready for us at any time and if we weren't prepared to leave at a moment's notice then we'd miss our opportunity. So Azif, the middleman's son, and I stayed put.

The view from the roof didn't amount to much: bleached-out flat roofs, a couple of uninspiring minarets and a hint of sea to the north. We passed the time pretending we were preparing for the interview. I read various books about him. Fairly dull gruel. The Father-of-his-People-type articles. The Monster at the Centre of the International Terror Conspiracy pieces. The Playboy. The Egocentric Power Freak. The Corrupt Crook posing as the Great Liberator but stashing billions in Switzerland. The Callous Murderer, etc., etc. All of it was fairly badly written and probably more or less true, but the problem with deep research is that the more you know the less interested you become in your subject. You know too much. What more have they got to say? Why bother meeting them? Why hang around in a crap hotel in the middle of Tunis hoping for a glimpse of the Great Man? Fuck him. Let's go home.

Azif was having none of it. His father had expended good capital arranging this meeting and his son was not about to skulk home, mission seriously unaccomplished, because his interviewer thought the interviewee was boring before he had even met him.

We hung around on the roof for a couple of days. It was never guaranteed we were going to get a meeting anyway. We were told just to come and they'd sort of see what they could do. I was deeply sceptical. But we'd got on the plane and here we were. 'Let's go out', I'd whine. 'No. What if somebody comes for us and we're not here?' 'So fuck 'em. They can fuck off. And then so can we. Back home.' 'No, no, no.' Days of this.

Azif called some number over and over again. 'It will be at night-time,' we were finally told. Great. Could we go out then and look around? No, because it might change to daytime. They couldn't say. I gave it one more day and then I was off. That night Azif pounded on the door. 'Get up, it's on, let's go.' 'What time is it?' 'Three. Get up.' 'Fuckinell.' 'Yeah, well, hurry up, they're downstairs.'

There were three Land-Rovers out in the street, the street I hadn't seen now for days. I was knackered, barely awake and very grumpy. We were put brusquely into the middle vehicle. I was in the front passenger seat and Azif, clutching the tiny and frankly unimpressive digicam, was in the back. There was a cackling of walkie-talkies. Hacking Arabic crackled back and forth. It was loud in the night streets of Tunis, but I suppose the citizens of the city had learned to curb their curiosity and complaints about their PLO guests by now.

I began to be a bit apprehensive when they handed us the blindfolds. We were not to see where we were going. Could we please put them around our eyes? Now, in those days there were a lot of kidnappings going on around this region. Not precisely in this part of the world, mainly in the places off to our right, but pictures of McCarthy, Keenan and Terry Waite kept appearing vividly behind my tightly tied white cloth blindfold.

I tried to remember every twist and turn of the road. I'd often seen this in the movies and it seemed to work. The fact that they were probably just going round in a circle and that the hiding-place headquarters was next door to the hotel did cross my mind, but I had to think of something to do to stop feeling so scared.

I had automatically assumed that Azif could speak Arabic. Unfortunately, this was way off the mark. Azif had a loud middle-classish north London tone with not a single word of the native tongue to his monolingual credit. Before we began our Night Ride to Terror HQ, he had asked professionally if we could just try to shoot a dramatic piece to camera travelling up the bumpy street. The escort was thrilled. Being media hip as all terrorists are, they wrapped their red check headgear around their faces, turned their headlights on full beam and gunned their engines belligerently. Poor sleeping Tunis. I turned pointedly to the back-seat camera and invented some dramatic-sounding bollocks as the headlights picked out the dust from the car in front. The guards asked, 'Okay?' We thanked them and they asked us to slip on the blindfolds.

We drove for a long time. I started to get worried. We were driving straight, the sound of the car no longer bouncing off the buildings beside us on the streets. Were we in the country? That made no sense if we were going to meet the Chairman. What would he be doing in the country, away from communications and contact? Maybe security. I chatted nervously to Azif. I didn't want to show the driver I was intimidated or scared. But I don't know why. He probably couldn't have cared less. If he wanted to shoot or kidnap us he could. What difference did it make whether we were crapping ourselves or not? I suppose it was a matter of personal dignity or some other nonsense. Azif was being falsely hearty. Probably for the same reason. Maybe the driver was a plant. Maybe he could speak excellent English or something. Better to show him our insouciance, our phlegm, our sangfroid. He didn't give a fuck. We hit a rock and banged our heads off the roof. 'Sorry,' he said in perfect unaccented English.

We came to a halt and were told we could remove the blindfolds. I have no memory of the outside. Just the usual mêlée of men with keffiyeh and guns. A lot of pistols in waistbands. Some camouflage or olive-green ex-army combat jackets. A lot of smoking and gobbing. In the lobby several people stood around or sat on benches waiting for appointments. It was a bit like a school corridor. Classroom-like doors led off the hallway with names and titles on them. A minister for this or that. It was interesting, this pretend government in exile. Of course, many people bought into the notion but it was empirically nonsense. Except that it did give this wandering dispossessed people a sense of a centre. A locus of power. This dull, scabby surburban villa in a scrubland was their capital city in exile, their presidential palace, the gravitational pull for their nationalist aspiration. A fantastic and useful trick of the imagination which everyone in that room and the millions outside believed in. But at 3.35 a.m. you couldn't fail to be impressed by the power of its imaginary and emotional logic.

Waiting to be summoned we were by turns ignored and cosseted. Then we were mostly ignored. We were brought hot, sticky, sweet tea. After half an hour the dawn was visible through the unclean barred and wired window. I was getting tired and pissed off again after the fright of the car ride. And then we were called for.

There was a long oval conference table. Some gunmen loafed against the walls chatting. Various styles of facial hair were sported. Some of them looked fantastic, exactly the image of the romantic freedom fighter, while others had the classic scruffy unshaven terrorist thing going on. Like me at that time of the day, I thought, hoping I fitted in. I looked at Arafat. He sat at the point of the oval signing papers and talking. Behind him, covering the back wall, was a huge photographic mural of the Dome of the Rock, the giant gold-covered mosque in Jerusalem. It wouldn't have looked out of place in *Coronation Street*. He didn't look up at us as we entered. We stood about awkwardly for a long time. Azif motioned, was it okay to film? 'Only the Chairman'. Okay.

He was pale, his lips slobbery. They were loose, floppy and wet. The famous stubble was out of control. Not nearly beard, not regular enough to be described as stubble. Just unshaved, scruffy and grey. I'd heard he had bad skin and couldn't shave. His cheeks were flabby and grey and the bags under his eyes were rolling mounds of puffy flesh that dominated even the bulbous nose. Above them the wet eyes bulged and popped as if in a state of permanent emphasis. Like a King Charles spaniel making a point. He looked fucking awful.

And so did I. Hauled from sleep and not having bothered to shave for two days out of boredom, we equalled each other on the ol' George Michael late eighties front. My thick lips, thick nose, hamster cheeks and baggy eyes mirrored his and were still sleeping and out of control. I was a complete, scruffy mess.

'You need a haircut,' the Chairman offered by way of greeting. It was true; my hair was crap as usual. Worse than usual. 'You need a new scarf,' I replied, pointing to the famous thing on his head. The Most Dangerous Man in the World launched into a peroration on the unique symbolism of his hat.

He pointed at the photograph behind him. 'Do you notice anything?' he asked coyly. 'Er, no,' I replied. He reached up. He was very small and chunky. He stretched but didn't quite make it. He got a stick and traced the line of the golden dome. 'Now?' he asked slyly, eyes wide with anticipation, willing me to get what he was on about, like a team-mate during a game of Christmas charades. 'No, sorry.' 'The dome,' he exploded triumphantly, slobbery lips wet and shaking with delight. He looked around the room, but they'd seen it before. One or two nodded. 'Look. My head. Is the same,' he explained. 'You cannot see? The dome. My head is the same. See?' His hand described an arc over his head. He kept repeating this half-halo motion, but I wasn't getting it. 'My keffiyeh represents the return of Jerusalem,' he finished, shouting gleefully. The gunmen continued talking loudly, smoking and clattering their guns around. I hadn't a clue what he was on about.

'And now look, my friend.' He pointed, smiling, at the map of

Palestine that took up the left side of the mural. 'Can you see now?' I really did want to see. I was desperate to get it. I kept looking at his hat. At the map. Back at the scarf. I didn't get it. It was late. I was tired. What the fuck was he on about? I wanted to help if only out of politeness. It was getting awkward, this not getting the Great Hat Paradigm. Azif was uncomfortable. 'Is the same,' he said exasperated, not smiling any longer. 'Is the exact same. See,' he said, agitatedly jabbing his finger up and down the Mediterranean coastline of Palestine. His finger scooted along the map then gestured feverishly at the side of his scarf. I shook my head. 'No. Sorry, Mr Chairman.' He jabbed at the side of his head, indicating the map with his eyes and now running his finger in a diagonal down his cheek. 'Oh yeah. I get it,' I lied. 'I see,' I said, while Azif fidgeted nervously. 'Hah, you see. You see!' he laughed delightedly. 'Is the same, no?' He flipped the edge of the headgear forward until it flopped down the side of his head. 'Now look, my friend.' He pinched it delicately between his fingers and pulled it back into a straight diagonal line, creating a point at the crown of his head. 'You see?' 'Aaah, yes,' I said, still nonplussed. He gestured at the map and the scarf. 'Is the same, no? My scarf is the map! My scarf is Palestine. See, it is same shape! I wear Palestine on my head. When people see me they know I am wearing Palestine on my head. In all meetings with world leaders they see Palestine on my head. And they see the dome is the top. The sacred dome of Jerusalem. The round dome.'

That was perhaps the time to bring this lengthy game to an end, but Azif heard me say, 'Hold on, it's not round, it's pointy.' 'No,' said Arafat emphatically 'you are wrong, my friend. Is round. Completely round. Like the dome.' 'Well, it looks pointy to me.' Why didn't I just shut up? 'It is not a point. I tell you, it is round.' 'Oh yeah, I see it now.' I gave in to the mad old trout. He licked the spitty lips and beamed around the room. 'Is round.'

The Burntlands

We had been travelling through the Burntlands for hours. We needed to get to the tuna factory before nightfall. There were bandits about and the manager would not answer the door after dark. Despite the heat I did not want to spend the night on the cool stony ground of the 'road'. The prospect of the tuna factory floor and a couple of electric fans seemed delicious. So we sped over the shale, through the gulleys, the dry river beds and over bumps towards Lasquaray in the quivering blister of mid-afternoon heat.

The army boys clung stoically to the wooden benches mounted on the back of the flatbed pickups with the ferocious 132-calibre cannon between them and stared unseeingly out at Mars. Tortured by an unremitting sun, the ground seemed twisted into impossible shapes. Nothing stirred in the vast space.

We screamed ahead, rocks pinging off the steel underframe. Sometimes I looked back and saw them bouncing through the gravel and shale that was the road, the dust of our Landcruiser smothering their Technical. 'They must hate me,' I thought in my air-con, upholstered comfort. I hadn't asked for them. They were a pain.

It wasn't so much an escort as a private army. There were thirty-four of them in various outfits approximating a uniform. The general look was hats, camouflage trousers, T-shirts, jumpers, flip-flops or ruined army boots and what seemed like a competition for the most preposterous shades. I liked the big white plastic oval Jackie O ones, myself. Especially when they were worn in the intolerable heat with the woolly balaclava, the slung bullet belts and the ferocious RPG grenade launcher casually cocked on the bouncing lap.

They were mad. And wired. All day they'd been chewing khat. Their mouths bulged with the wad of leaves wedged in their cheeks. Green dribble seeped from the corners of their mouth and when they took the shades off, their eyes were wide saucers of dilated pupils, darting, staring, wild white globes bulging from their lean, hard, narrow faces.

Arriving in Bosasso we had been summoned by the governor. Things were 'iffy'. The local warlord was in Nairobi for the 'peace talks'. They took our passports and did not return them until we'd 'talked'.

There were always 'peace talks'. 'Peace talks' were a warlord lifestyle choice. Someone pays you to stay in a nice hotel, free meals, staff, phone bills. You sit, talk with the guys – your warlord rivals. If you don't get what you want, you activate the lads back home, things kick off and there are more 'peace talks'.

The latest ones had lasted two years. There was some trouble about who'd pay the hotel bill. 'General' Morgan left the talks, gathered his hooligans and marched on Kismayu. He paused before taking the town and gave them one day until someone agreed to pay his two-million-dollar, two-year hotel bill.

The Kenyans said it wasn't their problem. Morgan could go fuck himself; they weren't going to pay. The people of Kismayu braced themselves for the killings and lootings that would enable Morgan to pay for his minibar and extras. Finally, as it always does, the UN gave the Kenyans the money to pay for Morgan and Kismayu was saved until the next unpaid lunch.

Up here in the north of the country, Puntland, as it was now called, was thinking about declaring independence if their boy didn't get what he wanted. Some of the clans didn't fancy the idea and if they knew I was around they just might like to have a go. It was complete bollocks of course. No one wanted to kidnap me; the governor just wanted a bit of cash. I was to have, for my 'protection' you understand, whether we liked it or not, eight guards at a hundred dollars each or else we could not move and they could not guarantee our safety. And oh yeah, we have your passports. Nice.

The governor's room was darkened against the glare. Outside, heavily armed men hung about. It is odd how quickly you become used to guns. After a while they seem to become part of someone's attire. What the well-dressed under-aged thug is wearing this year. AK47 is the new black.

The men lay stretched out on the steps, squatting, playing cards or brewing the endless sticky tea on an upturned satellite dish, the water pot balanced at the centre cross-hairs and the sun bouncing off the silver bowl heating the water to boiling point. No fires needed. Smart, in a country with little wood. A man guarded the door. In the room behind a desk was the governor, the vice-president of the interior, the minister of religion, the mayor, the head of the militia, and at least six others of various rank arranged in silence around the T-shaped conference table emanating from the governor's desk. The desk was the crossbar, with locals down the left and myself and companions on the right against the nylon brocaded wall hangings.

There is a curious, polite formality to these discussions. Time dragged on. Those not fingering Kalashnikovs toyed with their pistols or mobiles that exploded regularly throughout with improbable ringtones. The electronic notes of distant cultures pinged about the crowded space. 'Auld Lang Syne', 'Liliburlero', 'Lili Marlene', 'I Should Be So Lucky', 'We Wish You a Merry Christmas', 'Mission Impossible', a little bit of techno, Eminem, 'Smoke on the Water' and occasionally some cute Arabic quarter-tones interrupted our conversational flow. The phone, always held in the hand, would be scrutinised in exasperation for at least two beeps then cut off if the caller were unwanted or else barked at loudly before being hung up abruptly, seemingly always without a 'goodbye'.

We showed them our many papers and endlessly repeated our purpose, extolled the beauty and uniqueness of themselves, their town and country. All this is necessary. It cannot be avoided. If you don't do it, they will. The formality makes way to a false tone of friendship. 'Smiling never cost you anything.' Nothing was agreed. The mayor couldn't be responsible. They knew who I was, very honoured, great friend of Africa, etc., but ... where's the wedge?

The security chief told us things were particularly bad at the moment. In fact, the last mayor had been killed the month before, said the round, chuckling, bearded new mayor who, not very bizarrely where everything is mad, came from Acton in west London. He told us not to worry about the last mayor. 'He was a civilian,' he chuckled. 'I am military.' Afterwards some people said that he had done the actual killing. Which was possible. 'There are many doors in Bosasso,' he winked, 'but I am the door to Bosasso.' We got it. He had fond memories of Acton. 'You must be the only one,' I said. We were getting on famously now. The mayor was asking did I knew friends of his in west London. Someone else had been a chef in Croydon.

The following day the discussions as to my relative importance were interrupted by a lengthy conversation, conducted sotto voce by the governor, a weedy man with an unconvincing moustache, on the phone. The mood radically altered.

'That was the president in Nairobi,' intoned the governor, still rigid with respect and terror. 'You are to have complete access and you are to be protected at all costs. You are to have thirty uniformed men, two heavy-cannon-mounted vehicles and four personal plain clothes with you at all times. There is no more negotiation. The president apologises for his absence, welcomes you to our country of Puntland, is honoured by your presence and wishes you a successful trip. However, other parties in Nairobi are also aware of your presence and therefore the president commands us all to make your security our number-one task. There will be no further talks. The cost will be the same.' Rightho.

Our driver spun round to shower green spittle at me as he gabbled incoherently through his khat speed-high. He moved and drove frantically. He argued constantly with the guard in the front. They said the same things over and over again. Their voices shouted at each other. They pantomimed extreme rage in the barking, peremptory tones of Somali. They swilled extravagantly from our limited supply of Evian and, eyes bulging, raced on, mouth chomping on the hedge they had inserted into the corners of their faces.

Khat is a serious drug. It's four espressos all the time. It's chewable cocaine. Green amphetamine. And it's legal in Britain. Every night a full cargo flight leaves Dire Dawa in Ethiopia for Liverpool stuffed with freshly plucked khat wrapped in wet outerleaves to preserve its freshness. It's destined for the Somalian and Ethiopian populations in the UK where it's chewed throughout the day. Back here it's out of control.

Your average Somali makes around five dollars a week. One bunch of khat costs five dollars. Our brave lads were on three bunches a day – fifteen dollars. Three times the weekly wage in one day. There was a chance that these militiamen would receive some monies from their overlords, but as in most of Africa it's unlikely, especially in what is politely called 'failed states', i.e. basket cases. By any measure Somalia is a failed state. Indeed, it's a moot point as to whether it ever was a state. It is a huge empty slab of land in the Horn of Africa that has been parcelled up for centuries by competing clans. These clans are in an almost permanent state of feud over land, water, goats, camels (the big one), trade, whatever. They are brilliant traders, incredibly beautiful-looking, hard as nails and a complete hoot. I love being in Somalia but how do you make a functioning modern state, i.e. a politically functioning entity that exists for its citizens, out of hundreds of different competing claims? And why bother? If that's the way they want to do things, why should we care? The truth, I suspect, is that in our world we only know how to deal with entities that resemble our own. We may be incapable of negotiation with anything that doesn't fit our pattern. How does Britain complete a trade agreement with several different clan groups with different interests who will start arguing and killing the minute they feel they want more or they've been hard done by or whatever? It's kind of pointless insisting on statehood when the traditional state is anarchy and the gun. Sort of like Afghanistan without the heroin.

The police and the army are unpaid here. You get a gun, a sort of uniform, possibly a small daily meal and the right to bully and terrorise people into giving you money, when you're not actually holding them up, extorting or robbing them. Here everybody's got a gun and the law is the man with the biggest.

The women are sick of the men. 'We have to save the goats from two wolves now,' they say. 'The men are useless. Khat has killed them.' The women are exhausted. All day they care for the family and by night they keep watch on the goats. This was the man's job, tending the goats. Now they steal their own goats from their own wives, from their own families, from their own children. 'The women must be awake all night, otherwise the husband will come and steal his own goats! They steal to buy khat.' The word is a cough. It's a clearing of the throat, and when the woman says it, it is with such a depth of contempt behind the guttural noise that she spits fiercely at the ground to illustrate unnecessarily the emotion behind the noise. Like junkies at home, the men will ultimately do anything for the leaf and end up doing nothing with their lives.

It's a social thing, this khat chewing. It tastes foul. Bushy, in fact. Initially there's nothing, but eventually you can feel it. The little light bud leaves on the top are best and the rich discard the rest. Old men, their teeth completely gone from a lifetime of chewing, make a paste of powder and rub it on their gums. It's a nervy, jangly, mercury high. But you need so much of it. A bunch has maybe ten long stalks. They are often shared or constantly sifted and rearranged in bunches. It's casual. Some women do it. But it stops the men working. They become erratic, indifferent, sleep on the job from not sleeping at night. They become poorer. They rob their own families. They can't get it up any more. 'They are useless,' a woman spat and added with mockery, 'for anything.' And this is true. To be without children or goats makes you nothing.

The heat seeped under the roof.

The khat made the boys thirsty. The heat and dust and balaclavas and T-shirts, jackets and wellington boots made them thirsty. There wasn't any water left.

Things got iffy. We had been travelling for hours. The gunner mounted on the back of the flatbed Technical was required to remain standing throughout. He balanced like one of Nelson's sailors on a rolling poop deck, clinging to the steel handles of his cannon. He surfed the Burntlands anticipating the rocks and holes, flexing, bending and bracing as he rolled. On either side of him the grimly stoic, munching militiamen clung hands-free to their bouncing bench, their scrawny arses the sole suspension against the jarring scrub.

We wasted precious light at the enforced tea-stop – an awning at the 'roadside'. A mosque had appeared from nowhere. Built with Saudi Wahhabi money in the last three months. The mood grew lighter as the sky turned dark.

We were late. Occasionally the lights picked out something. 'Hyena'. There was a puncture. Punctures are pit stops in Africa. A puncture is not a possibility – it is a certainty. There were no jacks. The truck was lifted and rocks placed underneath. One of the various mix 'n' match spares was applied. We sped on.

'Lasquaray,' a rain of green spittle shouted triumphantly. A low adobe took shape in the dim. The tuna factory was big. There was, not unsurprisingly, the ubiquitous smell of drying fish. The commander pounded on the factory door with the stock of his gun – like in a film. Nobody answered. He shouted something at the cars which focused a semi-circle of headlights on the factory, the commander pinned against the light. He pounded again and then everyone leaned on the horns. My heart began to sink.

Eventually a tousle-haired man in pyjamas emerged and told us to go away. He knew nothing about us and we could all bugger off. We offered to pay. We begged. He didn't care about the guns or the soldiers, who were indifferent anyway. Sleeping on the stony ground would be a luxury after that trip.

There was a 'hotel'. It was beyond crap. Some women did their best but it was still crap. Some of us stayed on the ground getting bitten and inhaling the foetid fish stink that hung about the empty town. Four of us shared itchy iron beds in a sweltering heavy room. The people were kind. They did their best. There was no food. The soldiers drew water from the well and drank. They stripped and poured the water over their bodies then, wrapping themselves in anoraks, they lay on the ground and went to sleep.

Three guards posted themselves outside our room. We tore open our SAS cook-in-the-bag rations. They were ready in four minutes. Boiling Lancashire hotpot. I was amazed: the soldiers were amazed: we shared amazement. And stew. And amidst this sentiment of shared well-being these tough, drug-maddened boys kept watch over us while we slept.

The River

The river was too high for the crocodiles to take the goats or the people, so they stayed sleeping in the tall grasses on the islands and fed on whatever was left in the underwater larders.

The river was in flood. Fast and brown, it skidded between the clumps of mud and grass, and punched against the wooden bridge posts jetting through its gaps.

Coming back from Gambela, the dugout loaded with the weekly maize, beans, coffee and bright green plastic basin and useful tin cooking pot, was a thrill. Once you'd pushed off from the reed bank and negotiated the side stream, it was all a question of baling and balancing. The gunnels were about parallel to the stream waters. If the shopping shifted you were over. In this tide there was no recovering. Your boat was gone and your supplies were lost. All that money, all that labour wasted, and while you knew the crocs didn't like the flood, if they were hungry enough, if you were easy enough, if you couldn't make the shore against the tide, well . . .

Past the island the dugout catches the current. Paddle quickly from the shore to the still, fast centre. Lift the paddle. Feel the shifting supplies. Counterbalance with your body weight. Dip the paddle just a slip to adjust your path. Watch for bow splash and bale carefully. Feel the rush. Become the tide, a tiny hollow stick speeding home upon the great beast's back. A dart on the flood. Now gently ease across the flood path of the broad great river pounding down to Khartoum, seven days away, and on to the Nile, to the sea, and then, like a jet screaming through the Straits, out at last to the great vast ocean.

Such an adventure. Get lost in the heat of the day. The sun glaring off the water. The water sluicing, hissing beside you, alive and dangerously indifferent. At best what can you be to this living, raging torrent – a small nuisance, a tiny impediment to its unfettered free-flow? A bobbing speck on its dangerous wash?

Negotiate gently now through the whipping currents past the white splash of unseen obstacles. Gingerly edge across towards the village now a mile away but still hidden behind the tall grasses. Round the bend and be careful not to catch the water's turning spin. Now. Paddle. Quickly. Dip. Other side. Hold it, hold it. Other side again. One, two, three now catch the water bouncing off the bank and let it whip you under the overhang and smartly round the bend and out into the main mid-river flow in one mad, exhilarating flash of power, speed and muscle.

Hold it. Feel it. Feel the flow, the flood, the whole vast, tumbling tumult of power and . . . beat it. But careful. Not too confident. Not yet. You're not home yet. You know every speck of foam, every glint of wave, every tug of tide, every obscured obstacle and hidden danger. You have known these waters all of your life. Ridden on them since the day you were born, negotiated them as an infant, learning each move from your father and grandfather and uncle. Learned to respect it from your mother and aunts. It is as familiar to you as your house or village or friends. It is more dangerous than your worst enemy and will give you more than your best friend. It will carry you, feed you, wash and clean you, comfort and soothe you, play with you, amuse and entertain you and then it will take you in a moment as swift as an upriver rapid and you will be gone. In its depth are your worst fears. The trapping weeds, the killing jaws of crocodiles, their grey underwater shelves lined with the bodies of your people, the dashing rocks, the drowning floods, the drought-stuck shallows, the snapping fish, the dark pulling depths and the fast flood that will carry you away on a whim, never to be found or seem by anyone again. Yes, be very careful.

Become the thing again. Lose yourself inside it. Into it. Be it. Look up. There it is. Just up ahead. Behind the grass, the dot of thatched roofs. The thin stream of smoke from the open fires. Paddle right. Twice. Adjust. Balance, balance, rushing now too fast. Adjust. Paddle one, two, three now, speeding towards the bank. Paddle, paddle. Harder. Coming, coming now. Turn the head of the canoe. Quickly into the tide. Watch for bow spill. Good. Boiling along the bank, into the tide, slow, slow, nudge the shore, into the small cove, throw the string. The boy takes it. Makes it secure. Don't idle. The river's high and the crocs won't come. But you never know . . .

In one month the river will be a trickle again and then the crocodiles will come. They will wait patiently for the day when idly, unthinkingly, you come to the river bank with your calabash for the morning wash. They will watch you take just that half-step too far from the safe shore and the quiet circle of neatly swept huts where the whole world lives.

Falasha

Behind the village of Woleka, down a country path and across a pretty stream, lie the last remains of the African Jews. They are buried here in their African homeland. The others, after two thousand years, made it all the way home.

The modern world dislocates and relocates people. It might be damage caused by climate or environmental change that sets people on the move away from their previously fertile lands; it might be political circumstances like war. Both of these factors came to a head in the Ethiopian Highlands in the great famine of 1984 when more than a million people died.

At that time there was a unique group of people here called the Falasha (the word means 'exile'). They were black Ethiopian Jews who claimed to be the lost black tribe of Israel, direct descendants from King Solomon and the Queen of Sheba through their son Prince Menelik, still exiles after two thousand years.

The Israeli government heard about these people and asked the communist dictatorship governing the region at the time if they could airlift them to safety. After much negotiation and eighty million anti-personnel bullets and $26 million changing hands, the Falasha were finally free to go.

Altogether about fifty thousand of the African Jews left their homes and their Christian and Muslim neighbours with whom they had lived fairly peacefully for some two thousand years. And in a wonderful and funny anomaly, some of those Christians who were left behind gradually took over the old Falasha villages and began to pretend to be Jewish. They learned old Jewish phrases and some sentences in Hebrew and even learned how to celebrate certain Jewish festivals. And they did this in order to make a living from the tourists who visited. If you ask them they say, yes, they're Jewish, and they're waiting to go to Israel. But they're not.

The reality is that in this funny African Jewish Disneyland there are only two true old Falasha left, and both of them are waiting for their visas – waiting to go home, as they see it.

An Old Madman

There's an old madman in the khat market after everyone's gone home. He's picking up the twigs and tiny leaves that have been discarded or have fallen into the liquid mess that is the shit and mud of the market pathways.

I watch him for a while. Poor old bastard. He wipes the few leaves on his filthy rag of loincloth that covers neither his scraggly, dangling balls or his scrawny, flacid arse. It has been raining. He is cold and has no covering on his back. There is a slice of muddy, stained fabric reaching across his torso and tied in a knot on his shoulder. It keeps slipping as he painfully, awkwardly, bends to the ground. He chews the little leaves. Then he stops wiping them. Can't be bothered if they're clean or not, I suppose. He just roots around in the goat shit and puts them slowly into his mouth.

Can he still get high? Oh I hope so. I hope so, so much. What awful God would not let this cold ruin of a man not spend his sad, wretched life smashed out of his gaunt skull?

I hate it. I don't want to, but you know what? I take the fucking picture anyway. How often, in how many ways, do you disappoint yourself?

In the Land of the Mursi

It is not exactly cold as our light aircraft bumps to a standstill. The grass landing strip runs through the centre of the town of Jinka in the extreme south-west of Ethiopia. But it is overcast and none of the heat from the great high sun penetrates the cloud. This is not what Africa is supposed to be like.

The townspeople lean on the railings that surround the strip and examine us with a sullen curiosity. They watch, unsmiling, as we unload our gear and pile it into a small caravan of Japanese four-wheel drives, the ubiquitous mode of transport all across this mighty continent. I am wearing a blue shirt. 'Tsetse flies are attracted to blue,' one of the drivers tells me, with apparent seriousness. Shit. Or is he winding me up? I grunt ambiguously in response.

We set off for the long, long drive to the Mago National Park. We are to meet the Mursi, one of the few tribes allegedly untouched by the modern world. They live still by that slash-and-burn agriculture, which, we were taught at school, was the hallmark of primitive man. Everything we had heard of the Mursi pandered to that image. They live without clothes. The women have gigantic plates dangling from their lips and ears. The men are the fiercest warriors in Africa. Like so much about this mysterious continent some of it turns out to be true, and some of it doesn't.

For hour after hour we bump along a narrow, muddy track. The soil is a rich brown. The jungly vegetation crowds right to the edge of it. Orange-bellied parrots flash through the trees. Occasionally the shriek of a black-backed jackal cuts through the undergrowth. From time to time we come to a river, and the 4x4s push their way through the thrashing current. The water is the colour of the milky coffee they used to sell in what passed for the groovy coffee bars of my dreaming youth.

After a few hours we come upon the first clearing. The surrounding forest is a dense cliff of solid vegetation but for a few hundred square yards it has been roughly cleared, apart from the odd massive tree which has clearly proved too tough to cut down. In the clearing stand the withering remains of last year's crop – sorghum, to judge by the broken stalks. Dotted around the landscape every few hundred yards are abandoned watchtowers. In these, boys armed with slings and piles of stones keep vigil to drive away pigs by day and baboons by night, to guard the vital crops.

Then, we are upon it. A tiny village. A hamlet, really. A few huts by the side of the road, with no attempt made to clear the land between them. The shrubs and trees and creepers of the rainforest press in upon the small grass huts like the fingers of an intrusive hand. In the road there suddenly appears a naked man. He begins to run in front of us, as if we are pursuing him. Then, just as suddenly, he stops. He holds out his hands in supplication as our vehicle flashes past. He is stark bollock naked, apart from a string hanging across his shoulder that carries a gourd. Initiation scars, in little bumpy rows, march across his torso. Round his neck he wears a single row of red beads. The same colour as his mad, staring eyes.

'A wild man,' says one of our African guides simply.

'Drunk,' says another.

Alcohol is new in the land of the Mursi, but it is what many of them buy when they make their way into the local towns to barter meat from their cattle. That and the odd bullet for the ancient AK47s, which are the designer accessory of choice for these supposedly primitive people. 'What do you think of Western civilisation?' Mahatma Ghandi was once asked. 'I think it would be a very good idea,' the great man replied. It would be nice if the modern world had brought the Mursi something other than guns and booze. Still, I suppose they can use both. What use would a blender be?

After an unnerving encounter with a particularly deep, fast-flowing river, we arrive in a low valley, its sides steeply wooded. At its heart is a clearing. By now it is raining, not the torrential monsoon you might expect in the tropics of Africa, but that fine wetting drizzle so familiar to the Irish. We pull up by a little concrete hut with a corrugated iron roof. I almost felt at home. Drunks, drizzle and Kalashnikovs.

Then, out of the trees, a man appears. Two things are striking about him. Apart from a long cloth fastened at one shoulder and draped loosely in a diagonal across his body, he is naked. And he is carrying a small umbrella.

'G'day,' he says. He has the faint twang of Australian in his accent, but his English is perfect. His name is Olisarali Olibu, 'but you can call me Ollie,' he adds. He is a teacher. 'Teachers have umbrellas to carry papers in the rain,' he explains. But the collapsible umbrella is clearly a status symbol. It also stops the rain pouring down your naked body.

My ears have not been deceiving me. There is a touch of Australian in his speech. 'I learned to speak English in Sydney, mate,' he says. 'I lived there for nine bloody months.' A missionary brought him. Jinke–Sydney return. That's a lot of air miles.

We climb up a steep, winding track through trees to the summit of the hill. Our shoes slip wildly in the mud, which has turned to a quagmire in places. In his bare feet with his wide-splayed toes, Ollie moves sure-footedly ahead of us.

At the top of the hill the trees thin out. At the summit there are perhaps thirty little huts of grass and sticks, whose sloping thatch almost reaches down to the ground on either side. Interspersed between them are smaller huts, grain stores raised from the ground on legs to keep the termites out.

The women are bare-breasted but wear bits of hessian or animal hide round their waists, or sometimes hanging loosely from one shoulder. Round their ankles and wrists they wear a dozen or more dull metal bracelets, with a prominent brass one closest to the foot or hand. Each has a single row of beads around her neck. Their lips are huge and pendulous. A great sagging flap of flesh hangs down like an old tyre from their bottom lip. Not a good look.

Many of the women have painted their bodies and faces with a stark whitewash, not normal attire for grinding corn, which is what they are engaged in. Some of them produce large plates of baked mud – four to six inches in diameter – and insert them into their lower lips. They look like table-tennis bats dangling from their mouths. In Mursi culture these labial plates are signs – no one can explain quite why – of great beauty and wealth. Some say it began so as to make the women unattractive to the slave-raiding parties terrorising the area. There's only one problem with that theory: the Mursi think they look cute. Over time the slits in their lips are stretched wider and wider. Some women have smaller plates slipped into similar incisions in their earlobes.

Dogs roam everywhere. 'We have many dogs,' explains Ollie. 'They have good ears to hear wild animals or enemies. The Bodi are our enemy. Seven years ago we had a big war with them. The Bodi eat monkeys. Pah,' he exclaims in a 'can-you-believe-it' tone of incredulity, as if that is sufficient explanation for an enmity of immemorial duration.

Gradually the men start to appear – elegant, rangy, tall with the most extraordinary poise. A few are naked, or painted white. Most wear the coarse woollen cloth knotted at one shoulder, doing little for Western notions of modesty. And yes, they are certainly big boys.

Some drapes are striped, others plaid, others rough, undyed hessian. The men are from different villages and their drapes reflect different fashions in different groups. Either that or each village just bought a job lot of cloth. They wear copper bracelets around their upper arms; some have patterns shaved into their cropped hair, others wear loose bandanas round their heads that fall down upon their lithe shoulders. A few carry battered old rifles, often without bullets. One or two have Kalashnikovs. Most of the Mursi, however, carry spear-like sticks called *dongas* with which they engage in mad, punishing, yet graceful, stick-fighting competitions through which the young men display their bravery, establish their status and perhaps even attract a young woman to marry. Young men have been known to die in these contests. Serious injuries are common. Ollie pulls back his robe to reveal his *donga* scars. He smiles at our reaction and in his smile we catch a flash of teeth broken in the *donga* fights.

'Why do the Mursi like to hurt each other?' we ask.

'Why do the English like boxing?' counters Ollie.

It is a favourite rhetorical device of his. Ask why Mursi men and women have such elaborate scarification and body markings and he ripostes: 'Why do people in the West have pierced tongues and belly buttons?'

The men have been talking for a while. Now the conversation becomes heated. We will have to pay to film the Mursi, they tell us. Now they are arguing about which village should get the money, or whether it should be divided between them, and if so how. As they talk they spit. The Mursi are copious spitters.

As the men argue their children, shivering, naked in the rain, come up to us.

'*Charlie*,' I say, which is Mursi for hello.

'*Charlie*,' they reply, putting their hands inside our pockets.

'The Mursi have a singular attitude to private property,' one of our party suggests.

'No,' says one of our guides, 'they have just learned the negotiation that you call tourism. They will want one Ethiopian birr every time anyone takes a photograph. It's the going rate.'

The deal is done. A large wodge of Ethiopian birr is handed to the chief whose name is Olicoro. The Mursi men, in various states of disgruntlement, disappear whence they came.

We ask Ollie about the effect that contact with the outside world was having on his people. 'The government wants us to stay in this place and build a little town and have electricity and police and an army,' he replies. 'We don't want that so we said no.' Instead they will abandon their little settlement clinging precariously to the upper contours of the steep hill in a year or so, when they need to move on to fresh land. But not next year. Ollie points down to the other side of the hill to show us where the land has already been cleared and burned in preparation for the planting of next year's crop.

The Mursi have had contact with the Ethiopian state for a relatively short time. And the relationship is a fairly limited one. In return for paying taxes of twenty-five birr per head a year and refraining from hunting the wildlife that tourists want to see, the Mursi get food in famine years and health services when they are sick. 'It's a good deal,' Ollie admits.

He takes us to his house. In the yard his mother and mother-in-law are smoking a fag and grinding corn. One woman presses the grains of sorghum between two stones, a large flat one with a delve worn into it, and a grinding stone. The other bashes a second grinding stone with a rock to make it grind better. When she is satisfied the women swap stones.

A bucket of milk stands by the door. 'The cows are not here. They are two kilometres away,' says Ollie. 'The boys and young men are there to tend them. We use cow's urine to clean the bucket. There's something in it that helps keep the milk fresh.' Ollie smiles. He knows the kind of thing a tourist wants to hear.

The Mursi diet is mainly sorghum porridge, flavoured with leaves picked in the forest. 'We eat beef maybe once a month,' he adds. 'We season our food with salt which we buy from the Ari people. We don't use money. We pay in meat. It's barter,' he adds, educationally. Spooning the meat stew which has been prepared in our honour, we pretend to eat.

There is a tightly woven framework of grass around the doorframe, and beside it a grass door that fits snugly into the opening. 'In the dry season when there are no mosquitoes we sleep outside,' Ollie elaborates. 'But in the rainy season we take a brand from the fire each evening into the house and burn leaves. We fill the hut with smoke and then block the doorway with the woven door when the sun goes down.' Of all Africa's dire range of diseases malaria, from mosquito bites, is the single biggest killer of the continent's children. Four million kids die from it every year. Inside the hut is Ollie's week-old son. Ollie lifts a smouldering branch from the fire. He is taking no chances.

'But you will not sleep here,' he says. 'You should put up your tents in the clearing in the valley.'

'Okay,' we say. 'It's, er, safe down there is it? No wild animals or anything?'

'There are lion, leopard, cheetah, hyena, jackal, giraffe, buffalo and elephants hereabouts. But wild animals don't come here much. They hear the sound of men and keep away,' he says. We are not reassured. Then he adds: 'But keep away from the trees. A python dropped from one and killed a twelve-year-old girl last week.' Great. Well, yeah, g'night then. Bloody hell. We put up our tents and watch *Black Hawk Down* on the DVD. Beyond our gas lamp a group of Mursi gaze at us clustered round the tiny screen. 'Good movie.'

The night passes with nothing more dramatic than the whooping of a troop of black and white monkeys crashing through the trees. Next morning Ollie has already gone down from the hilltop. He has a meeting with a group of not necessarily welcome white missionaries who now employ him as a teacher and translator of texts. Like a minority of the Mursi in his area, Ollie has become a Christian, though, strikingly, the minority are all from the section of the tribe who will become the elders of the future. Opinion-formers . Ollie's father did not approve of his conversion, but now he is proud of his son's achievements. Ollie is currently working on rendering the Bible into Mursi, a language which, until seven years ago, had never been written down.

Talk of missionaries prompts one of our lot to repeat a joke told by Archbishop Desmond Tutu: 'When the missionaries came to Africa they had the Bible and we had the land. And then they said, "Let us pray." But when the prayer was over, and we opened our eyes, we found that we had the Bible and they had the land!'

Being a convert, Ollie has a more generous view. 'Until they came the Mursi were in thrall to some bad traditions,' he says. 'Many people still are. Just last week a boy died in another village because his family would not carry him to the missionaries' clinic. The old Mursi belief is that if you touch an ill person the bad spirits which have made him ill will be transferred to you. So they let him die when he could have been cured.'

Belief in the old spirits is still strong. 'The Mursi will not even cross a river at certain times because there is a river spirit who might be angered,' Ollie tells us. 'They believe that a sorcerer can curse you and you will die.' He had caused a stir not long before with his new-fangled Western beliefs. 'There was a sorcerer who was putting curses on Christians so that a lion would come and eat their cattle. I went to him and said: "Be careful; if you throw a stone at a tree it might bounce back and hit you." The very next day a lion came and ate the sorcerer's bull. Hah!'

Ollie has learned to tone down part of what he picked up in Australia. 'When I came back everybody said to me: "You smell terrible." I smelled of soap. But I'm all right now,' he adds, roaring with laughter. 'I smell of here again now, which I prefer. Sydney was big, with too many cars. I missed my family and friends. I didn't like living in one place. I want to move with my cattle and people. I came back to teach my people.' He is aged just thirty.

He has taught four other teachers, including his half-brother Milisha. They now teach sixty Mursi students in a school under the trees. For texts they use primers, which Ollie has written himself. Some are traditional Mursi tales, like the one called 'The Snake and the Monitor Lizard', which begins: 'A long time ago we Mursi shed our skins and there was no death. But death was given to us by the monitor lizard …' Others are health tracts, such as one on diarrhoea. 'Traditionally you keep diarrhoea a secret in Mursi culture,' he says, 'and the one thing your mother teaches you is that if you have it you must not drink anything whatsoever – which is medically 100 per cent the wrong advice …' He launches forth on a primary healthcare lecture.

He also writes a newspaper called the *Mursi News* every month. He produces a copy and reads out the start of a few stories:

'This one is about talks the elders are having with the Bodi about who can graze their cattle, and where. Some people wanted another war with the Bodi. The elders got together and killed a cow and had a meeting. They decided No War.

'This one is about how the Mursi had to pay the Ari people twenty cows in compensation after two Mursi men got drunk and killed someone from the Ari tribe.

'This one is about two Bodi men eaten by a lion. Hah!

'Here is a story about a man from the Surma tribe across the river who took a Mursi man's wife. The Mursi man had to pay the Surma a cow to get her back.' But that is cheap, he interpolates; the Mursi price for a bride is thirty-five cattle.

'Then there are stories about relations between Ethiopia and

Eritrea and the UN peacekeepers at the border. There's a warning about AIDS in Kenya. And a story headlined "100 die in air crash in Nigeria". I got that from the BBC World Service.'

Olicoro, the village headman, has agreed to see us. We climb the slippery mud slope to the village. Olicoro is a stately man with a ramrod-straight back, aged perhaps fifty. It's hard to tell. A figure of immense dignity, he had played no part in the argument the day before, but his ruling had resolved it. He is from the 'priestly' caste. Though he himself is not a priest.

The chief sports a wristwatch (which tells the wrong time) and an AK47 but his feet are bare and he wears only a drape of hooped cloth, which bears a label reading Made in China. 'When I was a boy we wore no clothes; now we do,' he says, though until they are eighteen the boys still go more or less naked. 'Then we fought with townspeople; now we don't. Things are better now. They will be better in the future.'

Olicoro has seen the future and he thinks it works. He was once taken by an anthropologist to the Ethiopian capital, several days' drive away, and an uncountable number of days' walk, not that anyone would have thought of walking there in the days when the emperors ruled the country. 'I have been to Addis Ababa. There I saw a house with electricity and water. It was fantastic. You just turn it on! I would like to live in Addis but I don't have the income to do that. Everything is there. People in the capital have no need to keep moving on to look for a place to grow food or good grass for the cattle.'

Intriguingly that is not the view of the one Mursi man who has experienced the so-called benefits of modern civilisation. 'We are much happier here than we would be in Sydney,' says Ollie. But there is nothing romantic about his worldview. 'That is not to say we do not want change. We would like a school building, and a clinic with doctors and nurses. We need education for our children so that they can argue with the Government. If that alters Mursi tradition over time that doesn't really matter. We will make our own choices.'

Indeed he has. His wife, Hoytigonyi, though she looks fourteen, is in her twenties, well past the age when she should traditionally have begun the process of stretching her lips by inserting ever-larger plates made from baked mud. Hoytigonyi's lips are untouched. 'We make our own choices,' Ollie says again, smiling. His new baby is called Solomon. Why did he choose that name? 'He was a man who above all else was wise.'

LANDSCAPE

Man has invariably altered the landscape wherever he has trodden. This is less true in Africa where the landscape has forced man to adapt to it. There are no imprints of man's passing here, except perhaps by accident. The deserts, forests, rivers and mountains remain unchanged, immovable, inviolate.

David Beckham in Africa

The River Nile gets serious up around the Blue Nile Falls. It tumbles in a vast gush over the rocks and launches itself on its long, long journey to the Mediterranean. It's a difficult place to get to and not many tourists make it, but if they do get there now they might be disappointed. They've built a dam upriver from the Falls so that even the mighty Nile can be turned off and on like a tap. If you don't time it right you could show up after hours of gruelling hardship and find a trickle resembling a domestic plumbing problem rather than the thunderous roar of triumphant nature.

I was there during the trickle hours. But that was okay because I'd seen it before in all its colossal grandeur. Now, however, the military helicopter crew from whom we were hitching a ride were getting restless. They wanted to get back to town to their girlfriends and already these bloody foreigners had held them up long enough.

As ever, a landing helicopter announces itself magnificently, even drowning out the sound of one of the biggest drops of water in the world. We had seen the local people running towards or away from us as we hovered down over their fields.

Some wore their togas and carried staves, others were in jeans or pants and T-shirts, and stood about while we descended. There is no particular curiosity about a helicopter. Like me they just like the noise and the magnificent ability to be a mechanical hummingbird.

Many years ago I landed on a plateau in the Ethiopian Highlands from which the people had never come down. They had lived and sustained themselves up there with maybe one or two of them occasionally going off somewhere else in that remoteness to get something they needed. After we had descended from the machine, they gradually approached us, undaunted by this thing dropping out of the sky but more agog and curious at the ugliness of the first white people they had ever seen. One said, 'I have heard of white people but never seen one.' She sounded disappointed. But the helicopter more than made up for that. They stared at us and we at them and then the girls did something wonderful and universally feminine: they looked at their reflections in the helicopter wing mirrors, hysterical at the sight of themselves for the first time in their lives. At first they laughed and then they became confused. They touched their own faces as they stared in the mirror. I didn't know what was up at first but then I twigged. The mirrors were all convex, so as to give the helicopter pilot all-round vision. In this fish-eye view these girls saw their distorted, funfair, trick-mirror faces. They clearly couldn't relate what they felt were their own features to their convex reflection; they couldn't understand how, when they looked at their friends they were normal, but their own image appeared hideously deformed. As the science of optics dawned upon them they collapsed into hysterical laughter, just as at a funfair, or they preened and admired their own beauty in the chrome side panels of the helicopter. The men contented themselves with checking out the rotors and the engines and examining our cameras.

Now here at the Falls some children stood around frankly staring at us in open curiosity. One whispered something. I said, 'Sorry?' He whispered again. The interpreter barked at this shy adolescent to speak up.

'David Beckham,' he said.

Bloody hell. You couldn't go anywhere and escape the Great Blond

One, I was sick of it. 'Wherrre rrr hyew frrrim?' we would inevitably be asked in much-practised, husky English. 'England.' There would be a pause of wonder, a sort of headshaking like Indian people do, as the lightening-bolt information was absorbed. Then would come the inevitable, 'England. David Beckham.' Yes, thank you very much, we know. That's very nice, thank you. And then, 'He miss goal Euro 2000.' Yes, we KNOW that, thank you very much.

The entire continent is gripped by the Blond Beauty. He is all over the place. He is without doubt the biggest brand in Africa, as the marketing men would say. Coca-Cola, BBC World Service and David Beckham. And of the three Beckham is probably the biggest. They listen to the World Service to hear the football and they drink Coke while listening to the exploits of their hero.

'He marry babe.' Look, shut up. We know all of that. Don't you realise I am trying to pretend that I am in this hugely and adventurously remote part of the world that no one has ever been to and you keep crapping on about David bloody Beckham.

Satellite dishes point straight up at the Equator. There's no pissing about trying to angle it to 35 degrees or whatever. Boosh, up it goes, point straight up at the sky, thank you very much, and bingo, Arsenal v Man U live.

More Beckham.

We are three hundred miles north of Timbuktu. There is nothing. Absolutely nothing for hundreds and hundreds of miles. There is no electricity. No satellite. No phone signal. We're standing around a well in the middle of nowhere, watching kids playing football with a ball of dried camel dung. I bet the interpreter that the kids here have heard of Beckham. He says 'No, it would not be possible.'

'Who's David Beckham?' he asks, in a language possibly spoken by sixty people.

A hand shoots up. 'Footballer.'

The interpreter and I are agog.

'Yes, but he does not know who he plays for.'

'Okay. Ask'.

A little chap of about seven shoots his hand up. The interpreter nods to him.

'Who does Beckham play for?'

'Mali,' he confidently pipes.

Everyone wears the T-shirt. Everyone has the poster. From the markets of Mopti to the lads in Lalibela they're worshipping at the shrine. He is huge. In the desert I saw the name. In the rainforest the picture. And now this git in a toga was waving a ragged piece of printed paper at me. It was in Amharic. What does he want now, I wondered.

'Prrremerrship,' he said, typically rolling the r's. Oh Christ, I thought, seriously considering rolling his arse. Can you never get away from it? He opened the page. Inside were badly printed photographs of people impossibly familiar to me, and also, unfortunately, to him.

'Rrrrooney,' he pointed in glum seriousness then looked at me for a response. 'Yes,' I replied heavily. The finger traced down. 'Sherrrerrr.' That's right. And so it went until the pin-up boy in the centre. 'Beckham.'

In Lalibela a fight broke out. I was asked by a boy of eleven with thirty-five goats if I was watching the match that night. 'Which one?' I foolishly enquired to their obvious dismay, as if every moron in town knew who was playing and was going to be watching. Which they probably did. And were. 'Arrsnl-Lvrrpull eight o'clug kiguff.' I should have ended the conversation there but I unfortunately asked in my best, most ingratiating, 'getting-along-with-the-natives' voice, 'And who do you support?' The boy looked around and said, 'Arssnl'. There was uproar. His friends jeered and spat. 'Last week he was Lvrrpull. They lose, now he Arrsnl. We always support Arrsnl.' My interlocutor was shamefaced and sort of shuffled and did the Tigrayan version of 'yeah, well...'

But I was in the middle of nowhere. A sacred monastic town of pilgrims, famous-ish for its eleven ancient underground cathedrals. There is barely power in the market town. This is the epicentre of the great recurring Ethiopian famines. Arsenal v Liverpool? What's going on? But it's fantastic, isn't it? We can talk together about something we both know and like. We can discuss through the medium of football the modern world. It is no longer the poor African and the well-heeled European; it's football fans. Beckham isn't white; he's a star footballer. Thierry Henry isn't a black African; he's a great athlete. Along the upper reaches of the Blue Nile, in the roasting bar shacks of Lokichoggio, where the blackboards on the street advertise the English premiership matches and the tribal Turkana and Toposi people mingle with the UN aircrews watching these teams battle it out on drizzly February afternoons in the north of England; where they sit under a hammer-blow sun shouting their team to victory across the sand and mountains and oceans and fields until it resonates like a huge Blue Nile Falls of tumbling sound around the Kop or Stamford Bridge or the Chief God's Old Trafford – this is where the modern world joins us together in despair or jubilation. In shared emotion. In shared fandom. It is where the chasm is bridged and we talk as equals a common language of understanding and appreciation.

But, bloody hell, I'd still love to go somewhere, anywhere, in Africa where they've never heard of David Beckham. Where the beautiful boy is not grinning winningly at me from every market stall or paper seller in the continent.

One day I tried this.

'Wherrre rrrr hyew frrrim?'

'Ireland.'

Now I have them, I thought, as the eyes glazed and the head began to nod, absorb the fact and locate the country. I waited.

'aRrroy Keane,' he said.

What can you do?

23 Pairs of Trainers

It was all very delicate. After all, these were serious killers. Or they had been a few weeks back. They didn't look it, mind. Just kids with an attitude, really.

Perhaps inevitably, it was the smallest one who was the most gone. The one who had been sitting on the doorstep feigning indifference whilst glancing sideways at us. The spookiest. The most lost.

The carers, big African women capable of anything, had told us it was difficult. These were the hard cases recently arrived from the war and not yet found homes. They were an unsettling presence to the older hands who had already left for their foster homes for the evening. They would return the following day to carry on their lessons, both academic and social. Old and new hands had to re-learn how to live amongst people without hurting or killing them. This lot varied in age from ten to eighteen.

The two we had asked to talk to appeared sullen and non-committal, but were also proud to have been picked out. Having first refused to have anything to do with us the others now began to demand payment, and in the end we agreed to interview all of them.

They were children after all. They were afraid after all. Some were getting the dreams, but most felt it was war – and you either killed or you were killed. But they didn't know if others would understand that. Their families. Their neighbours and friends. If any of them were still around or remembered them. Or would even have them near them. Most were afraid of a future in which they were fit for nothing. Their friends would be educated, could do things, could get jobs, whereas they had just fought, and could do nothing but kill. They would be stupid. People would laugh. What could they do, they pleaded. One thoughtful boy almost cried for his lost life and bleak future.

Their stories were all the same. Their fears were all the same. Their greatest fear was that all they could now do was kill; that they would be forced, by circumstance and by their inability to do anything else, to do again that which they had been taught since childhood.

At some point the small one marched towards us, stiff-backed and -legged in perfect military step. Snapping to a halt, he stared hard at us and said absolutely nothing. His body quivered with its taut rigidity. His eyes blazed. He looked a lethal ten-year-old. The mama calmed him and he spat something towards us. Meanwhile the others loafed about looking incuriously at this tableau. This guy was the boss.

He was fifteen and had been in the army for five years. He was a sergeant. He was fearless, unafraid, dead to understanding. He was a bush automaton. He killed, he ate, he shat, he slept, he marched, moved on, fucked, killed and ate. He had no knowledge any longer of what it was to be a person.

I didn't like him. Oh I'd met tyrants, torturers and thugs of all sorts before, and some I'd liked. Weird, I know. Revolting even. Had they not stunk of murder, one might almost have enjoyed the company. But this little one scared me.

The small sergeant was unapologetic. He calmly laid before us his many crimes. He unrolled his horrors unashamedly. He smirked at our discomfort and couldn't comprehend our scruples. He liked the army. Liked the war. Was prepared to give this civilian thing a go but if it didn't work out, well…

He slouched in a chair, legs splayed in front of him. There was no hesitancy in his reporting. It would be nice to say that his eyes were dead but the opposite is true: they purely sparkled in the telling. I was sure we hadn't heard the last of this one. It was only when he'd finished frightening us with his tale that I glimpsed the child and not the ageless killer.

The others were afraid of him. He would simply look at them and sometimes bark a peremptory word. They towered above him but he terrified them. Now he negotiated.

They didn't want money. Could we buy them some schoolbooks? No. Pens, pencils, clothes? No. They wanted trainers. Every kid wore trainers and they had army boots which shamed them or rubber Wellington boots which humiliated them. They wanted brand logo-ed trainers. Nike, Adidas, whatever. They wanted membership to the global confederation of teendom. They wanted to be cool – all of them. They told us to get them in the market. We asked if that was what they all wanted. They agreed. Yes, it was.

It was getting dark. We promised to return in the morning with the trainers. The small one was animated now. He didn't ask for more than the others, and he never once argued for himself – always for the group. He felt he had done well. He laughed with the others and glanced for approval at the maternal women standing watching by the veranda, hands folded on their aprons. One smiled at him. Suddenly he snapped one step backwards and flung his hand rigidly to his forehead in a perfect British Army salute. The hand quivered at his temple, the little finger poised delicately as if for afternoon tea. His face was taut. We smiled.

As we turned to go he spoke. Quite clearly. Quite calmly. 'If you do not return by midday tomorrow, we will burn this building.' The women remained impassive.

We bought shoes for all the children in the school. Twenty three pairs of trainers. I didn't return. I didn't want to see the little creep again.

The Boy Whose Parents Wouldn't Let Him Go to School

You cannot, as a white man, be alone for long in Africa. I was sitting one day on a ridge at the side of a steep, steep valley in the highlands of Ethiopia. The hillside fell away precipitously five or six hundred feet. Below, a vast vale in the mountain plateau stretched before me. I could see for thirty or forty miles or more. There was no one in sight.

Within a few minutes I heard a far-off shout. I could see nothing. Then I made out a tiny figure on the other side of the great valley. It was a man – or perhaps a child – with a flock of tiny goats. He was waving to me. Across the vast distance the voice carried as clearly as the tinkling of the bells around the goats' necks.

The figure left his goats and began to make his way towards me. For a long time I watched as he moved down the other side of the valley, then out of sight for a considerable time, before he reappeared at the bottom of my hill. Time seemed suspended as I watched him climb. A man. No, a boy. He was wearing a blue shift. A biblical figure in a timeless landscape. He climbed. He climbed.

'Where's yer goats?' I asked him as he climbed to my vantage point beside a lone, wind-bent tree. He looked perplexed, even when the question was translated. He sat down beside me, entirely comfortable with my proximity and strangeness.

'I hope you haven't lost 'em. You'll be in serious trouble if you have.' He looked even more perplexed.

Gradually the interpreter teased out his story. That was his job: goatherd. He spent most of his day, every day, looking after the animals. His ambition was to go to school. But his parents wouldn't let him.

In the West we have clear views on this. Kids should go to school. Parents who don't see the benefits are just backward. In Africa it's a bit more complicated than that. Mum and Dad don't want to lose the services of their goatherd. That's not in the family's interest. Kids have distinct and valuable jobs in African families.

People who bang on about birth control and the population explosion often don't understand this. There are lots of jobs to do when you live on the edge of subsistence. It takes four hours to walk to the places where you can gather firewood, so you need a kid whose job that is. It takes all day to walk the cattle to the far-off waterhole, so you need a kid to do that. It takes two hours to carry water from the borehole to the family home, so you need a kid to help Mum do that. It takes all day to plough a stony field, where rocks have to be weeded from the ground in huge quantities before you can apply the single-bladed plough pulled by the only ox you can afford to hire, so it takes two kids and their dad all day to do it. Take away the necessity to do all those immensely time-consuming chores and the birth rate falls naturally, as it has done in the developed world. Especially if social networks are in place to look after people in their old age; without them parents need large families as a kind of insurance policy, especially on a continent where four million children die every year before they reach their fifth birthday.

The young lad looked at me. Would he ever get to school, I wondered. Perhaps his parents feared, quite justifiably, that an educated child would find that no job was available when he or she left school – and would by then have been made discontent by the lot of his parents and forebears. And he was a boy. Had he been, like my four kids back home, a girl, I thought, his chances of schooling would be even less. But again, it is far from clear whether this reflects, as Westerners often assume, some deep-rooted African prejudice against women, or whether it tells us something about the deeper social changes that are taking place in Africa, as elsewhere, about how men feel increasingly marginalised and alienated and – as one African matriarch told me only days before – reduced to the status of 'a mere sperm bank'.

The boy looked at me. He had something very different on his mind.

'Can I have your bottle?' he asked. He was looking at the empty plastic water bottle I was still holding.

'Sure,' I said, suddenly understanding that my refuse would make his life easier.

So happy with so little. I hoped one day he'd go to school. Imagine all those minds we are losing among the goaty mountains of the world.

A Warlord

The warlord was beautiful. Tall, immaculately dressed in a crisp, clean, freshly ironed white cotton shirt, he wore perfectly tailored trousers, beige stretch-cotton socks and brown Italian loafers. He was about six foot three, elegantly thin with a lightly tanned, long, copper face, a straight, slightly hooked nose and grey wavy hair swept back from a fine forehead and cut at the collar. He was about seventy-five.

He waved me to a seat at the table on the roof terrace of the restaurant that looked out over the dusty town. The smell of fish drifted up to us when the evening breeze changed direction and eased in from the beach a mile away. It occasionally carried with it the heavy slurping sound of the slow waves of the thick, warm oily sea.

His English was perfect and his life had been extraordinary.

The English colonial powers had trained him to be a police sergeant. As independence approached, they offered him and a colleague the opportunity to be head of the police or the army. He chose the police and was sent to Scotland Yard for training. His friend, meanwhile, went to Italy, the other colonial power, for his military training.

The British had bought him an expensive air ticket which he traded in for a cheap round-the-world one. After completing his training in London he applied for entrance to one of the American Ivy League colleges. He was extremely bright and was accepted by

Yale or one of the others. Before he began his studies he embarked on his world tour, going first to Rome to see his friend in the military college and then on to Paris, Moscow and eventually New York.

As we talked, food continued to arrive. Stews, chewy goat meat, fish, spinach and onions, carrots. We drank a thin wine and an unspecified whisky, for which I was wildly grateful in this dry Islamic country.

He didn't monopolise the conversation. He spoke softly but proudly of his life. As one might expect of an Ivy League scholar, he was informed and erudite. The little fairy lights on the roof swung gently on their strings. Wood smoke curled up from the street. The scattered fluorescent tubes around the town blinked and flickered. Sometimes they fizzed and went out altogether. The power on the rooftop, however, remained on.

At the bottom of the narrow, white-painted stairs that led to the roof stood two men with Kalashnikovs. Outside were two technicals, the lethal mounted cannon on a Toyota flatbed jeep. This calm, elegant man with the impeccable manners dipping his bread into the communal spicy stew was engaged in an on-off civil war and a permanent feud. He told jokes and quoted scripture and the Koran.

When I had first arrived I had been taken from the plane and placed under house arrest. A polite letter was handed to me stressing that this was for both my comfort and protection. However, I was under no circumstances to leave the building. I stayed in that sweltering hotel room with the inadequate overhead fan for a while and got bored. 'To hell with it,' I thought and walked out of the door and past the man with the gun. He shouted something to me and I half-turned and said, 'Just going for a walk.' He shouted again, a little pleadingly this time I thought. At the entrance to the hotel were two other men with guns. Wiry little men. Black, black hair, piercing desert eyes. Everyone shouted. 'Just going for a walk,' I repeated as I passed them. They shouted louder, following me down the street, tugging at me. I was afraid but furious. 'Fuck off,' I screamed into the faces of one of the men. He didn't flinch but shouted right back at me. It was when they stopped following me that I got very frightened. I knew these men killed but they believed themselves to be soldiers. They killed for ancient reasons. Maybe they were unsure about me. Maybe it was a bigger mistake to shoot me than simply follow me. Perhaps they would be in serious trouble if I ended up being shot.

But I didn't know that. Though facing and walking forward, my back ached with the anticipation of a bullet. I dared not look back. My back arched forward, waiting. My legs felt ungainly, straight and stiff. I saw a café with two old men playing chess on a plastic table on the roadside. I tried to assay a casualness I did not feel and kicked playfully at the countless carrier bags that blew like plastic dust devils haphazardly down the quiet, dirty, dusty road. I sat down beside them. They looked up and nodded in greeting. I said hello and looked back. The soldiers had gone.

I felt very brave. One day I'll write about this, I thought, and it will appear heroically mad. People will want to have these adventures and think how much they'd like to come to places like this. But they'd be wrong. That was the compensation I allowed myself for my stupidity, my pride and this dead, fishy, smotheringly humid hellhole.

I asked for fizzy orange and sat back trying to collect myself, wondered what was going to happen next and feigned interest in the outcome of the chess game.

It was lovely up on the roof. The lights had all gone out below and, though the fairy lights obscured them slightly, if you walked to the roof's edge and looked up, the sky was pitted forever with the most blinding of lights. Big African sky. Big African night stretching all the way across the whole gorgeous continent. Fishy, dusty, briney, frankincense and wood night softly blowing around my cooling body.

'Somalia became independent,' the beautiful warlord explained.

'My friend returned from Italy and became a general.' The new independent Somalian president went to America to visit the president of the US. He was invited to dinner at the White House by President Eisenhower. But who should the Somalis invite along as their party? A quick trawl of notable Somalis in the US produced our friend studying in Yale. His invitation arrived unexpectedly but excitingly. He travelled to Washington and ate with the president and First Lady and their guests who included the young Senator John F. Kennedy and his beautiful wife.

The warlord paused and smiled at the memory. He sipped his water and refilled my whisky glass.

I was on my second fizzy orange and needing to get into the shade when the new letter arrived. The old boys had stopped playing chess now and were sitting silently, looking at the empty street and the plastic shopping bags gathering about the stick that held the fluorescent tube with the wires dangling worryingly off a nearby wall.

The runner waited, staring at me. What now? The letter was on the same paper as the one that had informed me of my house arrest. It was signed by the warlord General Whatshisname. Unlike the previous missive, which was at best peremptory in tone, this was effusive in the Arabic style and a thousand million greetings were pressed upon my noble forehead and all my ancestors in welcome to their unworthy country.

No mention of the house arrest. No mention of the previous note at all. Not a whisper about the Great House Arrest Bust Out I had recently perpetrated and the subsequent perambulatory 'chase'. No, all was immense sweetness and infinite light. They awaited me with barely contained delight and anticipation. Goats were to be slaughtered and several virgins deflowered in my honour. That sort of thing.

My new friend the general returned to Somalia and took charge of the police. His friend ran the army. Unfortunately his friend and his friend's clan had inappropriately undemocratic ambitions. Ones that involved a coup d'état. My general couldn't, with great regret, go along with this and when his old friend was successful in overthrowing the president with whom the general had broken bread over the White House Delft and cutlery, our elegant warlord had to do a runner. But now his clan was in trouble and as clan leader he had to return and summon a tol – a meeting of clan elders – who subsequently swore undying enmity to his old friend, now the illegal and ruthless new president. War.

He was caught and put in solitary confinement for twelve years. Twelve years! Solitary confinement in some desert hellhole.

His soft voice paused here, and almost in a trance he looked out over the roof for a moment, then at the stars, and sighed. There was a long silence, but not an awkward one, just a break in an epic that required consideration. The unexpected history of a country lived through an extraordinary life. One of the guards from the stairs came up to get some Cokes for the guys in the technical. The other five diners on the other tables had now gone.

One thing happened to him in prison that he can never forget. There was another man in the cell beside his. He knew he was there because of the occasional guard activity and because he would hear him singing the Koran. He had no sacred book with him. Nor was he allowed it though he begged and petitioned his old friend the illegitimate president. He never received a reply.

The years passed in the utter silence of the desert. One night – and he does not know how – a sliver of printed paper was pushed silently under his door. It was a page of the Koran torn from his fellow prisoner's book. He could hardly believe it. He dared not touch it. He had seen nothing for years. Heard no one but himself and his mutterings. Now, lightly caught in the underdoor draught, this sliver appeared to glow. The writing seemed alive. Words danced and shone. As in a religious drama the true word seemed literally to light the room. To burn and be incandescent. He snatched the paper. And read the suras. They were redemption. He pounded his thanks on the prison wall. He broke down and sobbed. He chanted and read aloud the words of the Prophet (may his name be praised). He shouted them from the top of his lungs and no one said anything.

One day they let him go. He did not know why. Apparently the illegitimate president had been overthrown by another. He asked who it was and was told it was a man called Aideed. This man, though he did not know it, had been his fellow prisoner for years. It was he who had given him the gift more sacred than water. He had been released years before although the general did not know this. Aideed was now president and had declared a general amnesty.

The general poured water for himself and ignored my attempt to refuse more whisky. He sat back. 'I will never fight him. That is my vow. I will never fight him. Although my friends and allies are arrayed against him, I will never forget. So now when you see the others, tell them this man you see here owes more than his life; this general owes his soul to Aideed. Yes, he is a bad man and, yes, he is not good for my land or my people and, yes, perhaps he will kill me. But that is his right. He gave me my life and he can take it. I will not fight him. When I had nothing he gave me everything. The others do not understand this but they must. Tell them when you see them.'

He paused. I was a little drunk by now. The air was freshening. The old, elegant, educated, learned and experienced gentleman who had fought wars, who had dined at the White House and trained at Scotland Yard, who had studied at Yale and visited the world lay back in his chair. He brushed some crumbs from his lap and reached into his breast pocket. He pulled out a worn, inscribed leather wallet and extracted from it a piece of paper. Carefully he unfolded it and laid it on the table. It was torn at one edge as though ripped from a book. It was creased permanently along its folds. It was dirty at its edges and worn from being interminably thumbed and it lay there on the table and shivered gently in the fish-scented night air, as if it was alive. As it must have looked that night in the general's desert prison as it lay on the floor fluttering in the underdoor draught.

The handsome warlord did not look at it as he rose from the table, hitched his immaculately tailored trouser legs and knelt down on the roof facing east. He bowed his head until it touched the floor and softly began to intone the words on the page that fluttered on the table in front of me.

I looked out over the roof towards the sea and felt the cooling breeze. I drained the rest of my whisky.

The Wheelbarrow

Inside the governor's compound the militia were loafing around. They were sort of sprawled everywhere, wearing a motley collection of jumpers, T-shirts and camouflage stuff. A few had new army-style boots, but most wore flip-flops, battered boots without laces or green wellington boots. This last, a touch of the Home Counties or Sloane Square, a little out of place in this part of anarchic Somalia.

When a superior arrived, those not asleep tried to look vaguely alert, as if they were just itching for something to do. But things had calmed down now the 'peace' talks were underway in another country a thousand miles away, so there was really nothing more for them to do than chew khat, get stoned, shoot into the air sometimes, lackadaisically patrol the port, man a sleepy roadblock, extract some money from a ship's captain or lorry driver. And try and stay alert to who might take control at any minute while the chief was away so they could switch sides on time.

The governor's office was quite grand. The heavy drapes were drawn against the sun and the walls were hung with a faded brocade, giving it the inappropriate air of a fifteenth-century Venetian palazzo. The governor, too, had to be alert to straws in the wind. How the talks were going. Who was up and who down, who in, who out. Maybe it was him. Maybe he was out. Maybe the chief away in the other country was being fed stuff by a real traitor in order to oust him, or maybe the chief thought he was getting too big in the chief's absence. All this one had to guard against. It got very wearing sometimes.

You certainly couldn't tell what those wired hopheads outside were saying or cooking up. No, the only way a governor could be safe was to surround himself at all times with his oldest trusted comrades, the ones he had something on. Or knew everything about. Who owed their position to him. Not that that meant anything. Ho-hum.

Two stick-thin boys with the inevitable well-worn AK47s scrutinised passes at the entrance to the governor's building. They examined the voluminous permission stamps. Refused, as a matter of course, to acknowledge that their newly autonomous province had an office in London, Paris or Brussels. They were right in a way. It wasn't really an office, more a kind of bare room with a table, a map of the motherland on the pale green wall and some papers, a typewriter and an official rubber stamp. A country is wholly illegitimate without its rubber seal and equally obviously cannot possibly exist if it has no official stamp. Clearly, then, everything was invalid, suspicious, and at least several hours of delay seemed called for.

We stood and waited. And waited. Suddenly there then arose the most dreadful shouting. Peremptory barked conversation is the norm in Somalia. This may have something to do with the fact that there is no 'please' or 'thank you' in the lingo but, anyway, it sounds harsh and, frankly, downright rude. Perhaps, it is inevitable with the absence of the normal courtesies present in the mother tongue. At any rate, the door was suddenly thrust open and a man in a wheelbarrow began shouting at the startled boys fumbling with the sheaf of papers.

He was a torso. An upper body in a wheelbarrow. He had on Arab headgear and a dirty white tunic that billowed out around what would have been his hips inside the garden wheelbarrow. The barrow was tilted forward ready for action and at a precipitous angle. The barking torso had his AK47 resting on the rim of the barrow, making

Toposi, southern Sudan

Boy in Timbuktu

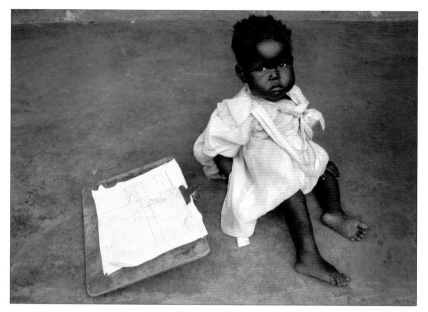

Her medical chart, Kitgum, Uganda

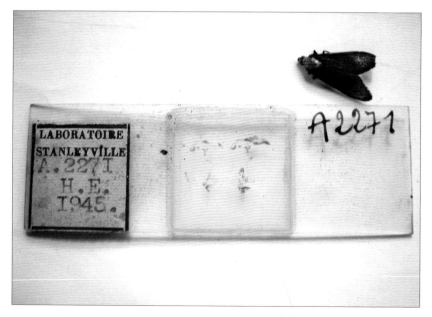

The suspect files of Kisangani

On the plane

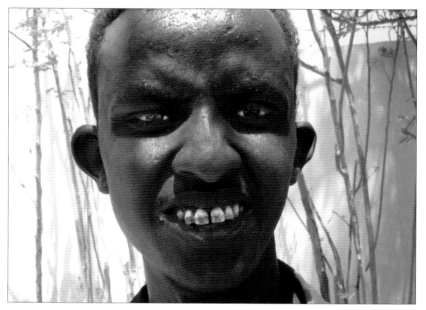

Wired Greeen Spittle

My Private Army

Cybercafe

Arouane, Sahara

Jinka, Ethiopia

Harriet and Harry Potter, child witches, DRC

The boy whose parents wouldn't let him go to school

Lalibela, Ethiopia

Grumpy Mursi teenager, southern Ethiopia

an exceedingly dangerous gardening tool. His beard was dyed a lurid red-orange, the same colour favoured by Russian hookers and much admired by ageing gents in these parts. He had one eye. He shouted some more at the thoroughly cowed doormen and was pulled backwards inside by the as yet unseen barrow handler. Before the door closed behind the retreating implement, he motioned for us to follow.

Inside was a shallow hallway. To the left was a corridor and on the right the door to the governor's office. The wheelbarrow was parked sideways flush to the wall and was now straightened. Its pusher had retreated to a corner of the hall and had lain down on a mat, his head propped on a hand. He gazed at us with dull indifference. Barrowman cradled his machine gun and squatted in the barrow saying nothing. We waited.

We tried not to stare. There was no sound. Just the pusher, the red-bearded torso in the barrow and us. We smiled a lot in his direction. He didn't respond. Once he hawked a gollop of phlegm down the hall away from us in one whiplashing motion of his head. The barrow pusher was asleep.

After what seemed like an age, the torso suddenly barked something at the door he was facing and the pusher roused himself from behind, tilted the barrow forward and pushed towards the governor's door. Barrowman knocked and was wheeled in. A few minutes later he came out with a tea tray balanced across the barrow rim. One hand steadied the tray, the other kept hold of the gun. He nodded to the tea and us. We grinned wildly and accepted. He masterfully lifted the tea, poured expertly from a height, stirred in vast amounts of sugar and, still holding the gun, still tilted perilously towards us, handed the glass cups around and was then pulled backwards into position. Nothing else was said and again we waited.

The governor eventually saw us. We paid him a fortune, on top of the one we'd already paid before arriving. Then he promised us thirty-four fully armed soldiers and two cannon-mounted vehicles to 'guard' us and we paid for that as well and then we left. The barrow guard was wheeled in front of us as we left, leading the way through the still-loafing soldiery who moved smartly out of his way. He glared at them and we could see their fear.

We heard later that night after the curfew, when only the dogs barked and the hyenas came in to eat the rubbish and make that awful noise, and nothing moved on the streets and our great metal compound was safely shuttered and the guards guarded, that Barrowman went to battle in his wheelbarrow. He was vicious and cruel. Sliding forward, he would charge full tilt towards the enemy. If, during the fighting, he felt he was being pushed too slowly, he would spin round and summarily shoot dead the laggardly pusher, sit bolt upright and threaten to shoot the nearest fighter if he wouldn't immediately push him running full speed towards the enemy. By definition he fired low, so equally by definition it was far more likely the barrow pusher would get shot. Pushing necessarily unarmed and upright as he ran, rather than the pushee. Let's face it, if you missed the torso who else was going to get it? It brings a whole new concept to the field of armoured fighting. Full-armoured garden-tool attack.

The torso lived for the governor. The governor for his part knew the torso was loathed and feared. He could never get another job. It was perfect for the two of them. And so day after day the wheelbarrow, and its half-man occupant, was parked in the tiled and marbled hall outside the governor's office with no other option but to sit there on the sloping, metal bottom cradling his gun and dyeing his beard and staring ferociously at the big front doors for the inevitable day when the traitors came and he would make his last stand. Or sit. Whatever.

The Border Post

I arrived somewhere from somewhere else. I was there for something or somebody else's business. The place didn't have a name that I was aware of. The pilot and I just sat at the GPS coordinates and this looked like it as we circled the blinding salt flats in the little four-seater Cessna. He found a spot, taxied to a halt, idled the engines, dumped me, revved the motors, took off and was gone in the whiteout.

My Ray-Bans, cool as I may have considered them, did nothing to stop the glare.

There was nothing on any side. The flats just extended in each direction until the land disappeared into the shimmering haze. After a bit, I could just make out a small box shape in front of me. I picked up my overnight bag and walked towards it, light bouncing up from the crystalline surface into my face.

The box shape became a gate and then I saw that it was a border post. A border post that seemed to hover in shimmering infinity. Alone. Unique. Solitary. No wires or fences stretching out from either side of the posts supporting the cross-pole. Just a border post, about three feet high, standing on its own. Being useless.

I had no idea what it was doing there. There wasn't supposed to be a new country here. There was no airport so it wasn't the entrance or exit to some flat piece of earth upon which I had just set foot. I hadn't seen any town, village or military base it could open on to or bar entry to. It was a stand-alone border with no one at it.

It was regulation barbershop, six feet wide with a rough painted red and white stripe and twin white uprights supporting the cross-stick. But what was the point? I could just walk round it. There was no one there. Just blazing salt flats and these three sticks.

I came up to it and dropped my bag. I didn't want to be shot. Maybe there were mines on either side. Maybe it was one of those random African roadblocks put there by yet more unpaid African soldiers. I peered over the pole. I leaned against it. The heat prickled my chest and stabbed at my back. No one. Lots more white stuff and nobody.

I picked up the bag and moved to the left post to go round it. I suppose I could have climbed over the thing but it seemed rude – disrespectful – and, anyway, I might have broken it. Besides, the effort was too much in the heat.

I had barely put one foot over the imaginary line abreast of the left upright and stretching into the boundless infinity when the most dreadful whistling started up, blowing and hallooing from my right. From absolutely nowhere, a scruffy, gun-toting militia guard appeared.

He ran towards me in a fumble, dusting his shirt and trying to smooth his trousers. He was officious and standing on his dignity. He had clearly been asleep and was now at pains to show that, despite the embarrassment of being found wanting in his vigilance, he was the authority in these parts. Wherever these parts might in fact be.

With his gun he motioned me back over the imaginary line. I withdrew my right foot and stood on one patch of ground while he stood on the patch in front of me. In his eyes, this was a more distinct, if not actually better, patch than mine, and it would only be after due examination, deliberation and by the authority invested in him that I would be able to join him on his clearly, though imaginary, delineated ground.

He assumed the weary air of customs officials all over the world. He looked around vaguely at the huge nothingness that surrounded us as though he were manning the busiest immigration line of the largest and most attractive-to-immigrants-wise metropolis in the world and made an irritated, beckoning motion with one hand. I reached into my breast pocket and produced the purple passport with the golden harp emblazoned proudly on its cover. He glared at this as though I had handed him a wodge of used lavatory paper.

Had I made some awful mistake? Was Ireland in fact the sworn enemy of this outpost of north-east Africa? Had I uncovered the secret shame of that most anti-imperial of nations? Was this some dreadful scene of hidden Irish imperialistic excess?

He examined the blank back cover of the passport, staring at it, daring it to give up its awful meaning before he wrung it forcefully from its flexible, fabric-woven, moisture-resistant Euro-conforming cover. He turned it slowly to the front again, the while staring at me balefully. It was scorching and I tried to affect nonchalance.

This lunatic could do anything. What was he doing here? And where was here? Someone was supposed to meet me, for Christ's sake. I shouldn't have landed until we had spotted the car. He stared at the Gaelic on the inside cover demanding passage for me or else the Paddies would getcha. And we fucking well would, I'm tellin' ye.

He nodded sagely at the incomprehensible language. Looked at the frankly flattering photograph of the quietly tousled, sober-minded, grimly serious and responsible face therein and then rather unflatteringly held the photograph up to my own now scorching red, sweating mien, the lank, badly cut hair dangling stringily around the greying, unshaven half-beard as though he couldn't see any resemblance whatsoever.

Eventually he found the monstrous stamp with the imperial eagle clutching a Marxist symbol in oak leaves, or something similarly inappropriate to whatever barren shithole this place lay amongst. The Great Stamp of Entry. The Hugely Important Ink Stamp of Immensity. The size of the rubber stamp increasing, of course, in direct proportion to the anonymity of the nation state concerned. National pride, thy name is Rubber Stamp.

He laboriously traced the permit dates and signatures with a stubby, bitten finger. These were the golden runes that would finally allow me to move over that imaginary line to the magical side upon which the guard now stood. It was all so real in his head. Here, it was clear, stood a Berlin Wall of imaginary concrete. A virtual Maginot Line. He'd been hanging out his washing on this salty Siegfried Line and there was clearly no space left for anyone else's dirty laundry. Failure to meet the required number of seals, stamps or, indeed, seriousness, would mean I would be stuck this side of the six-foot-wide gate in this nothingness until the next plane arrived back at the same point tomorrow. I tried to exude solemnity. I radiated respect. I tried to be helpful and to point things out.

This was a mistake.

He snatched the document away from me, turning sideways with it, staring manically sidelong at me and sneaking furtive glances at the passport, like a cheating schoolboy at the summer maths exams.

Eventually he closed the thing and smacked it down a few times in his palm, as if Jesuitically weighing up the advisability of allowing such a suspicious character as I into his sovereign motherland. The burden of authority lay very heavily on his already rounded shoulders at this point. He was, when all was said and done, the first and last guard against this foreign virus standing impertinently before him. It was down to him now. No one could help him. There was no one to turn to now. This was what it was all about. All the training. The years of struggle. It was on his head and his head alone. To this he, and only he, had been entrusted. This was his job, his honourable but onerous responsibility. No one had a clue who he was or, indeed, where he was, or what it was, but, sure as hell, he was going to do it. Whatever it was. But he and he alone knew that the 'it' was that if he hadn't been there, alert and ever ready, this ferengi, this azerene from another country he'd never even heard of, would simply have sauntered, bold as brass and twice as useless, up to this clearly visible border post and simply walked around it, cool as a bloody cucumber if you don't mind the how's yer fathers and kept fucking going!

The thought stunned him afresh. What was the point of even putting up a border post in the first fucking place if it was going to be ignored by every Tom, Dick or Harry who happened to fly by, in a Cessna C-190 mind you, in the middle of nowhere? Why bother? Let's just ignore the internationally agreed proprieties and allow everyone into the whole bloody country without so much as a by-your-leave-thank-you-very-much. And what about him? What would he do, for a start? He'd have no job. He'd be out of work, thank you very much. Oh no. Oh no, no, no … I smiled at him.

He said something in international guttural. He gobbed a remark at me. I tried a name. Someone I was supposed to meet. Someone who was supposed to mean something in this dump. Someone who had allegedly killed quite a few thousand people in excruciating circumstances. He smiled sardonically, I could have sworn said 'wanker', then nodded meaningfully and went 'Tch, tch, tch'. Had I made a serious mistake or was he just sucking his less than Californianly even teeth? He sighed suddenly.

It seemed he had come to a decision and, although it was with great and immense reluctance and, subject solely to the proviso that he'd keep a hawk eye on me during every step that I took in my visit, with a heavy heart he let me pass. He waved me on, my passport still in his hand. I stepped forward, utterly relieved. As I moved he went ballistic, slobbering incoherently with rage, and pushed me back forcefully with both hands. I was staggered. He screamed in my face from his side of the imaginary wireless, fenceless line and pointed at the pole beside us.

The tirade lasted two minutes and I realised with dawning

incredulity what it was he wanted. Wearily, I lifted the overnight bag again and moved six paces to my right. I now stood in the middle of the waist-high barbershop border pole. I put my bag down again. From his side of the imaginary line and standing at the left-hand-side post, he glared at me. Then he moved opposite me in the middle of his side of the border post. Standing pointlessly in this vast salt plain, in the middle of nowhere, flat and even for miles in every direction – front, back, from side to side – with three tiny sticks plonked arbitrarily somewhere on it; standing pointlessly in all this immensity on either side of the pole. Millions die for these things. Politics alter geography.

He nodded gravely and returned my passport. I said 'Thank you'. He saluted expertly and rigidly and said something like 'Welcome to Shitholio'. He smartly marched the one and a half paces to his right and heaved laboriously on the stone weight balancing the striped pole. The pole rose slowly, perfectly, until it juddered to a halt at the top of its arc. The gateway to the exact same piece of ground that I was already on was now open.

I dared not move. I stood on one side of the opened gate blinking behind my glasses at the 'lone and level sands' stretching far away. He shouldered his gun and, standing not exactly to attention, motioned me through to the land of plenty. I sighed and reached down for my bag again. I stood there clutching it, seized suddenly by an unexpected air of apprehension and expectation. I paused momentarily and then, with an elaborate pantomime of unconcernedness, I sauntered through.

Riveting

Even here there's a wrong side of the tracks.

To the left of the single-carriage, narrow-gauge track was the ruin. You could almost see it being slowly pulled apart by the enveloping greenery and carried off, grain by crumbling grain, by the various ranks of purposeful ants.

On one side of the track people loafed about the elegantly arched brick shelter that served as the train station for 25K. At some point some minor Belgian administrator, rotting away in the forgotten damp density, had decided to build himself a little Beaux Arts folly in the middle of the African jungle. Perhaps from imperial zeal, or to inspire awe for the colonial authority, or simply because he was longing for home, comfort and civilisation. And perhaps when he had finished, he had felt less lost. Less lonely. Less abandoned.

The station-master, or whatever he was, lived in an almost derelict grand manor house down a beaten path a few yards further up the line. It was rather like coming upon a living scene from some American Civil War movie. A plantation house after the Yankees had come through. And in fact this house was built at pretty much the same time. And despite all the decay and dereliction and shrapnel scars this house indubitably remained very much the right side of the tracks.

25K, as its name suggests, is twenty-five kilometres up the track from the central station at Kisangani, or Stanleyville as it was then.

This is where the great man came to after hacking his way into the centre of the huge continent in pursuit of glory and wealth (though I suspect that if it had been just glory alone, Stanley would have settled for that). Insanely but bravely, stupidly but heroically, preposterously and extraordinarily, in a genuine triumph of will – and with all the attendant baleful consequences which that phrase suggests – Stanley and his followers carried by hand and on their heads lumbering tonnes of Victorian engineering. Great sheets of heavy steel and cast iron plates, vast turbines, massive bolts, rivets and heavy machinery, hefted by fractious subordinates and rebellious porters through one thousand miles of malarial swamps, rivers, ravines, mountains, impenetrable jungles and hugely hostile peoples and labourers, to this very spot. Whereupon they assembled the lot, and steamed another thousand miles down the wondrous, vast Congo River until they reached the sea.

Stanley opened up both the river and the continent to the outside world, and in the following 150 years as much misery plied its way up and down the waterway as did trade. And Stanley was to blame for that. He had tried to sell the possibility he saw first to the British, then to the other powers, and finally to Leopold II of Belgium. And indeed Leopold took over the vast area, but not as a Belgian colony, as a private company, and proceeded to turn it into his own personal slave state. By the time he had finished with the Congo the original population of 20 million had been reduced to 8 million, and the glory that is Brussels had been built with the proceeds.

Stanley had presided over a lot of this and, understandably, there is little love or fond memories squandered on nostalgia for this Victorian adventurer. We moderns can recognise and admire his drive, nerve and determination and we can even understand and forgive the monstrous egotistical ambition. But we are thoroughly repulsed by the motive and the resolution, and completely abhor the greed, stupidity, cruelty and ignorance of it all. It is no use arguing that it was another time with different views and morals to ours: we cannot indulge in either historical romanticism or revisionism, for the sad, simple, unavoidable truth is that this great explorer knew what he was doing. Worse, he often admired the very people he was doing it to.

I found Stanley's little steamboat in the backyard of a padlocked, disused museum on the crest of a small hill overlooking the river he had plunged down. The museum is located on the outskirts of Kinshasa (neé Leopoldville). The Belgian king himself is still on a horsey plinth and stares morosely and big-beardedly away from the river over a shady little valley towards the town they built on his rubber riches. It's a well-kept place. There are a few caretakers still around and in the dusty hangars are rows of wooden, tribal artefacts that are familiar to us from the ethnic shops and auction houses that dot our own cities.

There's no big deal about Stanley's steamboat – the boat that opened up the scramble for Africa. The boat that ushered in the horror. That introduced Kurtz to immortality, that introduced the modern to the eternal, that imposed the state over the clan. That paved the way for the long catalogue of inept, unscrupulous, tyrannical, murderous, criminal thugs who have postured as leaders, both European and African, while ripping the heart and soul from the people who have suffered under them throughout this whole continent.

It's so small really. Ridiculous of course, to take it flat-packed as if it were an IKEA boat from Birmingham or wherever, and cart it across vast unknown lands. Huge and heavy of course, but when it was assembled with hardly a bolt missing it was pretty small. Cute even.

The bolts were loose and I took one. Another white man stealing something from the Congolese. Maybe I'll be arrested. But they didn't care about the boat anyway, and they can have it back if they want it. I just brought it home.

Think of where it's been, that rivet. Carried on porters' heads across how many terrors. Ploughing up and down one of the mightiest waterways in the world. And now here it is. On my bedroom window-sill alongside the whistling thorn from the Laetoli gorge in Tanzania and the kola nut from Ghana and the voodoo ring from Benin. A Birmingham rivet. Home again after 150 years.

So arrest me.

The Catholic Ummah

At mass in Lokichoggio I am overwhelmed by familiarity. Perhaps it is the exotic location but it is strangely and unexpectedly affecting to see or hear the rituals of my childhood re-enacted among the tribal peoples of the Sudanese/Kenyan border.

There is some warm-up preamble – lusty, haphazard singing – until Father Tom, their priest of forty years, emerges in his cope, chalice in hand. How odd that same priestly cadence, the same slow note rise at the end of the West of Ireland sentences. But now the mass is being celebrated in fluent Turkanan. Turkanan with a Limerick accent.

Children shuffle and fidget while their grandmothers glare at them until, exasperated beyond reason, they give the children their marching orders and send them peremptorily out of church – which is what they wanted in the first place. I should know.

Old ladies, young mothers, younger girls sit on the long benches in the breezeblock hangar that is their church, looking like they're backstage at some Vivienne Westwood fashion show from her late seventies tribal 'look'. The young mothers' children who are treated in Father Tom's clinic wear shirts and trousers while the young boys wear 50 Cent and Beckham T-shirts.

During the sermon, the familiar, vigorous nose picking among the elderly ladies, the examination, the cleaning of the nails. Harsh singing. Ostentatious coughing, spluttering, sniffing, snorting and gobbing straight after the consecration.

The part they like best though, unlike us, is the mortifying and frankly suspiciously Prod-like, Vatican II, shaking-hands-with-your-neighbour-as-a-sign-of-peace bit. Cripplingly embarrassing at home, here they launch into it with immense vim, vigour, and not a little gusto.

They don't just shake hands with the people beside, behind and in front of them; they do it to everyone in the church. No one escapes and it can take a long time. These stern, tough people crack a smile of welcome, the young girls beam, the children, released from their faux piety and boredom, dart around playing tag. Father Tom waits with the patience and understanding that forty years of knowing these people and their families brings. It's like midnight on New Year's Eve, just short of the stranger's snog.

And as they queue for the communion – their tongues, ears, lips, noses and eyebrows jangling with fabulous adornments, the huge weight of the necklaces, including discarded Bic lighters, strung decoratively along the bead strands – Father Tom tries to find some unimpeded passage to insert the Host. And then the beauty of the offering. What have they got to give? And yet they do. A few coins, saved and chucked in. For what? We knew ours back home were for the Little Black Babies, i.e. them. What are theirs for? The Little White Babies?

Nice idea. Nice to think so.

Here it is, then, the great universal boredom of the mass. The restless crowds, the communal gathering, the ritual of belonging. Belonging, like me, the lapsed unbeliever in Dun Laoghaire; or Father Tom, the kind, patient missionary in Limerick or the Turkana people of Africa; or all of us together in Lokichoggio. The Catholic Ummah.

Welcome Welcome Welcome

Someone clearly knew what was going on, but no one was telling me.

We had arrived in Somaliland to do a bit of filming. 'But first you will film and interview with the president,' an official said at the airport.

Er, no, we said, as politely as we could; that was not what we were here for. We wanted to go to the coast, to film at the spot where one morning, umpteen millennia ago, a group of early humans broke camp and set off walking north. You see, we explained, pre-historians reckon it happened somewhere by the shore of the Red Sea. But in those days there was no sea. What is now the continent of Africa was joined to the rest of the world by the Sinai peninsula. From that group, those first few individuals – the group may have been as small as fifty men, women and children – everyone in the rest of the world is descended. That's what we wanted to film.

'Very interesting,' said the official, very uninterested. 'But first you will film and interview with the president.'

Which is how we ended up in the office of the president in what looked like the kind of school they built in Ireland in the 1930s, interviewing the president – a very nice chap, it turned out – about a load of things we weren't really interested in.

'Now we will give you a feast,' he said, generously.

We went out of his carpeted air-conditioned rooms into the sticky

Hargeysa night. In the yard tables had been set out at the back for the minor dignitaries. At the front was a row of velour-clad sofas which, sitting out in the open, looked like a load of junk from a second-hand furniture store. We paraded along them and sat down in front of a tiny rickety stage.

'It is a Somalia tradition before eating,' explained a luminary from the Ministry of Culture, 'to sing a song to welcome an honoured guest. The tradition is that the performers improvise the lyrics as they go along.'

On to the stage came a group of disengaged looking musicians. They rambled up to their instruments – keyboard, bass and drums – and looked at me. Oh God, I thought, they're going to ask me to sing. Only they didn't. They just couldn't think of anything to sing about. They were traditional praise singers, but they couldn't think of anything I had done that was worth praising. Instead, three glammed-up Somali women bounded on to the flimsy podium, followed by four men in yellow sateen shirts and, for some inexplicable reason, a person in a Disneyland Mickey Mouse outfit. Somebody'd better praise something. In desperation, one of the gelled, yellow-bloused boys leapt forward gamely, grabbed a microphone and bellowed:

'Baaaaarb Geeeeeelduff.'

It spat and crackled in the approved overdriven electric sound of Africa, while the others grinned at their fellow praise-givers in admiration and relief. But what next?

'Baaaaarb Geeeeeelduff,' shouted praise singer 1 again, all inspiration evidently dried up and reaching desperately for his opening gambit.

They quickly got the hang of this and, in what can only be described as loose harmony, as one, *con brio*, they bawled:

'Baaaaarb Geeeeeelduff.'

The girls, catching on quickly, for there were no flies on them – except there were, millions of them, zooming in the fairy lights –

responded in a fair appropriation of a Somaliland Supremes, chimed:

'Wilcum, wilcum, wilcum.'

'Baaaaarb Geeeeeelduff,' they sang. 'Wilcum, wilcum, wilcum.

'Baaaaarb Geeeeeelduff. Wilcum.

'Baaaaarb Geeeeeelduff. Wilcum, wilcum, wilcum.

'Baaaaarb Geeeeeelduff wilcum.'

And that was just the first verse.

And so it went on, interspersed with one other line which I couldn't quite make out but which included the words 'Breeetish pop seeenger'. That was it. Over and over. I smiled in fixed appreciation.

The luminary looked at me for approval. I smiled more fixedly. He looked again, questioningly. Eventually, desperate for something to say I muttered: 'Actually I'm not Breetish. I'm Irish.'

The luminary looked horrified and clambered up on to the stage, or what approximated to a clamber for a man of his girth. He whispered urgently into the ears of the singers. They looked bemused and carried on singing:

'Baaaaarb Geeeeeelduff. Wilcum, wilcum, wilcum.

'Breetish!

'Baaaaarb Geeeeeelduff. Wilcum.

'Breetish!

'Baaaaarb Geeeeeelduff. Wilcum, wilcum, wilcum.

'Baaaaarb Geeeeeelduff wilcum.'

I kept on smiling and glanced surreptitiously at my watch. They carried on for another fifteen minutes before finally coming to a close with no real ending apart from a burst of giggles.

'What was so funny?' I couldn't resist asking afterwards.

'Your name,' the translator replied. 'In Somali geel means camel and duff means looter. Welcome, Sir Geel-duff, most honourable Breetish camel-looter.'

High praise indeed.

DOWN AT THE BAR, LALIBELA

A bar is indicated by an upturned can at the end of a stick, otherwise it looks a normal house. The beer is home-brew, i.e. disgusting. The liquid content is in inverse proportion to the material at a ratio of about 1:9,650. It is an almost solid stew of twigs, bits of burnt bits, leaves, islands of mud-churned foam, swirling amidst a dense, muddy, grey colour served in a used tin as above. The barmaids resemble Tanita Tikaram and Yasmin le Bon, respectively. Hmm. Two pints, please, and two more for the ladies.

Camel Bones and Antibiotics

It looked like the usual story. A pokey old hospital with no money, no drugs and an impotent and demoralised staff. I had seen them all over Africa. But this one was different.

In a dimly-lit room, with paint peeling from its walls, sat a man in his forties. His name was Mohamed Hassan and his leg stuck stiffly out from the thin blanket which was wrapped around his waist. His leg was healing. The bone had been shattered by a bullet. He was deliberately vague about how this had happened. He had gone to one of the other hospitals in the region but had been told his leg would have to go.

What was different was how his leg had been fixed. The man in charge of the little hospital, Dr Hussein Adan, explained. 'I took a bit of camel bone and sterilised it using a mixture of camel milk and a paste made from the bark of a desert shrub. Then I put it into his leg where his old bone had been, set it, and stitched him up. I gave him antibiotics to fight the infection.'

Dr Adan was both a traditional healer and a Western-trained doctor. His hospital mixed both traditional and modern medicine. He spent five years training in Somali folk medicine and seven in Western scientific medicine. He had been practising a combination of the two disciplines for thirty-four years. In that time he had performed the camel-bone trick thousands of times.

Okay, very impressive; but mending a leg is not exactly brain surgery. In the next ward was an eighteen-year-old girl. Her head had been crushed in a car crash. 'Her brain came out on the road,' the doctor explained. 'We brought her in, removed the stones and grit from her brain, and then used a mixture of frankincense and camel milk to clean it. Then we covered the hole in her head with a piece of goat bone.' The girl was sitting up in bed. 'She's not well but she's improving.'

All this was done on a black, plastic-covered bed beneath a single rotating ceiling fan. It was illuminated by an energy-saving bulb in the overhead fitting and one of those handheld lights which was a bare bulb encased in a metal mesh – the kind of thing car mechanics use to look under your chassis.

From this unlikely setting Dr Adan performed operations of great delicacy. In the next ward sat a fourteen-year-old boy who had been attacked by a hyena. His jaw had been broken in four places, which the amazing doctor repaired before stitching the boy's tongue back into his mouth. He used camel milk for that, too. 'It has great healing properties because the camels eat from different trees and the herbs are all absorbed into the blood with their healing properties. Camel milk is particularly good for the brain.'

Camel bones and goat bones, frankincense and antibiotics, and camel milk with everything. It sounds preposterous. But, like so much else in Africa, amazingly it works. And the striking thing is that tradition and modernity were not opposites, or a starting and a finishing point, but something which has fused to make a singular African solution.

We saw that in politics, too. And in the same country, if you can realistically call somewhere as autarchic as Somalia a country. The hospital was not in Somalia but in neighbouring Somaliland, whose people have declared independence from Somalia though no government in the world will recognise the fact. On the ground the fact is inescapable. Somalia is a place of violent anarchy and Somaliland one of modest but ordered prosperity. There are many points of contrast but one of the most striking is in the role of a system called the Tol.

For centuries Somalia has been a place of feuding clans. These clans policed themselves using the Tol, a word which literally means 'my clan come to me'. When a Somali was in trouble he would shout 'Tol, Tol' and the members of his tribal group would fly to his aid. It is an ancient and complex system. One key aspect lies in the self-policing mechanism it has developed. Under the Tol responsibility for crime lies not with an individual but with his clan. A victim does not seek recompense from the criminal but from the traditional court of the tribal elders of his clan. This creates social pressures to prevent crimes against even members of rival groups. For if a man steals a camel his clansmen will say, 'Where did you get that?', and when he is forced to tell them the clan replies, 'Well, take it back, or else his clan will come to us and demand that we all pay compensation.'

But in the parts of Somalia where feuding bandit chiefs held sway the influence of the Tol has been abolished over the past few decades. By contrast, in Somaliland it has not only been retained to maintain order between the area's five rival clans, but it has actually been elevated to the status of the second chamber of parliament. Few there doubt that this is one of the key factors in the relative stability of Somaliland.

It is not a system which any bright young Harvard politics graduate would have thought of inventing. But there is no doubt that it was an effective system of peer-group pressure which, alongside the 'one-person-one-vote' first chamber of parliament, was responsible for an odd mix of African and Western systems of governance which clearly worked. The challenge is to find such hybrids for the rest of Africa.

In the West there is an implicit supposition that development is a linear progression from tradition to modernity; it is about Africa 'catching up' with us. But the evidence shows that tradition does not inevitably precede modernity. It is the interaction between the two that in Africa will bring change and progress.

Outside the hospital it was dusk as we left. Vertical neon strips were nailed to trees at the roadside in lieu of lampposts. Across the road was a ruined theatre. On one of its walls a childlike hand had made a pictorial record which told the story of what had happened there.

The scene was of domestic normality. A woman sat in a chair by a tree in full bloom. Another figure pushed a baby in a swing. Beside them a television had been switched on, showing two footballers exchanging passes.

But then, above them, a large black plane roared across the sky. Bombs rained down from it on to the scene of happiness below. A line of handprints, black then gradually fading, spoke of the dying of the light. All around lay the concrete shards of the bomb-shattered theatre, its columns stark and skeletal like the wreckage of some ancient civilisation. It set the daub in a chilling frame. The fruits of a brutish modernity.

In a shack, by the ruin, a group of people huddled round a radio. They were listening to the BBC World Service, enthralled by the live commentary of Crystal Palace v Man City. Tradition and modernity, side by side. And I'm not talking about Palace and Man City.

The Jesus Thorn

I thought they were Jesus thorns. They were everywhere and they were beautiful, but barbarously savage. In the scrub landscape the hostility of every growing thing is apparent. They have had to do so much just to survive. There is hardly any moisture. If they do grow among the concrete-grey shale and rock, every living animal or insect will try to eat them. Anything to sustain oneself. Anything for nourishment. Anything to develop a mechanism that gives you the advantage over the other creatures, even if it means eating two-inch dried spikes to live.

I do think of Jesus when I see these things. I see the plastic bags that wash across the African continent spiked on their thorns. I see scraps of togas caught as some Masai or Songhai Toposa or Turkana have passed by, snaring the threadbare threads and occasionally ripping the sole article of clothing. I do think of them penetrating the thin flesh around the crown of the head.

Once, I carefully snapped a piece of Jesus thorn. It was surprisingly green and flexible at its centre. It snapped smartly initially, but then there was a lot of bending and twisting and backwards and forwarding. I was getting bored and was about to leave it when it finally came away. The spikes were perhaps an inch long, some longer. I didn't bother to make a Jesus-type wreath or wrap it in any form of girdled crown. I just pressed it softly to my forehead and the side of my head. It was excruciating. Of course. The thorns are widely spaced but as the head moves it encounters not simply the ones at the point of contact but the others growing on either side of the spike, drawing blood. I didn't draw blood. I just pricked the skin and that was the end of the experiment. But they are forever associated with a dreadful sad, leering, knowing cruelty. And they look at home on the grey ranges of scrub and shale they are native to. Hard, cruel land.

STICK FIGHTING

The young men were ferociously and dangerously pounding each other about the head, face, neck and body with long, thick poles. The crowd cheered and when one of them no longer got up from the ground, the fight was over. There was a lot of skill involved. It reminded me of Japanese stick fighting but more vicious. What bare-knuckle boxing is to our more sadistic gloved version.

'Why do you do it?' I asked.

'Why do you box?' came the eminently sensible reply.

The young boys wear elaborate sisal protective headgear about the neck, head and face. These are worn at some fights but are considered a little bit girly. People are killed quite a lot but more often they are left a pulpy mess of bruised, purple flesh.

Just as in boxing.

The Acacia and the Giraffe

A ranger in South Africa told me once of the battle between the giraffe and the acacia thorn. It may not be true – I'm not a naturalist but it is extraordinary and desperate and funny and moving. And weird.

To gain advantage over other creatures on the savannah plains of Africa, giraffes became vegetarian. There were heavier, more savage competitors for the low bush dotted about, and you do not fuck around with hippos and elephants. The giraffe, therefore, over millennia, gradually grew taller. At first the neck and then later the legs, until he had no competitors for the high trees, which had in turn grown tall to escape the attentions of the ground-feeding animals.

The acacia, at first benign, had developed its height as a safety defence, but now found itself under attack from the long-necked, elegant, eyelashed beauty of the giraffe. Not cute if you're an acacia. It in turn developed long, hard, sharp thorns that will cut your palm open if you seize a branch. Momentarily stymied evolution-wise, the giraffe soon came up with a thorn-beating leatherish palate and tongue. It could not be stung, spiked or cut. It could curl its elegant lips round a whole branch and rip the buds and leaves from a stem without a twitch. The acacia seemed doomed.

Desperate and alarmed, it took the work of mere thousands of years to invent a foul poison in its leaves. It was designed to be utterly revolting to the giraffe. They got over it. Even if it tasted horrible, the giraffe cleverly figured it was a lot better than starving. Ad it seemed that not knowing when the giraffe would suddenly appear and start eating them, the acacia never had the chance to produce enough yucky stuff. Slightly put out of their evolutionary stride but unbowed and undeterred, the acacia next did something extraordinary. It developed an early-warning system.

When a giraffe began to feed upon a particular tree the acacia would, incredibly, send a chemical signal downwind to alert its brother trees. They, equally incredibly, would immediately begin to produce copious amounts of GiraffeBeGone or whatever. In theory this should have deterred the loping, doe-eyed tree destroyers. But no. The giraffe quickly twigged over mere dozens of years what was happening and began to feed downwind and work their way up the tree line away from the prevailing breezes, thus catching the trees unawares. Checkmate. Again.

What's the state of play at the moment? Stand-off.

What will the acacia do next? Tune in to next millennium's instalment.

The Whistling Thorn

My favourite thorn, though, is the whistling thorn. It sounds so lonely. I noticed it in the Laetoli gorge in Tanzania where man first stumbled out of the stinking, belching sulphurous dioxin world of three and a half million years ago. It is a barren place with old volcanoes on the horizon, occasionally emitting thin wisps of smoke. In that emptiness stands the whistling thorn.

When the breeze blows through the gorge it really does whistle. You have to be very silent but when you stop talking you realise that the background noise to your conversations has been a thin, oscillating quavering. It is impossible to detect where it is coming from and being a stranger you would never find it. I was saying 'Shhh, shhh' to my colleagues and bending down because it seemed to be from the ground. They thought I was mad. And it was in fact driving me mad, because once you've detected an irritating noise it's very hard not to hear it, even over engine sounds. Then they heard it and it started driving them mad. If you turned in a certain direction it would be loud, slightly in another direction and it had gone.

The two Masai sitting on the rock started smiling at each other. I looked at them, made a cupped-ear gesture towards them and at the same time gave a questioning shrug. One of them stood up, took my hand and led me to a stick-dry, brown-dead thorn bush. Through his teeth he made a whistling sound that was exactly what I had been hearing. He motioned to me and I bent down towards the thorn. And there I heard it: a soft, almost imperceptible lullaby. It whispered with the breeze and multiplied a thousand times through a thousand bushes throughout the valley. It whistled a lonely, sad, thorn-like sound. It actually seemed to me to be the sound a thorn might make if it could speak. Sad, shrill, lonely, pointed and barbed. A curse from God for what its brother had done to His son? A lament for its dry lands? A longing for the cool waters of a stream? It was all those things and I looked at my Masai friend in wonder and smiled. He looked back, nodding and gesturing, telling me with his eyes that, yes, this was the source of the soundtrack of their lives.

Besides its keening lament it was beautiful. And it was its beauty that allowed it to sing. And the beauty came from an extraordinary bargain with nature. A bargain like that of the giraffe and the acacia born out of necessity and the harsh land it grew upon.

The thorn in its early genesis had been disturbed by ants, which would attack it. How, I have no idea. Perhaps they destroyed its root system. So the thorn and the ants made a deal. A bargain to their mutual advantage, to ensure their survival. The ant comes equipped with, or has developed, a poison, which it injects into the thorn. The thorn, thus poisoned, balloons into a hard, hollow ball at its base where it joins the stem. When the balloon has blown up to its optimum size, the ant will bore a hole in the hard, nut-like shell and make its home inside. It is this balloon that catches the wind and makes the thorn bush sing. It is the number of balls and their separation that makes the quavering, thin, oscillating notes of the whistle scale. An orchestra of gently keening, poisoned thorn bushes lamenting their lost, untampered-with selves. Their rape by nature.

The ant protects its home from other insects and the whistling thorn is safe. But it has been violated by its protector. Its lonely pity speaks eerily over the dried-up lava flows of long ago.

The German Tarzan

Wolfgang was born beside Lake Eyasi in the shadow of Mount Oldeani. His parents had moved there in the late seventies, looking for the perfect hunting grounds, and when they saw this remote garden of the Rift Valley and its soda lake, they built a house and had babies and became friends with the people who lived in the area. These are small, lithe hunter-gatherers and they are called Hadza.

Wolfgang grew up with the Hadza children. He can extract raw honey from the beehives halfway up the tamarind trees. He can light a fire from friction sparks in seconds. He can talk in clicks and burrs like they do. He shoots bows and arrows, can shoot and kill the monkeys that scamper through the high tree canopy overhead and then he cooks and eats them. He can graduate from university and do brainy stuff. He can go online while his Hadza friends click and burr and chat about him, wholly disinterested in the activities that don't concern them. He can watch satellite television which bores his hunter-gatherer compatriots who sit outside on the porch by the soda lake and smoke small bamboo pipes and make arrows while Bayern Munich thrash Bayer Leverkusen in the damp of Hamburg. He is Tarzan. A German Tarzan. Tärzan with an umlaut.

It is so beautiful. The house hidden in a shelter of palms behind a small lawn in front of the lake which dries in summer leaving a blinding white crust, over which hippo or deer wander leaving delicate clover prints and deep splat marks behind them. The mountains stand behind the palm groves that become dark green forest and stretch away to the hills which rise to the clouds that shroud their covered peaks. The sun is hot but not oppressive and when the winter arrives the lake fills milky blue because of the sun bouncing off the white floor and brilliantly leaping back up through the shallow warm water. Then the lake fills with Capitain or some other fish and the Hadza and Wolfgang paddle their dugouts, leap into the water, spear or net the fish and swim the vast bowl that holds the lake. If it seems like a description of paradise then that is what it felt to me.

Wolfgang was lucky. He met a beautiful girl at university named Eve and she agreed to marry him. She was hardly dismayed when he told her where he lived and of the life she might expect if she accompanied him to this remote place, for she had been born and raised on an isolated farm in the high pampas of Argentina and craved the space and beauty that such an upbringing demanded. They have two small children blonder and whiter than Eve, who romp through the woods with the children of the Hadza. They are looked after by their grandmother, their mother, two Hadza ladies and everyone else in this small collective. When they are of age they will be sent to a decent boarding school in one of the big towns relatively near so they can come home easily and often.

What is extraordinary is that all of this life happens a bare fifty kilometres from both the Laetoli and Olduvai gorges in Tanzania. What is exceptional about that is that the entire evolution of man occurred there within that tiny circle of Africa. For those who remember Stanley Kubrick's *2001: A Space Odyssey*, this would be the place where early man realised the environment need not shape his destiny. Rather, he could manipulate the world around him to his own needs and, standing up, symbolically hurl the large bone tool he held in his hands towards the heavens. That was a film but all that stuff actually did happen here. Well, maybe not the bone-throwing moment exactly, but you know what I mean.

Laetoli is weird. It actually does look like the Dawn of Man. It is grey and rubble-strewn. The rocks look like they are still flowing lava streams except now cold and grey. Little ancient eddies and wave forms are smoothly visible. Down one end of the narrow valley and in the distance is the cropped peak of an extinct volcano whose top was blown away three and a half million years ago.

The world then and Africa specifically was exploding with geothermal activity. It is said that the continent at the other end of what was to become the Rift Valley was joined to Europe and Asia. Familiar animals wandered about foraging, but something was brewing down here in nature's kitchen. An evolutionary stew burbled away inside this Frankenstein's lab of nature. A new thing was trying to get made. It was never quite right. Various models were sent off the production line to wander about in the choking poisonous volcanic smoke and acid rain which were not really equipped to deal with the older, wilder animals that hunted anything. But one day something cropped up that wasn't bad, that just might work, that was different enough and equipped enough to get traction on the greasy evolutionary foothills.

Laetoli man was a hominid, a near human. He stood upright and had a big brain but he wasn't quite there yet. He wasn't exactly us. He was a Missing Link. In the end he didn't make it. He just wasn't smart or strong enough but he left us a heartbreakingly beautiful souvenir to remember him and his family by. To let us know that without him and his woman and kid there wouldn't have been us.

The mountain had been coughing and spluttering for days. It was more than the usual smoke that rose ceaselessly from its core. Then it erupted again, spewing stone and ash and gas over the whole area and streaming lava down its sides. After a couple of days it eased off and the ash was allowed to cool. A few weeks later it began to rain and the ash turned to mush. That afternoon a couple of hominids, hairy and naked, walked through the cool sludge leaving their footprints behind them in the volcanic ash of Laetoli gorge. These were human feet. Unbelievably, they were those of a man and a woman. Adam and Eve. And even more touchingly they were a family, for scientists have told us by gauging the slant and depth of Eve's prints that she was carrying a small baby on her right hip. It is profoundly moving to stand where they stood. To go back to the end root of man. To stare at those feet and marvel at how similar they are to those other famous footprints made by Neil Armstrong in the volcanic ash of the moon some three and a half million years later. And then look up and see the spectacular Masai herdsmen in their red plaid togas leaning tall and thinly on their spears looking at you in open curiosity, magnificent in their command of their landscape. Baby, you went far.

It took about a million years but finally *Homo Habilis* – us more or less – popped up over the road in Olduvai. If there was a garden of Eden this was it. This was where man finally got his act together. Now it is rocky, brown, pretty bare and unattractive. Then this place was beside a lake with grass and wood. Animals roamed everywhere and man was the game being hunted. He was far weaker than everything aligned against him.

His teeth were small and blunt, not the tearing and pointed killing cleavers of the tiger, lion and everything else. His legs, though nimble, were slow and tired quickly – he would never outpace the wild creatures. His muscle mass was puny compared to the other creatures who shared his hunting ground. For man, life was touch and go.

But he was warm here in his des res lakeside Olduvai home. And typically, once settled in somewhere, he began to mess around. Which is why the scientists called him *Homo Habilis*. Handyman or maybe DIY Man. But, crucially, it was here that the Big Leap happened. The thing that makes us uniquely human was the application of abstract thought into the realm of actuality. He may not have thought it through exactly but *Homo Habilis* certainly intuitively understood that he was too weak against his fellow competitors for life. At some point he reasoned, and that's the critical advantage here, that in lifting a stone or recently skinned bone by hand, and, here's the nub, understanding that he had created a third object – a tool – he had made the final great leap to modernity.

What man had done out of desperate necessity was externalise his weaknesses – his lack of strength, speed, claws, teeth or wings – and using his greater cognitive strengths he had rationalised the speed/weight ratio of arm muscle, grip, hard object and speed and made a weapon and tool a hundred times more powerful than anything he could do with his own frail body. He had used reason and logic. He had thought. He had used his brain.

All over the Olduvai gorge are the evidences of this thinking. Various degrees of stone axes, some crude early lumps, some later extremely refined pointed blades, lie scattered about all over the site. You can see some embedded in the valley walls. You can pick them up. You're not meant to, but how can you resist holding your ancestor's tool in your hands – so to speak?

We hung around here for about another million years using this technology. One million years banging away with a piece of bloody stone. What the hell was *Homo Habilis* up to? Stone axes for one million years. Civilisation is only ten thousand years old from the beginning in Babylon or wherever. The Egyptians were three thousand years ago. The Renaissance five hundred years ago. My fucking iPod's already had it. What were we doing for a million years?

We were sitting pretty is what. But like today in Africa and elsewhere, climate change eventually forced Handyman, B&Q guy, out of his cosy valley. The lake dried up, the forest declined and man went off to pastures new.

He found them over the hill in the southern part of the Great Rift Valley that splits its way up through the African continent north to south. The Rift was the reason for the volcanoes that gave us Laetoli's signature and still today, it grows steadily apart at the same speed as our nails grow. Someone told me that but I don't believe it. It'd be as wide as the Pacific now if that were the case. Anyway, it is growing like all the great geological faults around the place. But the valley then as now was lush and fertile. Man had become like the other animals. He moved to follow the food and water he needed. He didn't settle. That would be borne of necessity later. He became a hunter-gatherer. He gathered berries, roots, fruits and honey. He hunted everything, and unlike his fellow creatures he was extremely cunning. Following the herds over millennia, he wound his way slowly up the Rift Valley, leaving little outposts of humans along the way who in turn would branch out in other directions.

One day, a group of hunter-gatherers wound up at the north end of the valley somewhere around the present-day Horn of Africa in north-east Somalia or Djibouti. They were camping there in what was then a wet part of the world. There was water and game in abundance. Their numbers grew. Africa was then joined to the Middle East and early one morning science tells us that fifty of these hunters set off from their campsite and kept moving towards the north-east. Towards different and dangerous unknown worlds. I considered the bravery and curiosity of those people and then I marvelled at the exceptional and staggering fact that all of the people in the rest of the world outside of Africa are descended from those exact same original fifty who set off that fateful morning to conquer, pioneer and populate the planet. How extraordinary is that? I stood at that place too and gazed out at the oily red sea slurping the shore and wondered at all of this. At Africa. At its total beauty. Spiritual and physical. How it exercises that same mind that formed here. How the ancient memory and smell of it draws you back. Draws you home.

And some stayed behind. Some stayed right where they were. Within forty miles of where man first appeared. Where he first reasoned. Where he won the right and the means to exist. All of it within a tiny circle of possibility, a forty-mile radius at the southern end of the Great Rift Valley. They didn't bother to move up the valley. They're still there. There are only about 450 of them left and in 340,000 years they have successfully lived in precisely the same way. They are the Hadza who swim, hunt and watch telly side by side with Wolfgang, the German Tarzan.

Check Your Spear at the Cloakroom

The Masai are an extraordinarily successful people. They occupy a land that straddles Tanzania and Kenya. They are pastoralists; that is, they follow their herds of cattle from pasture to pasture. They have done this since time immemorial and they have survived well. Indeed, they have thrived. They generally ignore our world and, though they know they live in modern states, the map of the country they truly occupy is the one that exists inside their heads and on the maps of the tourists who come to stare at these exotics in their beautiful territory.

The Masai only participate in our world inasmuch as they want to. They pay taxes if they have to and obey state law when they move outside their lands; they adhere strictly to their own codes while within them. They participate in the modern on their terms only, without any reference to those of us in the Western world. They are not disconnected; they simply prefer the way they live to anything we have to offer. Globalisation, Iraq, whatever; it is academic to them. They are aware of these other worlds but have consciously chosen to remain as they are.

And yet the Masai are an entirely twenty-first-century people. They just happen to prefer wearing red plaid togas, unfortunately not made by them but in China or India, carry spears and knives and live in houses made of cow shit. It provides good insulation, decent fire fuel and is readily available when you up sticks and hit the road again.

At the weekends the young warriors slope off to town. That can often be very far away but they don't care; they can walk for days without tiring. At night they curl up in their capes and togas and sleep. When they hit the bars and discos resplendent in their curiously shaved heads and extraordinary hair-dos, jewellery and weapons these lean, tall and beautiful men hand their knives, spears and rifles over to the hat-check girl who politely provides them with their cloakroom tickets for collection on the way out. Then the lads hit the floor. Barefoot. They don't do any of that leaping-straight-up-in-the-air-from-a-standing-start stuff that they do back on the ranch. These dudes get down to the latest grooves and dance like toga'd Travoltas.

Many anaemic-looking German women can be seen strolling hand in hand with these guys; no doubt the *Fräuleins'* fevered imaginations have them wandering this 'untouched' land with their pet 'primitive'. A daring shag with the wild untamed. They look awful on the beaches of Mozambique, these unlikely pairings of the elegantly thin, barefoot, plaid-draped warriors and the floridly sunburned, sweating *Mädchen*, dumpy in their hideous purple and yellow diagonally patterned Spandex pants and disgraceful sandals complete with 'tribal' necklace. The Masai know exactly what's going on and don't really care about being beach gigolos for a few days. They think it's great. And then, rifle and spear slung, they hotfoot it back home to the cattle. Home on the range.

It is a fact that for the Masai cattle are everything. They are not just a livelihood as they are for, say, a rancher in Europe or America. They represent wealth, status, food; they have spiritual value and they give meaning to the Masai existence. They are a life.

When the terrible events of 9/11 took place in New York in 2001, the Masai heard about it. Like everyone else in the sane world they were appalled. Their response was overwhelming. They presented to the people of New York something that was most precious to them, which had most value and yet was beyond price. Because the scale of the tragedy was so enormous, the Masai – a people who wear togas and live in houses made of cow dung, who have nothing material save cattle – gave to the city of New York not one but *fifteen* cows to honour the dead and as an expression of shared sympathy and universal shock.

Serious people.

Two African Jokes

These excellent jokes were told to me by the inhabitants at either end of the continent. It's the knowing fortitude and fatalism that is so funny.

What did they use in the Congo before they had candles?
Electricity.

And the one they tell in Sudan...

A scorpion goes down to the river to see if he can get a ride across. He goes up to a sleeping crocodile. He taps him on the snout. The crocodile is not pleased with this intrusion, and asks the scorpion what the hell he wants.

'Excuse me,' says the scorpion, 'but as you know, scorpions can't swim and I was wondering, could you give me a lift across the Nile?'

'Fuck off,' replies the croc peremptorily, and tries to go back to sleep.

Undaunted, the scorpion tries again.

'Look, I've already told you to fuck off once,' says the crocodile, 'now fuck off.'

'What's your problem?' asks the scorpion, somewhat naively. 'I just want a lift.'

'What's my problem?' demands the croc incredulously. 'I'm trying to have a kip for a start, and you come whinging up to me looking for a bloody lift. Go on, mate, hop it. Bog off.'

The croc closes his eyes again and is attempting to settle down when, unbelievably, he hears the scorpion's reedy little voice again.

'Look, it's simple. I'm a scorpion, I can't swim. You're a crocodile, you can. I want a lift. I need to get across the river on urgent family business, and if you won't do it out of fellow animal kindness then fine, I am quite prepared to pay you.'

'Fellow animal kindness!' explodes the croc. 'Don't make me laugh. Are you mad? You're a bloody insect, man! A stupid bloody scorpion, and no, I don't want to be paid or give you a lift. Do I look stupid, or what? Listen, matey, scorpions and crocodiles don't get on. We hate each other. Always have. Ancient enemies. If I gave you a lift I would be going against every tenet held sacred by crocodiles all over the bloody world… And besides which, you'd only sting me when we were halfway across and kill me or something.'

'Oh don't be so bloody childish. And ridiculous,' responds the scorpion after this outrageous outburst. 'Do I look thick, or what? I'm not going to sting you. Why would I do that? If I did and I killed you, how would I reach the other side? I'd drown as well. Use your bloody intelligence, man. Go on, it'll only take a minute.'

And so it went on for hours. Eventually the scorpion (scorpions are well known for their persistence) persuades the crocodile, who relents, if only to get some peace.

'But I'm warning you,' says the croc, 'no funny business on the way. No stinging. Remember, I'm warning you!'

'Yeah yeah,' says the scorpion sighing, 'don't be ridiculous – I have no intention of dying just yet, thank you very much.'

'Alright, go on then,' relents the crocodile. 'Jump up.'

The scorpion hops up onto the bridge of the crocodile's snout, so the croc can keep an eye on him. The croc launches off into midstream, and is just ploughing through the main current when suddenly, and for no apparent reason whatsoever, the scorpion leans forward and stabs the crocodile on the bridge of his nose with his lethal poison.

The crocodile is in agony and dying. He begins to thrash wildly about in the water, dislodging the scorpion in the process, who, unable to swim, begins to flounder and drown himself.

'You idiot!' screams the crocodile with his dying breath. 'What did you do that for?'

And the drowning scorpion replies with a shrug,

'That's Africa!'

The Forgetting Tree

As the slaves walked, shackled and bound, down that last dusty road past the gently stirring ocean towards the waiting ships they saw a tree.

At first they didn't pay much attention to it. At the back of the line there were many hold-ups. The steel neck braces cut the flesh and each person sought the most comfortable position in which to stand and which caused the least abrasion. The person in front might suddenly be jerked forward on his chains and cause you to stumble forward, gagging and chafing. Someone behind may not move and you would be pulled back, your neck suddenly and savagely choked. In among the confusion and the terror you had to keep your wits about you.

The line moved on. People called out in strange languages. The white men said nothing but let their African partners handle the unpleasant business of ship loading whereupon they could take over. Some of the more terrified wept with fear and loss. Some keened with longing. Others moaned, still more wailed and the rest were as quiet as the ghosts they had become. Living ghosts.

Near the halfway point of the road they could see the tree. It was curious. Groups were being led to it still shackled and they were walking round the tree in a circle. That was the cause of the hold-up. What did it mean? Eventually you arrived yourself.

'This is the tree of forgetting', you were told. 'You will walk around this tree seven times. On each turn you will forget something different.

'You will forget your land.

'You will forget your village.

'You will forget your people.

'You will forget your wife.

'You will forget your sons.

'You will forget your daughters.

'You will forget your name.

'You now belong to your master. You have no memory and have nothing to forget or lose. In many ways you are free. Chained, yes, but free. Your past life will be gone. You must forget it. Your new life will begin immediately.'

And so you walk. And you cry. And with each turn and with each memory you say goodbye. You cry over each thought and smell and touch. You cannot continue. Your chain jerks. My wife. My children. And as each memory comes you break and the memory runs. It scurries, not out of reach, but burrows down deep into the mental cud for when, sick with longing, it can be regurgitated and chewed upon afresh on the thrashing seas and the shacks of Louisiana.

And I will not forget and I will never forget.

And my beautiful wife is my wife and she is …

And my children, my fine children are beautiful and strong and free and they are called …

And they are now, this instant, playing in our village and the sun is bright above …

In my land of …

In Africa, in Africa …

And my name is …

And my name will always be …

And I am …

The forgetting tree trick worked for some. It was a powerfully profound and sophisticated piece of psychological understanding. But, whatever it is about the shackled thousands who walked around it on their way to forever, you are filled with the sensation that this old tree has remembered everything it has seen and heard. It is too full of sorrow. The only way it could help people to forget was by remembering, by absorbing all their hurled-away thoughts, taking them in for when they could be reclaimed by their owners and the tree drained of its intolerable burden of stored pain. Today it looks old and bowed with the weight of its sorrow. It is not a grand tree. Perhaps it has been stunted by a surfeit of anguish. Does it long for the memory-erasing amnesia of the axe?

Standing beside it now, I defy you not to walk around it seven times. I bet you'll cry.

A STORY FROM THE CRAZY COUNTRY NEWSPAPER COLUMN
Circumcision traps man

Mbale – A man who has been dodging circumcision recently revealed he wasn't circumcised after an angry mob suspected him to be a thief. Godfrey Masaba, a boda boda cyclist, recently hit the lamps of a parked car . . .

The Bungalow of Goo

The high priest was a builder. He got a lot of work. Not surprising really. New house with free add-on spiritual protection guaranteed at no extra cost.

He waved his divining string to and fro, a bit of fishing line with some flat leaves made of lead on it. Then he got out his bag of tricks and emptied the contents on the floor. The old crones sitting around him clucked and tsked. Frankly, I had expected a little more than the worn-out shells, half-used biro, empty cigarette packet, hair clip and small change that tumbled from the small off-white cotton bag that held these presumably powerful magic totems. Even the shells were prosaic: no fabulous marine exotica here. There was simply no getting away from the plain reality of these chipped and faded, basic common or garden whelks plus two black/brown cowries and a white one.

I was asked to take the shells in my hand, put them behind my back, divide them and then hold the two closed fists holding the shells out in front of me. What was going on? I was expecting the full horned beast, dance with the Devil, Aleister Crowley, pentagonal star stuff. Voodoo my arse; this was a parlour-game magic trick. Twice we did this, to the audible dissatisfaction of the ol' biddies and the clear dismay of the high priest himself. What was up? Apparently he kept choosing the wrong hand, fer chrissakes. He shook his head and sighed.

Now you would think that being in one of the great temples of Voodoo in the town of Ouidah, the Vatican City of Voodoo, in the country of Benin (which, again, is what Italy is to the Vatican), in the presence of the high priest, the gorgeously beautiful seventeen-year-old high priestess, their acolytes, and the walls adorned with mysterious symbols, I would have been a tad apprehensive. Well, yeah, I should have been, I suppose; but, you see, the thing is, it was all a bit naff.

This temple dedicated to the war god with the distinctly unmartial name of Goo was in fact a bungalow. A bungalow with a little compound perhaps, but there is basically no other word for it: it was a bungalow.

It was the afternoon when we arrived but they had the fluorescent lights on, which, as night fell suddenly, as it does in Africa, cast a decidedly unspooky and ghastly public-toilet-type glare over proceedings.

It was so not what I wanted. I was totally geared up to the whole pounding drums and perspiring bodies lit by the ghostly glow of the fire thing. Faces leering in sweaty ecstasy. Eyes rolled back into skulls. Nakedness and trance. Blood sacrifice and frightening fetishes, smeared in the blood of still-beating hearts. You know the stuff. You've seen it in the movies. *Indiana Jones and the Temple of Doom*. I got Bob Geldof and the Bungalow of Goo.

Like everywhere else in the world, religion in Africa is a great new political force again. Islam, paid for by fundamentalist Saudis, in the north; evangelical Christianity, with links to the American Pentecostalists, in the centre and the south; and an unprecedented rise in the old traditional religions. People in Benin say, 'We're 60 per cent Muslim, 40 per cent Christian and 100 per cent Voodoo.' And that's true and typical of Africa – the assimilation of new ideas and bolting them on to the old. A continuity rather than a rupture. They can believe in both, so why shouldn't they? It's particularly easy

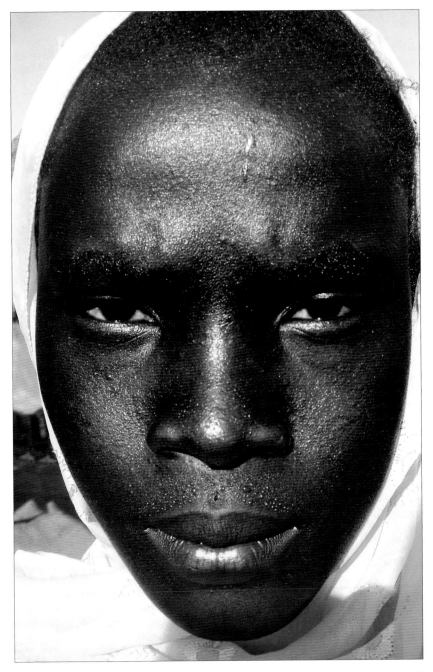

Mopti, Mali

Kinshasa, Congo

Power supply, Dogon, Mali

Football fixtures, Lokichoggio, north Kenya

Garage, Timbuktu

The Polythene Tree

Rubbish girl, Djenne, Mali

Morning wash, Jinka, Ethiopia

Random municipal art

Bouj, Tuareg desert guide, Timbuktu

Baobab Tree, Dogon

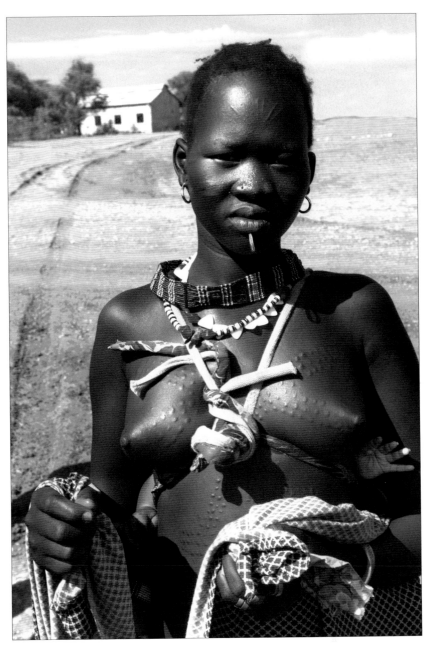

Mother and baby, Kapoeta, south Sudan

Masai, Tanzania

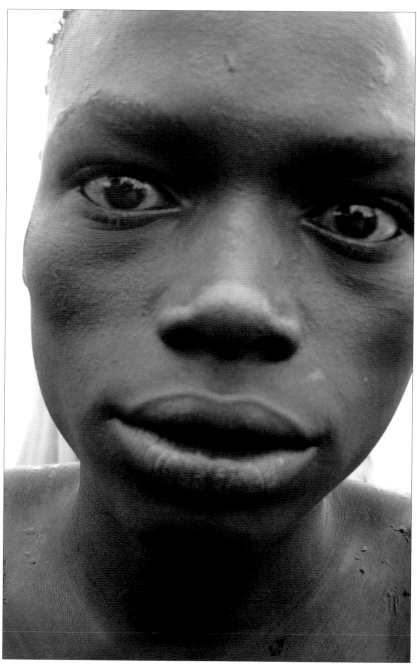

This country is full of ghosts

The Sacrifice to Goo, Ouidah, Benin

A Muslim Mona Lisa

with Christianity.

I looked at the symbols on the walls of the Temple of Goo. They were randomly and crudely painted in the naive style. The central idea seems to be that, like the big three religions, there is one universal God. He may be called by various names and he is represented by a chameleon. A nice idea. Being a chameleon, he can be anything you want him to be. He can blend into anything. He is all-seeing and ever-present. So far, so familiar. There are lesser gods, undergods, so to speak, in charge of different things, like old Goo here, busily in charge of war inside his bungalow. These lesser beings are familiar to us also. They are a bit like our saints. You can pray to them to intercede with God about their particular speciality. Unfortunately, Goo has had a lot to bother the African God with lately.

The sun and the moon represent life and the forces that nourish us. They too are manifestations of the Supreme. Various complementary forces were represented around the room so that, for example, Goo could easily co-exist with Aidoi, the god of peace. They often did stuff together, apparently, and could be prayed to jointly or separately. In the same way, for example, that a Catholic on a journey who had lost something precious would pray to St Anthony, the patron saint of travellers, and to St Jude, the patron saint of lost causes, for its safe return. A sort of double indemnity in exchange for a promissory 50p each into their respective collection boxes in church.

But peace counterbalances war and vice versa so, interestingly, these twin deities have a constant dialogue going. Goo and Aidoi are bound together eternally inasmuch as they are two sides of the same coin. Goo always had to stay on the good side of Aidoi, for war never lasts: it is usually fleeting. So Goo has to get a good deal when he quits. In the balance of the gods it is Aidoi, peace, not the war god, who weighs the scales. How elegant. A spiritual representation of Churchill's maxim, 'Jaw-jaw is better than war-war'.

The high priestess sat in the middle of the room, unsmiling. She had been chosen for her role when still a baby by the elders charged with the task and under the supervision of the high priest of the time. She was picked from among the children of the nation and the selectors were in turn guided to her by the Divine. Once chosen, she could never leave the compound again. She could marry and bear children but she could only choose her mate from the men who entered the compound to worship or study or simply to visit. As her spirituality grew, possible suitors could be daunted by her power. Often the priestess would die, untouched by a man and childless. She looked like a normal, lonely girl. She was not allowed to participate in the ceremony. She sat quietly, unsmiling, on her low stool, looking bored. She had no curiosity about me and was entirely indifferent to my incessant photograph taking, enamoured as I was not by her supposed spiritual power but by her beauty in this dull little room in the back streets of Ouidah.

This girl was greatly feared and admired. There was only one other woman in the country with anything approaching her level of pure spiritual power. The two women were never allowed to meet, for if they were ever in the same room the spiritual intensity would be such that the entire universe might explode. Wow.

Around her, like a court, sat the old ladies staring at the high priest, a well-built thirty-five-year-old man. They looked no different from other old holy ladies whispering their prayers in empty churches on empty afternoons, or like the priest or vicar groupies self-importantly twittering around the patronising men of the cloth as they served them tea and cakes in the sitting rooms and presbyteries of the Western Christian world. Ladies who long ago substituted piety-through-cake-baking for sex as approaching death focused the mind. God – the last love affair.

Above the priestess's head and on the wall was a small red disc – the sun. Facing it on either side were two chameleons and over the sun was an inverted crescent – the moon, arcing a roof over the sun –

and above them all a small cross. A crucifix.

In the 1920s or 1930s – I can't remember which – a local bishop came here to learn the theology of Voodoo. An open and enlightened man, he understood this belief to be more than 'pagan superstition'. He saw it as a functioning, living force inside his otherwise Catholic parishioners' lives. They accepted Christ. Christ was the chameleon nailed to the cross. The blood sacrifice. They got it. And in getting it they did not see why they needed to relinquish Goo and the others. If anything, it confirmed and broadened their own theologies. The bishop sat and listened and then he spoke. He found surprising theological similarities in the twin religions and when he explained the blood sacrifice of the Son of God in atonement for sin, the reparation for human corruption and the final triumph over death in the concept of an afterlife, the voodooers instantly understood the implication in an almost Jesuitical way.

There was really nothing new here. As every African understands, the ancestors – that is, all those who have died – are an immediately accessible but invisible reality. They are not dead as such; they have merely slipped through to the immaterial and insubstantial. It is not a question of triumphing over anything; it is an exchange of one actual existence for another and neither is capable of denying the other. Indeed, the opposite for both, like the eternal tango that characterises Goo and Aidoi, forced to work alongside and with each other. The ancestors are annoying and can be annoyed but, crucially, they are also the medium of negotiation between the substantial material world and the gods. This spirit world daily impinges upon the material. It is there to be recognised and to be negotiated with.

Well, the voodooers got the plot straight away and incorporated the + into their mythology. Its more extreme form it can be seen in Brazil and the Indies where Santeria, the bastard child of the old African and the New World thing, is almost a state religion. You know: bloody saints, snakes 'n' nails.

Meanwhile, back in Ouidah, in the Temple of Goo, the auguries are good. I have been asked, am I a warrior? I say, no I am a pop singer. They stare, dismayed, at the shells, the biro and the empty cigarette packet. They say, what about my father? I say, no, sorry: he sold towels. Something's up. They look bemused. To help things along I tell them I have been knighted by the Queen of England and that a knight is an ancient warrior. They brighten. They love it. They smile at each other knowingly and say stuff like, see, told you, and other things in their own tongue.

And then I remember a weird thing. Two days earlier I had been made a king of Biseasi, in Ghana. I tell them this. They gasp and stare at me. One of the crones puts her hand to her throat. 'What is your kingly name?' she asks. It then strikes me that I was called Nana Kofi Kumasah 1. 'Nana' means king or chief; 'Kofi' is Friday, the day of the coronation; and Kumasah was the great warrior of the Ashanti kingdom that is now Ghana. They are speechless. They shake their heads in wonder. And I am, in truth, a bit freaked out too, cos, let's face it, it is a bit weird, isn't it? It has now been definitively decided that I am descended from warriors and that, as a result, Goo wants the full ceremony of war. Cool. Except it will cost about thirty quid. That's fine; it's less than the cost of a funeral or baptism or whatever the priest charges you back home.

The drums beat, a goat bleats and a fire is lit. Three old wooden fetish dolls, like those you see in interior design magazines and which populate the homes of the fashionable metropolitan crowd as well as the homes and churches of the Beninois, are placed by the fire. The priest and his assistant strip to the waist. They have magnificent bodies and they wear loose, baggy pyjama-type bottoms. They begin to do a dance just like the Funky Chicken. Elbows flapping, arses stuck out, necks jerking like … well, like a chicken. The old biddies chant, the drums pick up a little, but the drummers don't seem to care and the results are, frankly, disappointingly desultory. Not much sweating there. No ecstasy and precious little in the eye-rolling department either.

The goat I had heard bleating is hauled out and summarily despatched, its throat peremptorily slit and the blood poured into an enamel kitchen utensil. We are given a swig of vodka and the blood gets poured on to the fetish representing Goo in the corner of the room. You can no longer see the original figure: it is caked in yellow tallow and dried blood. That looks spooky, I suppose, but it doesn't really feel it. Nor, bizarrely, does it stink. I stick my nose against it but it just smells waxy. The goat is hauled off and it's the chicken's turn. Slash and grab. More blood collected and distributed; another swig of vodka. Out in the yard a boy is burning the hair off the dead goat and chopping it up. Then the chicken is dismembered and both animals are put into the pot of boiling water which is bubbling over the fire. I'm beginning to wonder, is this some arcane ritual or have we just paid for everybody's Sunday goat stew?

We bite some kola nut and spit it into a pan. The ladies sigh and cluck loudly. Eventually, we somehow get the spit pattern right and everyone is satisfied. They can divine in the spat out kola the runes that tell us Goo is pleased, happy with our ceremony; nice of him, really. The beautiful priestess is still sitting alone and removed from everyone, too high, too great, too remote to be allowed to participate or speak. She looks so sad.

The infernal drums finally stop. I can understand now all that G. H. Henty stuff, books like *Sanders of the River* in which some chap is being 'driven mad by those infernal native drums. What could they mean?' Well, it meant there were plenty of shite drummers out there and they could drive anyone mad. We leave as they begin tucking into the goat stew.

Our religions are great because we could transport them and study them. We wrote them down. We exported them and with them our idea of the world. But there are no Bibles, Talmuds or Korans for

Voodoo and the thousand other wondrous ideas of the universe and our place within it that exists throughout Africa. But there will be.

One day in London people will be going out to get a ready-slaughtered chicken to pour over the household god. Hell, they're probably doing it already. Whole regions will be Gooist. Fantastic.

Milton Keynes, City of Goo.

An African Venice

There is only one place the slavers couldn't go. It is unique in Africa. It is an African Venice. Built in the middle of a vast lake on stilts of wood, it is called Ganvie.

People escaping the rampaging Amazon army of the King of Dahomey ran to the shores of Lake Nokue and rowed out to the submerged forests in the middle of the water. The slavers were forbidden by their Voodoo religion to cross the water. They feared it.

Knowing they were safe, the escapees began building a village raised above the lake; they called their haven 'Peace At Last' – Ganvie.

The inhabitants and their descendants then, as now, work their lake efficiently, planting branches in the shallow waters to produce artificial thickets that trap the fish for extraction or breeding. The people move about in small boats. Even the market is on the water and the people carry out their various enterprises by dugout also. There are churches and Voodoo temples built on the stilty streets rising out of Canale d'Amoureuse and the other names that remind one vaguely of Venice, that other watery place built to escape another war on another continent.

The Complex, Unexpected
Story of Slavery

It had been going on for a long time anyway before the white man showed up. But in that coldly efficient way of his it wasn't long before he'd turned it into an industrial science.

The Arabs and Chinese and Indians had been visiting the east coast of Africa for hundreds of years before the Portuguese showed up one morning in the 1500s off the coast of Ghana. There are bits of Chinese porcelain and Indian pottery and shells and tons of Arab stuff littering the earth down the eastern seaboard. They were serious traders but they were also taking the stuff the Portuguese wanted as well. Gold, frankincense, ivory. And, of course, slaves.

By the time the Europeans hove to it is estimated that 60 per cent of the domestic economy of Africa was slavery. Everyone was at it. The Arabs raided inland for a thousand miles to get their captives and ship them on vast dhows out of Zanzibar and Bamagoyo and other ports north. These people were then dispersed throughout the known and unknown world. Some even came to thirteenth- and fourteenth-century Europe by that roundabout way. Vast fortunes were being made by the Arab slavers and their African counterparts until eventually the Arabs colonised the ports from which they were working and stayed there until they themselves were unearthed from their Islamic strongholds by newer powers.

If the Emirate Arabs moved inland from the east coast their cousins in North Africa swept south through the Sahara where they bought vast numbers of people to herd through the desert wastes and be sold in the souks of the north. The slave markets of Arouane, Timbuktu, Djenne, Mopti and many other cities resounded to the jangle of cash and the mingled mongrel cries of the sellers and their hapless shackled victims of many nations alike.

It is as pointless for Africans or their American descendants to adopt a morally superior tone of denial with regard to their culpability over slavery as it is for whites to deny their own guilt over the prosecution of that sickening trade. The terrible truth is that when the Europeans came to do business with the Africans, to their undying shame all they had to sell were their own people and to our undying shame we bought them.

Slavery is trade. It is a business whose commodity is people. It will always have a market because other people always want free or cheap labour. Today in Benin five thousand children a year are sold into slavery by poor parents who have nothing and who cannot feed their children. Since I have been coming to Africa 100,000 slaves have left that one country alone. And there are many other places involved, too. The adults allow themselves to be fooled into believing they are doing the right thing by their kids. That at least they'll have clothing and shelter and nourishment and possibly even a career. In fact, the children disappear into domestic slavery or the chocolate plantations of Ghana and Côte d'Ivoire, among others. The girls will eventually become prostitutes when at fourteen they become raucous, uncooperative teenagers and get thrown back out on to the street. The boys become street thugs doing whatever it takes to make a living. Should they go home they face possible rejection by the very parents who tried to forget about them years earlier and who feel acutely embarrassed within the community that the youngsters have shown up again. Or they may simply try and resell them. I have met all of these people. Poverty really does pervert everything. It is a form of social pornography.

We had come for gold. The Arabs had written that gold grew in the fields of Asante (Ghana) like carrots. One had simply to stoop down and pick it up. It was true. It was everywhere and, possibly because of its ubiquity, it hadn't much value for the kings of that vast African empire which was already rich from conquest and slavery. The Europeans were extremely interested in the fact that the Africans were prepared to trade their gold for the Europeans' copper, measure for measure. The profits back home were enormous. And the Ashanti in turn valued the copper more. So, great, everyone was happy.

But then they saw the Europeans' guns and wanted some of those. The Pope, being suspicious of an armed Islam, wasn't happy and forbade it. Sound familiar? *Plus ça change…*

The Ashanti fancied the Portuguese horses, too, but the wretched animals could hardly withstand the rigours of Africa and would die within a year of malaria, tsetse fly, exhaustion, etc. The Africans refused to trade further. There was nothing the Portuguese could give them that they wanted. Yeah, they liked the cloth and nails but, ultimately, they were boring. However, there was one thing they did want. People. They wanted people to work. Slaves.

Maybe they were trading them with the Arabs or maybe they wanted them for themselves; whatever, they wanted them. And so the Portuguese sailed further down the unexplored coast to Dahomey where they had heard there ruled a ferocious king with an empire of terror and brutality that stretched far inland. Here people were eviscerated and crucified; hideous tortures and sacrifices were the order of the day. The Portuguese had heard about places like that in Europe too, so they weren't that put out. When they showed up off Ouidah in present-day Benin, the Dahomey were eager to trade people for guns and the Pope didn't care if the black Africans had them so long as they didn't go near them pesky Ayrabs.

Bizarrely, the Portuguese had become the middlemen in the slave trade between what became known as the Slave Coast and the Gold Coast. Africans selling Africans to other Africans.

But Europeans were doing that to other Europeans as well. When the Black Death of the 1300s finally abated, the AIDS of its day had decimated the population leaving only one-third of the workforce alive. That one-third could name its price in wage costs and the kings and landowners didn't like it. These peasants were naming their terms and beginning to dictate political policy. That could not be allowed to continue.

There was a new fad going round too. The crusaders had eventually limped home from Palestine demoralised by their failures and the lack of interest at home. But they had brought back more then their wounds and tattered flags and relics. They had developed a sweet tooth in the lands of sticky, sweet espresso tea and Turkish delights. They were hooked and needed their fix. The Portuguese – smart cookies (no pun intended) – began growing sugar beet and cane (I think) in the Algarve and Malta, Sardinia and Sicily. But where to get the labour? They were never going to pay the prices that the lazy oiks they normally employed were now demanding in the labour shortage. They turned to the slave markets of the east. There they found the Turks and the Arab traders eager to sell them defeated Slavic people as cheap, chained, unfree labourers. And so from these people, from the word Slavic, we get slaves.

Whenever there is labour shortage there are slaves. Whenever there is low population density such that communities cannot produce enough to sustain themselves and develop, then there are raids on other people for labour and increased birth rate. When fertility is low because there aren't enough women, they will be raided for, the children taken for work, the men for the fields.

Thus it was that St Patrick was taken as a boy by Irish pirates to work the fields of Sligo far from his native Wales. Thus it was that the

Vikings or whoever plundered the coasts of Britain and Ireland. And thus it was that the Barbary pirates raided Cornwall and made off with three hundred stunned villagers to disappear into the markets and harems of the Middle East.

Thus it began in Africa. Bedevilled by underpopulation due to the extremes of climate, disease and environment you took people when you found them. You sold them. You kept them. There are today whole tribes who are slaves of other dominant tribes and have been for centuries.

I have met the Bella, a nomadic group who are slaves of the Tuareg and their relatives in other groups. 'What is the relationship between the Bella and the Tuareg?' I asked the blacksmith who was the chief of the Bella I met camping under the Bandiagara Escarpment in Dogon. 'We are their slaves,' he said simply. We sat under the shade of a Shrek-like baobab tree. I thought about this for a while. He was about sixty-five and his four-year-old son worked the goatskin bellows of the little charcoal fire that made the steel glow. He sharpened a new knife he'd made. It was like a razor. 'Why?' I asked him. 'Because it has always been like this. It is the tradition.'

At some point in the past the Bella, under terminal threat from drought and famine, turned themselves over to the will of the Tuareg forever in exchange for rescue and life. That undertaking is still being played out today. The Bella are required to do whatever a Tuareg – any Tuareg – asks. Usually it involves camel or goat herding or domestic chores. The Bella must ask permission to move. If they see a Tuareg they must bow and may only rise when a hand has been placed upon the shoulder.

Some societies used slavery to get rid of their delinquents by sentencing them to be sold. Often the charges were trumped up simply in order to get the cash from the sale when the unfortunate innocent had been 'sold down the river'. The simple expression is literal and derives from the corrupt practices of the Congo tribes.

Others would purposely, like the Bella, become another's slave. There's a parallel in our own countries where a homeless person will ask to be arrested in order that he may spend Christmas in a warm cell with company and food and, if refused, will commit some petty crime in plain view of a policemen so that he can be taken in. In the same way a starving African would break someone's precious jar or steal a trifle in order to be taken into slavery and therefore 'safety'. They would eat at least.

There were as many forms of slavery as there was treatment. In underpopulated groups it was normal for the slave to be accepted into the family. Even to marry into it. Some slaves could become free. Some were cruelly treated. Some were considered less than animals. All were bound to the will of others. All were unfree human beings.

When the European world expanded and colonisation began it was the lack of population, the lack of labour, that fuelled the demand for available people. And the most available were Africans and the most underpopulated were the Americans who needed workers for their booming economies, which were being fuelled by the demand for the products of their vast cotton and sugar plantations. Thus began the baleful commerce that still resonates today through our psychologies and our politics.

It is true that African labour built American wealth. At its peak sixty thousand people were being shipped across the Atlantic annually and from the beginning of the trade in the 1500s to the 'end' of it, eleven million people had been wrenched from their homes and taken across a vast ocean to a distant continent in the most brutal conditions imaginable. They were to be stripped of everything. They were to be non-human. Bound and shackled, whipped and tortured. Their families were to be broken up, their children taken from them and dispersed. It is unthinkable what occurred before finally it was stopped.

Add to that eleven million the four million who had been shipped north out of Africa over the previous three hundred years before the

Europeans even found Africa. There are slaves today in Mauritania, Sudan, Mali, Ghana, Togo, Benin, Côte d'Ivoire, Congo, etc.

Some commentators have speculated that the terror lasted so long and was spread so wide that not a single village on the continent was safe from the slavers' ravages. These raiders were all Africans for the whites could not move inland for fear of disease. The only safe Africans were those who lived along the coast. Because they were the ones who did the raiding, or paid neighbouring kingdoms or mercenary tribes to 'go fetch'.

Things got so bad in 16-something that a Portuguese sailor standing one morning on the slipway at Elmina, watching children playing on the sand, saw a woman walk over to a youngster, pick him up and offer him to a seaman for sale. Even that was too much for our hardened slaver who, piously shocked, recorded the incident in his diary.

All of this brutality took place over hundreds of years. Experts say it has left a lingering fatalism at the core of the African psychology. 'Consider,' says John Reader, the African scholar, 'the extent to which the Second World War, of just six years' duration, has pervaded the consciousness of the developed world for two generations, and imagine how four centuries of slave-trading might have seized the entire social and cultural ethos of an underdeveloped continent.' Leaving it with a lingering fatalism.

It is quite possible and utterly understandable, for no other society has experienced anything like this in any other period of history. And slavery was then immediately followed by the removal of the Africans' lands by the colonial powers and the dispossession of all they had. This in turn was followed by the disastrous and enthusiastic mistakes of independence, the puppetry of the Cold War and the consequences of being the butt end of the world's economic motor.

How have they withstood this? How are they so resilient? How can any society continue and be so full of grace and dynamism? So sure of themselves? Not cowed. Unbowed. Dignified. Proud. Exemplified not by this year's pathetic tyrant but by their Mandelas, Tutus, Soyinka and the rest. What amazing people. We owe them a lot.

Salamander

There was a lizard in my bathroom.

It was early. About six in the morning. I turned on the overhead mirror light. I looked like crap. I stared at myself. I leaned into the mirror to stare at the wrinkled, brutally baggy eyes in the unforgiving fluorescent glare. Suddenly this fucking thing seemed to erupt out of the side of my fucking eye.

I must have woken it. It jerked out from under the small light. Pale cream, blending with the wall, the shower tiles. It freaked me out. I thought, in the mirror, it was coming out of my ear or my head.

It darted up the wall and hung upside down in the corner looking at me. Cute. Maybe it lived there. Yeah, that would explain the colour and why I didn't get bitten doing my teeth or something, I thought in a too-early-in-the-morning sort of way. It ate the flies. It was a bathroom lizard. Or a salamander. Maybe it was a salafuckinmander!

Salamander are weird. And chameleon. And general lizard in fact. People are always going round worshipping them. What's that about? Jim Morrison – the Lizard King? Who wants to be king of the fucking lizards? Up in Benin and Togo and other Voodoo countries they see the salamander as the symbol for the universal God. Or a chameleon, which also makes sense. And then, of course (and this was beginning to occur to me), the salamander is the canary of the universe.

Miners always used to carry a canary in a cage when they went underground. If there was any escaping gas the bird would croak, allowing the miners to get the hell out of there in time. A feeble last chirp I suppose, and the boys were exit, stage right. Well, they say that about the salamander. If you see a salamander dying it's game up. Imminent universal extinction. This one looked okay. Like he wasn't predicting anything. Like the universe was safe with him around. Relax, paranoid human man, I'm just hanging upside down to keep my head warm. Ogling me sleepily with his heavy-lidded swivelly eyes, big bags, elephant-hard and crinkled flesh. I looked closely in the mirror. Yeah – just like my eyes. Then he fell asleep.

Next day I didn't see him. I freaked out again. I know what a dead one means but what does a disappearing salamander mean?

Gingerly, I looked behind the mirror. I didn't want him darting out at me. Nothing. There was nowhere else he could live. There were no cupboards. No loose tiles or stuff. Where had he gone? How did he get out? I never saw him again. I didn't want to either, mind you. But I sort of missed him. It was only a bathroom salamander, I suppose. Anyway, maybe there's something in all that universe dying stuff, cos the day he visited me was cool but the day he disappeared turned out to be one of the worst days of my life.

What's that about?

O Great One

Outside the palace of the Dahomey kings is a low, squat god. He crouches beside the roaring lion, the symbol of the kingdom. Behind him is a green telephone booth powered by a solar panel that sticks out of the roof of the booth. In front of him are the gates to the immense walled compound of these once-fearsome kings who ruled over a vast territory, made a fortune from slavery and whose reputation for grotesque cruelty was maintained by a standing army of twenty thousand women. Perhaps that may be why the sole apparent attribute of this blancmange-like deity is a huge, permanent erection.

Legba, I was told, is quite a powerful god but he overstepped the boundaries of heavenly propriety when he shagged the chief god's missus when the Great One wasn't looking. Being God No. 1 from whom nothing was hidden (you'd think Legba would have copped on), and having no flies on him, nor having come down with the last shower, nor having just blown in on the east wind etc., etc., the Big Enchilada began to notice something was up when his wife/goddess (and she was) began to bulk around the middle.

To cut a long (geddit!) story short, old Legba was hauled before the Paradisical Court and sentenced to an Eternal Stonker from which there would be no release. He would never again be capable of ejaculation. Just the pain of a permanent hard-on. Infinite frustration with no possibility of relief.

The awful, considered cruelty of it all. We had a boy in school who had the same thing but I don't think he had gone around shagging the wives of the gods. Mind you, he was only eleven.

It is weird how all these myths are repeated throughout different cultures. This one is the African version of the Greek legend of Priapus, which is, of course, where we get the name for the painful but nonetheless humorous condition of priapism that so afflicted my classmate.

I don't know why they have to keep Legba mollified, but when I saw his tubby little fetish it had been recently covered in an offering. Each morning someone pours a milky millet porridge over his head, which spills over his chubby face. Unfortunately, it looks like someone has done to Legba that which he is incapable of doing himself. Poor sod. Must drive him mad.

Coffins, Gates and Beds

All down the road were the big beds, the gates and the rows of coffins. How does that work? You're driving home and think, 'You know what I fancy? A nice new pair of giant metal gates?' Or, 'Whoa, that's a good-looking king-size over there. Tell you what, mate, sling it up on the back there.'

And it's not just one or two shops. It's mile after mile of them, interspersed occasionally with the Clap for Jesus Nail Salon stalls or the beautiful globe bottles once filled with Nigerian cooking oil and now cork-stoppered petrol set on high tables that pass for service stations in this neck of the woods. Or your bog-standard He Sees All Vegetable Spot or Evil Shall Not Tempt Me Deep Fry Snack Shack.

The coffins line up half painted, a cross on the top third, leaning against the workshop door in various sizes and, ominously African, with more little ones than adult-size.

The gates are propped in various states of finish right at the kerb. Some lean half raised against boxes. Some are wire-brushed shiny, others painted with a rust-coloured undercoat and the rest are simply rusting. But these are serious gates. More like metal barn doors than garden gates. These things are solid heavyweight security barriers. But who stops on some African back road and buys them? Or puts in an order for them? Who's got a house big enough? Who's got the land? Where are the compounds that require these things? All I see are the shacks and tukuls – the little round thatched or palm-fronded houses. What do you need these things for and who are you afraid of? But there they are, between the coffins and the beds. Thriving.

Maybe the same person who bought a set of these monsters moves smartly along next door, opting for the 'Gates and King-Size Bed too' option. These aren't beds, they're Behemoths of the Slumber Kingdom. They're Monsters from the Planet Bed. They're the Mighty Beds from Oversize Hall. These aren't for sleeping on, they're for bed football. For building a housing estate on. Half the rainforest edging the road must have gone into just one of these babies. Where would they fit? What house, never mind room, is big enough for them? Is it the same house that gets the gates? Do they order coffins as well? All these things are a mystery.

People sleep out in the open here. The heat is too oppressive. Naked single iron bed frames lie alongside the shacks with their springs exposed. Mattress, sheets and blankets are redundant. People just lie on the springs and sleep.

Once I slept on one of those big beds. I was in the King of Biseasi's house. His name was John and he had a house somewhere in London. He made me a king too in front of his people. It was fun and the local kids got the day off school. So I slept in his place. In the big bed. It was King John's bed so, y'know, literally a 'king-size' bed. He insisted I sleep on it before going off to stay at one of his subjects' houses. King John's palace was still being built when I was there. There was a lot of marble, brass fittings, wall lights and faux rococo three-piece suites with heavy brown brocaded upholstery in the posh African style.

There was a nice kitchen – all mod cons – but his sister, the princess, preferred to do all the cooking in the yard on a wood fire instead of the gas cooker inside. That's why we missed the plane in the morning – cos it took so long to cook breakfast. We didn't know what was happening until I went to the kitchen to try and jolly things along and found them waiting for the water to boil out the back over a damp fire.

I thrashed around in the vast space of King John's bed. Around me were the samples of kids' clothing he'd brought back from his last trip to Thailand and China. That's what he did. Sold kids' clothes in Accra where he had another house. He told his people I was going to be his King of Development. They cheered. They sang songs. They dressed me in togas and gold. A gold crown, necklace, sandals and many, many rings. So many rings it would make Puff Daddy blush. I looked a twat but they don't think like that. They loved it and because they loved it so did I and so then I didn't feel a twat. And when he announced over the mega overdriven huge PA system, with each sentence bizarrely punctuated by the noises that you get on one of those toy digital space-ray- guns, that I was going to get Tony WHOOSH Blair BEEEEP BE BEEEP to give Biseasi lots of money to develop WHIRRRRRR and that's why I was being given my full Ashanti title of Nana (King/Chief) BURP BURRRP Kofi (Friday – the day of the coronation) Kumasah (the great hero-warrior of the Ashanti), they all went crazy. King John winked at me. I had been co-opted into his scheme to drag his people out of poverty. TWIRRRRBEEEPWHOOSHRATATATBLURPBLURPKOOOSHH. Fantastic.

That night I went to the bar in town. As I entered, the bar rose and respectfully murmured 'Nana' and the women bowed and when walking in front of me walked backwards in a low bow. Even in the street. Cool.

Back in the palace in the nylon sheets. Everyone in Africa has nylon, the miracle fibre! Just so you can get extra sticky, I suppose. I fell into a restless sleep. It was like I was in infinity. A world without edges. No visible parameters. Like a child needs. Like when they feel reassured when you tell them what they can or can't do. Borders. Limits. Security. Gates. GATES. That's it! I floundered awake and tried to find the edge of the vastness and stumbled out to the porch where King John's friends had spent the night in chairs to keep me company in sleep. To keep watch. To stand guard! Gates again!

But who else except a king would buy one of these beds? Where would they fit except in John's modest palace? A guy with several wives? Maybe. That's sorta normal in this part of the world. But I don't think so.

And the coffins?

Death is a big thing here. I mean, it's a big thing everywhere but here it's a BIG deal. I suppose because life is so impermanent, so transitory, and death always so imminent, that while both eyes are kept firmly on the business of being alive, the secret eye of the interior is staring wide open into the Home Call.

There is a great exuberance in life here that stems from the awareness and the proximity and the daily reality of premature death. The beds and the coffins side by side. So many children are made in those big beds. Children that will provide you with continuity and status and labour and care in age. Children that are the social safety net where the state provides nothing. Children that are as individually precious and loved as anywhere else . . . and who die so often and in such numbers and who must be replaced. And because they die so easily here and because the emotional hammer blows are so great, one must do something to protect oneself against despair. One celebrates. You sing and praise and laugh at the joyous Home the little ones have gone to. You understand perfectly through joy and loss God's seemingly voracious appetite for the innocent and precious. And thus when death does finally come a-knocking it is celebrated as fabulously as life itself. What else can you do?

You can pay a fortune for the right coffin. Sometimes $750! People save more for their own funerals than they do for anything else. It's serious party time. There are roadside places that have mobile phone coffins for the thrusting businessman. It is an exact facsimile of a

Nokia 6210. In full colour. There's a Nike trainer coffin with wooden laces for the athlete or shoe salesman, or maybe rapper. There's a Mercedes SSL coffin for the boy racer or car salesman. A Boeing jumbo coffin for the pilot or steward, a wooden butane gas tank coffin, a sack of grain coffin, a Coke bottle coffin and all sorts of large wooden animal coffins representing your tribe or attributes and into which you will one day fit and be carried Home at last.

Just as the well-lived life can be a work of art, this is art in death. It is spectacular. Otherwise, it's the black-painted pine casket with the cross like everyone else. Most buy in advance when they're flush and keep it stored someplace, mounted on bricks with water round the base to keep the termites away.

The newspapers keep themselves alive by pages of the deceased. The Home Call adverts. The bigger the ad, the greater the honour, the more important the individual, the more loved the person. Precious money is well spent on the Home Call announcement. They have pictures, times of service, a mini biography and a list of the family that is endless. Most people, like their coffins, plan and book their own ad years in advance of the actual event, always choosing the glamorous or flattering photo they wish to be represented by at the death.

There are Home Call posters plastered on walls or pinned to trees or lampposts with the same photo and text as the papers but even more lists of family and, crucially and finally, the names of the chief mourners.

Everyone wears bright clothes to the funeral. Bright and best. There is singing, feasting, dancing and laughing. In death there is the celebration of total exhilarating life. Home, Lord, finally home. Imagine the cost. Africans spend at least as much on their funerals as they do their weddings. They have the right priorities.

Nor do they believe they are actually dying. Christianity dovetails neatly into the traditional religions here. The deceased are simply changing dimensions. For the traditional religions, the ancestors are a daily presence and influence in your life. They can be extremely annoying but they can also help affect things to your advantage. They occupy a zone somewhere between the deities and the corporal living. They need to be honoured. They have eternal virtues which must be maintained for the sake of the clan or else they'll make things unpleasant and they generally mooch around at night which can be scary when you bump into them.

The biggest expanding market for mobile phone telephony in the world is Africa and a lot of that market is driven by the need of people who have migrated to the cities to stay in touch with their villages and find out who has died. People transfer credit over the cell phone to their parents to whom they have given a phone in order for their relatives in the villages to stay in touch, perhaps just using one which they can all share. That phone credit has become a form of e-currency, much more trusted than the national banks with their inflationary monies and corrupt practices. Virtual currency is readily understandable to an African. Indeed, there is a clear appreciation of anything virtual. Like the ancestors themselves who are unseen but present and wielding huge influence. And when infrastructure does not exist here is something that functions without it – a virtual infrastructure.

To most Africans the invisibility of the real is simply an inconvenience. It is clear to them that there is stuff happening everywhere invisibly that impacts upon us and determines life as much as that which is seen. And they're right. Moneyless societies exist throughout the continent. Trade and barter is ubiquitous. E-credit is simply an invisible exchange of values that cannot be perverted by the crooked state or its institutions. Bizarrely, as a result, Africa is leading the way in this form of virtual money and e-technology. Phones have become a leapfrog technology. Africa is connecting big time, driven by culture and necessity. And death is both.

When the state provides you with nothing, when you derive no benefit from the notion of a state, why should you give it your loyalty? No, your trust is to that which protects and sustains you, your massive family which is the clan, and the group of related clans, your tribe. That same vast family network will care for you throughout life as a mutual obligation. It is the key area where Africa differs from us.

Since the Enlightenment our part of the world has operated on the basis of individualism. And it has been relatively successful for us. Paradoxically, individualism only works when the individual works collectively for the common good. The opposite is true in Africa. Everything is done through the collective. Which is why whenever our world has tried to interfere in Africa, whether in an aggressive or benign manner, it has so often gone wrong. We have transplanted ideas developed under one notion of life on to another contrary view. It can't work and it never has. But should you come from the collective idea then death and who is dead is important. For when someone dies, a dangerous tear appears in the societal substrata and social safety net that is the tribe, and it must be repaired immediately.

Coffins and Home Calls are everywhere because death now is everywhere. Like never before, the social structures that allowed Africa to withstand the shocks of history and environment for millennia are stretched now to their limit. In one place so many are dying they steal the brass water taps off the irrigation pipes to make the obligatory brass handles for the coffins. It doesn't matter that the pumps no longer work without the handles and that nothing grows as a result. It only matters that they went with dignity. They went properly. As you should. With brass handles on your coffin.

Coffins, beds and gates. Everywhere, all along the road. In the end, if you think about it, I suppose it's all there really. Love and birth in the big bed. For the resulting family, safety and security behind the big metal gates. And finally the coffin, the big glamorous fuck-off coffin to get on outta there in serious style with the wives, the kids, the neighbours and friends cheering you all the way Home.

GO PLASTIC

It's the small, unnoticed things that change you. Plastic has not only provided most Africans with footwear and impermeable building materials, but also the revolution that is the plastic bottle. It is the children's job to collect water. Wells can be perhaps five or eight kilometres from the village; in the past, children had to walk, carrying the heavy earthenware jars to this source, returning home heavily laden. Thanks to plastic bottles the journey to the well is light; coming home more can be carried and less spilt.

The boys can stay out longer with the cattle, goats and camels, bringing their endlessly used Evian bottles over which they scrap when one of us thoughtlessly discards ours.

Go plastic.

The Sound of Freedom

When we Europeans first encountered Africans, we met more or less as equals; we both wanted to trade, and in their kingdoms and empires we recognised arrangements not dissimilar to our own. Besides, slavery was known and practised on both continents. But it was in the discovery of the new colonies of the Americas and their need for labour that that original understanding was perverted into the grotesque mass trade of human beings that still resonates today through our psychologies and our politics.

There was, however, one gloriously bright moment amidst all this tragedy, one that convinces us again of the historian's view that the great genius of the African is his adaptability and survival.

Forbidden everything, including their humanity, these new slaves understood that they could only keep that which was invisible, their spirit, their essence, their mojo – as one of their languages has it. Forced into hiding, Voodoo, their religion, remained secret and feared by those who didn't understand it.

But there was one place where these unfree 'non-humans' could practise their religious drumming. Every Sunday on Congo Square in New Orleans, crowds would gather to hear the drummers invest every beat with an infinite soul. Soon others joined in, watched by the ladies of the town with their sweet, perfumed, jasmine scent. And it was from the beauty of these women and their perfume that the musicians took the word for their new music. From jasmine we get the name 'jazz'.

It is ironic, isn't it, that these enslaved, dehumanised, shackled people invented the sound of the roaring, young, free, new country of the United States, and the background noise to the democratic twentieth century. Out of unimaginable brutality and in an act of creative defiance unmatched in human history, these Africans had created the music of a soaring glorious prayer to the unbowed, free human spirit.

The Kola Nut

The Arabs were prepared to put up with the immense danger posed by the Sahara for a few things. What lured them south into black Africa was trade. In no particular order of importance they were gold, ivory, slaves and the kola nut.

The kola nut. How innocent that seems when you consider the misery wrought upon the world by the first three on that list. And yet for the ancient world as for the modern the kola nut was considered just as vital and lucrative as the other more dubious commodities.

The gold and the ivory and the slaves may have been more readily associated with the wealthy but the kola nut was considered to be just as valuable. It was in its ubiquity rather than its scarcity that its true democratic value was to be found. Everyone wanted it; everyone could have it. It was the pick-me-up of the common man.

This West African nut has been chewed for centuries in coastal regions from Senegal in the north through the Bight of Benin to Angola in the south. It was exported by camel train across the dunes into North Africa and there was a cult surrounding it among Muslims in the Sahel even as far east as Sudan.

Historically it was used as currency. Even today it can still be regarded as wealth. Go to a market with your store of nuts and you will be able to trade them for other goods. Its addictiveness created a huge demand but, because it could be kept fresh for weeks while wetly wrapped in leaves, it was an ideal export crop. From its home in the equatorial rainforest packed and repacked in damp leaves every five days, it would reach its marketplace just beneath the Sahara and already be trading at forty times its cost.

The Arabs loved it. It was an astringent. A thirst quencher. Very useful in the waterless wastes of the desert. It is an appetite suppressant, which can be helpful when there's little food either in your own country or on a long journey. It is used as a digestif, a healthy clear-out after a hearty meal. And, most importantly, it is a stimulant, in much the same way as coffee or tea. Indeed, in the seventeenth century Europeans did try and make a drink from it at around the same time we discovered the plants that would become the society-altering beverages of our culture. It tasted disgusting. And it still does.

Among the Yoruba in northern Nigeria it occupied the same sort of mystical and religious place that coca leaves had for the Inca of South America. It was used as a symbol of friendship and hospitality. It was offered to guests when they entered the house. The nut symbolised everything that was civilised and peaceful in the world. It can be compared to the Native American peace pipe or the religious idea of breaking bread. In Sierra Leone the people thought that chewing kola could prevent malaria. This belief spread to the Europeans when they arrived in the guise of slave traders and resulted in many deaths among both black and white. It is still believed to prevent malaria. It doesn't. It is thought to render putrid water drinkable. Powdered kola is applied to cuts. In Ghana I'm told it's great for menstruation pains or as a contraceptive and even for headaches (possibly the same thing?). You rub it on your forehead! It is a valuable nervine agent, beneficial to the heart and a good all-round tonic.

Wow. So what's in this miracle thing? Kola is 2 per cent caffeine and has traces of other stuff that is valued as a heart stimulant. It's 10 per cent protein – for all the Atkins freaks in sub-Saharan Africa – 2.3 per cent fat, 80 per cent carbs (Atkins!!) and 2.5 per cent fibre. If you were to use kola as a major part of your diet you would begin to feel very uncomfortable. Your pulse and respiration rate would increase, you would suffer insomnia, hyperactivity and the diet would be thinning. Just like coffee. But bite into it and it tastes woody. No. Worse. Like biting into an unripe chestnut. Disgusting.

It has spiritual properties, too. It is used everywhere for divination purposes. Like a nutty version of a horoscope. For most sub-Saharan peoples divination rites are an essential part of their daily life. Just as we read our stars in the morning papers here an individual will cast pieces of kola nut in order to determine what to do to make his way successfully through the day. It is used in Voodoo rites in Mali where the nut will be bitten and spat into a bowl to be interpreted. Or scattered by the fox diviners of Dogon who lay complex astrological-type patterns in the sand, which a nocturnal fox will wander through. The feet patterns and nut displacements will then be read for what they reveal.

Anyway …

Though huge in Africa for millennia, it wasn't until the late 1800s that kola got its big break.

Enter John Pemberton, an American chemist making a living selling his elixirs, tonics and pick-me-ups to the crowned heads and popes of Europe. These drinks were in effect alcohol- and opium-based alcopops *du jour*. When America banned alcohol from medicinal liquids Pemberton was in trouble; any royalty actually partaking of Pemberton's quack medicines weren't benefiting from their supposed healing properties at all – they were just pissed. Business collapsed. In desperation Pemberton hunted around for an alcohol substitute to give their royal high(literally)nesses their kick. He heard about the kola nut.

He tried it out, mixed it with a sugary syrup and added for good measure a *soupçon* of cocaine. Just in case.

He sold the ownership rights to his drink ten years later for $25,000. Within another ten years it was worth millions.

This week six hundred million people all over the world will drink Coca-Cola. The 'coca' bit refers to the non-existent cocaine, the 'cola' to the kola of the nut. When they drink that delicious beverage all these people will be imbibing a tiny part of the African rainforest. They'll be drinking history. The kola nut is the real thing.

Coca-Cola make a 27 per cent profit in Africa per annum, a bigger percentage than any other of their territories, including America.

I presume the Arabs made a similar sort of profit.

This Country is Full of Ghosts

This country is full of ghosts. Handless ghosts are everywhere. The forest whispers them. They brush against you untouchingly.

The tyrant's palace is full of ghosts. People will not enter its decaying rooms. They say he is alive. He lives among the ghosts of the children he killed and ate in blood sacrifice. It was this that gave him his great and terrible power. Leave the gates locked. Let him think he still rules. He does not know he is dead. Inside he cannot escape. Do not enter.

On the river the ghosts of the slaves. Centuries of ghosts forever travelling to horror and exile. They rattle in their shackles, clank in their chains. Still shuffle, yoked, along the pathways. Still moan from despair. Still the children weep, the women keen. The water carries those 'sold down the river' and it laps their wounds still, on its worn, tired banks.

In unseen clearings are the many massacred. Their ghosts still plead, still call uselessly for help. The *chicotte* still scourges, the panga chops, the club keeps falling. The blood lust is not abated. The ghosts are frightened.

The mansion house on the river bank resounds with the echoes of the glamorous foreigners. Their laughter and their singing are here. From the empty ruin of the rooms an old glass string hangs from a half-fallen ceiling. The film they made here flickering ghostly still in dark rooms outside this country.

The ancestors hover. Everyone who ever died must be addressed. They are irritated easily. They will upset your day and can damage the harmony of your life. They can be cruel and unkind. They can cause trouble. Keep these ghosts happy. It is a chore but they are demanding.

All real, all alive. They cannot be forgotten because they are still material, still tangible, still here. The air is choked with them. The night blocked. The day an endless negotiation of their numinous presence.

The Policeman in the Hotel

As soon as the door swishes closed the weirdness stops. Looking back through the plate glass the hawkers still shout and push, still hold up their unbuyable crap for your attention. The money changers, waiting since 5 a.m. for the new colonials, clustered round the best hotel in town, clutching bank bundles, serious in their large, gold-rimmed sunglasses, waving calculators and wads of dollars at the shut door. They are silent now. Everyone's mouth moves, flashing gold fillings, pink tongues, red throats and white, white teeth. The street thug who accosted me makes biting motions with his teeth. He is saying he will eat me when he sees me next. Unsettled, turn away now. Their shouting is unable to penetrate to you. This unbridgeable gap between me with everything and them with an absolute of nothing. The unequal scrabble with the doormen, the blue-uniformed, whip-wielding, gun-carrying security, ends again and the street traders are pushed back once more off the pavement on to the road where they wait for the next guest to arrive. Some still stare. Huge drug-bulging eyes. Scared. But it's okay, you are in your world now.

It doesn't stink in here. The carpet is soft. There is no fog of clapped-out car-exhaust fumes. No pall of dust from the stinking dry city. It's beautiful. Calm. The air is perfumed and sweet. It is cool. The air conditioning hums. The chairs aren't worn or tattered. The desk clerks are reassuringly inefficient; you can become tersely irate without being threatened by broken bottles. There are many lights and it is bright. You have a special pass for the lift. The waiters smile. They, like the desk clerks, are relaxed in their secure, paid employment. They are not deferential and they are not rude. They, like me, are in their place in this coherent world inside the luxury hotel lobby.

Past the copyist contemporary art, on the banquette, is a policeman. He is from the threatening world outside the door. He sits uncomfortably forward, that place between the top of the thighs and buttocks perched, cuttingly on the rim of the sofa.

The policeman feels out of place. He is sitting nervously, he feels he doesn't belong. This place is as alien to him as the anarchy outside is to me. That is the world he swaggers through. Where he is sure. Of himself and my fear. Of himself because of my fear. Here in my world, I am effortlessly confident in this air-conditioned luxury with its fine-art comfort. Though, of course, I neither feel nor am aware of this. It's where I'm supposed to be. But he feels it. All of it. It is overwhelming.

Unusually for a policeman he doesn't meet your eye. Normally so arrogant in their certainty of power, here he must know that it is meaningless. This is where the money is. This is where the law comes from. This is where the power really lives. It's like it's suddenly struck him. The power is not in his whip or gun, it's in what allows him to use that whip or gun and for what. And that's in here. It's in the atmosphere. In the attitudes. That minister. The land where the leisure suit never died. That beautifully suited businessman. Those glamorous women trailing their scent and indifference in the overwhelming security of their beauty and sexuality. He can't shout at anyone here, can't use his whip. Can't molest or even approach you. What's the point of him? If I beckoned him to me, he would come. Twenty yards away, out on that frightening street, he'd stare at me with dismay and contempt at my arrogance and assumptions and then, humiliatingly, I would have to approach him.

What's he doing? Who's he protecting or waiting for? Some hotshot in the restaurant, I suppose. Waiting. Absorbing things he can tell the wife and friends. He pulls in his leg as I pass and fumbles with his watch, staring about, sitting at attention. Poor guy. He can't order a glass of water. Can't buy a coffee. He's probably not been paid for months, like all the police here. Unpaid for months in his pretty, pressed-perfect, camouflage-blue jumpsuit, his beret twisting nervously in his hands.

Bits of Diary

Shit, a dead dog. Hens picking at the fruit peels and shellfish on the shoreline. Pigs truffling among the fishing boats. Selecting what? The mud is filthy and stinks. Women scrape scales and slice tuna heads in two. Children playing on the beachfront of slavery which still continues among the fishermen they play alongside. Outside the Fuck You Hairdresser's a woman is walking with a sewing machine on her head.

At 8.30 we went to Mopti. There was a milky-grey sky and the sun was a grey sphere at its centre. We took off into the Sahara. It was in the sky. In the air. It had left the ground and now hovered 5,000 feet in the sky. The air is thick with material. We are 250 miles from the desert, but it comes to us. Sand, red in the early-morning light, covers the cars. Thermals stir the sand in a thick, burdened sky. A red fog. A driving wind that flaps your trousers. The effect is to be in a disembodied, claustrophopic cocoon, not a pea-souper, much thicker, more viscous. Like a bean-souper if anything. Sound is muffled, like at the seaside. The sun pale through the haze. Visibility two hundred yards max. Wraith-like figures, headgear flapping, move distantly through the odd atmosphere.

The modernity imposed on Africa is of the shakiest foundation. Divorced from the Western culture that produced it and in conflict with the culture that it inhabits, it is a recipe, like in Arabia, for cultural schizophrenia and the confusion and anxieties which follow from that.

We tend to portray Africa as being in a parallel universe of inexplicable horrors. In fact, it has parallel cultures where events are wholly understandable within their own conditions and circumstances, but seemingly alien to ours.

The Lubumbashi Road

The biggest market for mobile phones right now is Africa. Not surprising really when the stuff you need to drive them and computers comes from here.

I was driving back from the copper mines of Likasi to the coltan heaps of Lubumbashi. The Congo is so vastly wealthy even its river could supply the planet with one-sixth of its entire electricity needs, never mind the other stuff that's in its ground. Sad, then, that because of this wealth the Congo has been convulsed for seven years in the biggest conflict since the Second World War, involving nine countries and four million dead, though of course, and needless to say, we've heard very little about it.

It's odd, isn't it, that the poorer a society, the more peaceful it is and the wealthier a state the more conflict. I suppose that's because in the former there's little enough to share around but in the latter there's a lot more to fight over.

This has been the first pan-African war. In general, unlike us, Africans rarely have cross-border conflict. Most of their fighting is combined within the crudely and arbitrarily drawn boundaries of what constitutes their nation states. These were drawn up, ignoring the ethnic make-up of the new countries' inhabitants, most of whom occupied their own territories prior to the arrival of the Europeans and now, at a pencil stroke, found themselves separated by a 'line in the sand'. For others it forced them alongside their traditional enemies. As a result, many African countries have been riven by internal ethnic conflict since the countries were conceived of in a map room in Berlin in 1884.

These ethnic wars do in fact cross boundaries, virtual boundaries if you like, ones that we don't recognise but which have existed for ever inside the heads of the different peoples who live within them. We call this tribalism, as if we can somehow dismiss that as being an incomprehensible, primitive concept. As if we can ignore our own Yugoslavias and Northern Irelands; as if we can forget the Basques, Catalans, North Italians, Alsatians, Sudetens, Flemish tribes – as we blithely raise eyebrows and hands in exasperation.

The Congo, actually the Democratic Republic of Congo, is a doozie. It really takes the biscuit. Since its beginning as a national identity it's had problems, all caused by its vast wealth.

At first it was the Congo's rubber we wanted.

John Dunlop, the Scottish engineer, wanted to invent a soft wheel for his daughter's new bike and came up with the pneumatic tyre. The price of rubber went berserk. The motor car followed, as did the rubber raincoat, the macintosh (named after Charles Macintosh, another Scot. Talk about tribal) and, how ironic in the country out of whose impenetrable jungles, we believe, AIDS emerged, the rubber condom.

By the time Leopold II, King of the Belgians, had finished with this private slave state he had created, Brussels had been built, and the population of the Congo had fallen from an estimated twenty million to eight and a half million. It was, in reality, the first Holocaust, the first knowingly and indifferently planned mass murder of entire peoples. And, like the current barbarity, most of us knew little or cared less about it.

Joseph Mobutu, Congolese President from 1970, wasn't much better. He looted the state he lorded over into paralysis. He took everything for himself and stashed the money in the banks of the West. He was a brute and a killer. Many people in Kinshasa, his capital, believe his ghost still walks his palace, that he still controls and maintains power through his spirit. As a result, this vast building, which should be used as a hospital or university or even luxury hotel, remains locked and barred and people very carefully skirt its perimeter.

He took all the diamonds, gold, copper, coltan, zinc, etc., and stuffed it into his back pocket while terrorising his people. It must have been a big back pocket. The mines were vast.

Today, amateur miners burrow, dig and scrabble at them with their shovels, pickaxes, even with their bare hands. It looks like some vast Pharaonic undertaking. Around them lie the giant, rusting bones of Mobutu's excavating machinery, abandoned when he absconded. The people claw at the mines' still substantial carcasses but at least they can keep the rewards of their labour – as long as they pay off the otherwise unpaid police, the army, official and unofficial roadblocks and everyone else. Still, at least now the money is being unofficially spread around, and is being used to support families and pay for their education. I met three doctors working as self-employed miners, and several more medical students, as they lug the huge sacks of ore up the steep gradient to the waiting cars and trucks that then speed off illegally to the nearby, porous, border with Zambia.

I didn't want to stay in Likasi. It was a clean, well-ordered, quiet little country town but we'd being travelling for days and I really needed to stay in a half-decent hotel and get a bottle of beer or drinkable wine with a lavatory you could sit on as opposed to hover above.

We had to hurry. We'd been filming longer than intended and now we had to rush before night fell and the curfew closed the red laterite road that ran a straight 100 kilometres and joined the country town to the provincial capital and its pleasant hotel. I was not staying in Likasi.

We were too late. The night collapsed in on us as it does in that part of Africa. A gluey equatorial night, one that falls like a heavily draped velvet theatre curtain. In all the small low-voltage towns the paraffin lights or palm oil lamps splutter and sparkle on, if they're lucky. But on the country roads that penetrate the bush or forest it is pitch black.

That is when and where the army, unpaid and maybe getting one meal a day, change into civilian clothes and lie in wait in the bush that lines the roads in the hope of prey. They take off their helmets and camouflage gear but they keep their rifles. Two months earlier, on this same road, two South Africans had been ambushed and killed.

Maguire, the director, asked, 'What do you think, dude?'

'I don't mind either way' I said, 'Fuck it, let's go for it.' Two people dead in one year didn't seem too big a risk. And, anyway, I could hear those glasses clinking already. The rest of the crew were in the other Landcruiser. We walkie-talkied them. They were a little more circumspect but didn't fancy Likasi either. Everyone just wanted to wash the red dust, copper and sweat off their bodies and have a long drink followed by a longer sleep. But there was unease. You could feel it. You could sense it everywhere. Even on the walkies.

The driver was extremely alarmed, telling us again of the recent ambush. I was in the back so feeling a little more secure than the others, which was stupid because, unlike in Hollywood movies, a high-velocity bullet can penetrate sixty Landcruisers – never mind one – pass through vehicles, bodies, come out the other side and keep on going. Still, never keep a tired man from a comfy bed.

The driver expressed his deep concern again. 'This is extremely dangerous. It will be me who is killed. They aim for the right-hand side headlight, you know, and then they raise their sights slightly and fire blind into the windscreen towards the driver. That is me. Then I will die. The car will crash and they will rob and kill you.'

'Okay,' said Maguire. 'Keep going anyway.' Maguire, a laconic Irish Brummie, spoke into the walkie-talkie and told everyone to bunch up tight, top speed, not to fall behind, to stop for nothing and to drive with lights off until absolutely necessary.

The driver took his rosary beads off the rear-view mirror and wound them tightly around his fingers, clutching the crucifix and praying aloud. At one point he broke into song. It was a hymn. Maguire affected unconcern and lounged against the passenger-side door. In the back, hidden from the others, I sort of moved away from behind the driver and shrunk down into the seat as if I just wanted to have a kip. I moved my camera into the right-hand breast pocket of my shirt and held my mobile which, unbelievably in the darkness and immensity of this deep, deep jungle, still had a signal. As I lifted it in the pitch dark the screen lit up hugely and suddenly. I stuffed the phone over my heart. This was ridiculous, of course; if we were to be shot, a bullet was not going to be deflected by this tiny little phone that held at its core a precious little piece of the Congo earth we were busily, frighteningly, plummeting through. Still . . .

The night and the dark and the bush crowded us. We could see nothing. Maguire tried to keep up his bravura show of unconcern. It was an Irish equivalent of phlegm, sang-froid and indifference to danger. It's called bollocks in Ireland. And everywhere else for that matter. However, there was no going back now. Occasionally the walkie-talkies crackled . . . 'you're too far ahead we can't see you . . . keep up . . . we'll have to turn on our light for a bit . . .' The great fear was puncture or breakdown. It wasn't worth thinking about. We settled into a silence that had a kind of shimmer of fear along its edges. Sometimes the driver swerved suddenly as an animal darted out from the pressing trees. We left the radio off. The reception wasn't good and we didn't want noise. The driver sang a loud hymn again. Maguire said, 'Ferme la . . .' He shut up. Out there, out there . . .

I began to doze. JEEEZUS. Suddenly the car all but swerved off the road, the driver struggling with the wheel. Magure had his hand on the overhead handle but just looked ahead. I started awake. 'Answer the fucking thing, will you . . .' he said. 'Whaaaa . . .?' My phone had leapt into life; it glowed in the breast pocket like Kryptonite and vibrated against my heart like fear itself.

I wrenched it out, simultaneously irritated, embarrassed, afraid and amazed that in this absolute black, in the centre of this dark jungle, on this mud road where wild creatures, animal and human, lurked and roamed, my Nokia was instantly operative.

'Hello...?' 'Hey, Dad, it's Pix. Can I stay at Xantha's tonight?' 'What?' The line from Battersea was clear as a bell. As clear as the night sight on a sniper's rifle. 'Can I stay at Xantha's?' I struggled to adjust to a parallel teenage universe of sleepovers, homework and bedtimes. 'No, absolutely not. I've told you, not on a weekday.' 'But it's the weekend.' Was it? I was beyond time, in the twilight zone of the mud road between Likasi and Lubumbashi in the province of Katanga in southern Congo in Equatorial Africa and I was going to be killed at any second. 'Have you done your homework?' 'Yeah, I've done most of it and I'll bring the rest.' 'Okay, but no staying up late. Promise.' 'Yeah, cool, thanks, Dad. Love you.' 'Yeah. Love you too . . .' Very much.

Battersea. Lubumbashi. The light went off. Maguire turned, grinning. We shook our heads. Fucking amazing.

There was no shooting that night. The army was in bed and so would we be soon. After that excellent bottle of wine.

Africa has the fastest growing mobile phone market in the world. Thank God.

Latifa's Adventures in the Deuxième Monde

In the evening Tete, Latifa and Davide change into dogs or another animal and slip away to the *deuxième monde* – the second world – which is underground and also underwater. They will then rush to Bagoma, Bukavu, Kinshasa, America and Europe. When they get there they will make a child ill. That child will die and they can eat it. It's great fun and it tastes delicious but it's hard work. When they get back to their house in the countryside around Kisangani in the early hours, they're pretty exhausted and find it difficult to rise in the morning and get exorcised.

The children are between seven and ten years old but some of them in this school of witchcraft, this real-life Hogwarts in reverse (i.e. they don't learn to be sorcerers – they already are), are as young as three. One father cuddling his little boy explained that he operated 'African science'. He was a witch. It seemed improbable to me, but there were witnesses who had seen this very child kill other children. In fact, all five of his kids were witches and he'd brought them here, to this ramshackle building, where they could be cured of the devil along with the other sixty or so children who were there with their concerned parents.

None of this is new. It is a commonplace for there to be witches in Africa, people who at night can become animals and usually go to a parallel, underwater world where there may be universities and airports and roads and shops. I have often heard of the witches who meet at the tops of trees at night. They spin a web (a world wide web?) all over the world. The strings are attached to every door handle so that, if the humans within leave their house at night, the string will twitch, the witches will feel it and be able to catch and eat them. But what is new is that this is the first time children are being accused of witchcraft and simultaneously believing it.

The children are cute, like kids anywhere. They are matter-of-fact about their shape-shifting cannibal activities and their parents and they absolutely believe that what they say they do actually happens. Except that it doesn't.

Most parents will say that they try to stay awake at night so as to prevent the children leaving the house, whatever shape their offspring have assumed, but that they either fall asleep from exhaustion or a spell is put upon them to make them unconscious. Whereupon the 'African scientists' slip off to Idaho or wherever to terrorise the shopping malls of the Midwest.

It is interesting that the children do not differentiate between the local towns they name and the more exotic, distant locations of their activities, because the local places which they include in 'other countries' are the areas most troubled by conflict. The Western world is the one they either aspire to or believe to be the source of the wrong.

This part of the Congo is the area in which there is fighting for control of the diamond wealth, what the agencies call 'conflict diamonds'. The town is full of carpet-bagging Lebanese, Greek and Israeli dealers; men in rags sneak into the shops with gaudily painted fronts and rummage in their bags and pockets for a handful of cloudy yellow diamonds to sell. It must have looked like this in the Yukon or the Klondike in the old days. Except then they didn't have men in shades with Kalashnikovs standing outside the front doors of the assay offices, I suppose.

Sahara

The Great One

Les Sapeurs. Congolese 'mods' who pride themselves on their extravagant dress with no visible means of support

British slave fort, Cape Coast

The coronation of Nana Kofi Kumasah I (King Bob) with King John of Acton on the right

Bosasso, Puntland

Lokichoggio

Bosasso, Puntland

Timbuktu

Mursi

Arouane desert night
(Copyright © Tim Cragg)

Sisyphus

North Congo

Lubumbashi mines, Katanga

Mursi, southern Ethiopia

When you encounter the fleeing children in your headlights it is like coming upon an army of wraiths. Kitgum, Uganda

Imam, Djenne, Mali

The Great Mosque at Djenne, built in the 13th Century

Djenne

Salt miner's family, Arouane, Sahara

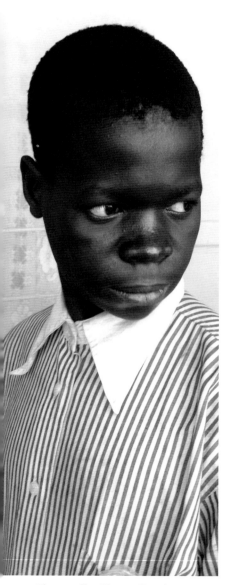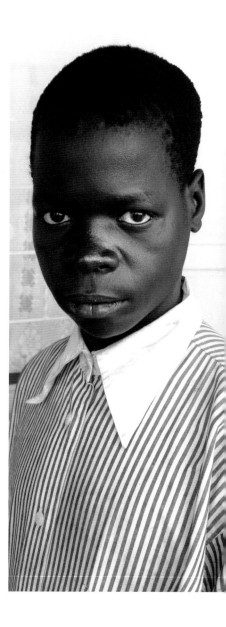

The egg seller, Kitgum, Uganda

The diamonds are bulk-smuggled out of the Congo and sold illegally on the diamond markets. Vicious fighting has been going on in this lawless region for years. The UN are here now but, having initially preferred to take a back seat, they have decided to shoot back. There are 17,000 of them and it's the most expensive UN operation in the world, costing, $700 million each year.

Africans, with their inveterate love of wordplay, parable and metaphor, refer dismissively to the Congolese UN mission which goes under the acronym MONUC, as Ma Nuc. My Fuck. Or, because the Democratic Republic of Congo is a French-speaking country and the UN in French becomes Nations Unies, the initials reversed now become NU, as in Nude or Naked. Which is another grimly apposite response to the UN's ineffectual stance hitherto. As in the emperor's new clothes ...

Kisangani is a thousand miles from the nearest ocean in any direction. It is the epicentre of Africa. The river took you in or out and it still does. Anything can go on here and no one will ever know. And it does. And no one knows.

Africa has held itself together recently throughout the appalling shocks of history, through the social security net of the clan. But it has almost buckled. Particularly in parts of the Congo, where the phenomenon of child witches can be seen as an expression of that partial collapse.

Within the traditional religions of Africa of which most people are adherents (as well as being Christians or Muslims) many believe that life, the world, has become so unbearable because all of the spirits have become, for the first time, uniquely evil. For these people this must be the only reasonable explanation for something for which they otherwise have no explanation.

Life has become intolerable. AIDS has ravaged and decimated the continent, perverting the normal social patterns of family and clan and, as a result, social and economic life. War rages across several places and specifically here in the DRC. Hunger is perennial. Medicine is unaffordable or non-existent, stability, government and education forgotten or imagined luxuries.

There must then be a great evil abroad and everyone knows the devil can possess the innocent child more quickly and more easily than he can the knowing adult.

Approximately 50 per cent of the African population is under fifteen. That's 350 million children. And it's a lot of children without families. It is, of course, one explanation why armies can readily pick up these orphans and give them a perverse sense of community and belonging and, of course, food. In exchange for killing.

AIDS having destroyed families, wives or husbands remarry. Often the new wife will discard the children of the first marriage. They will be abandoned on to the street where they must survive. Some of them are exceptionally young. In order to rid herself of these expensive and unnecessary mouths to feed and care for, the new wife will often accuse the child of witchcraft. Society will shun the family, often stoning the children; this continues even after their eviction from the household.

In other houses there simply is no food. Either that or the parents have died. AIDS affects primarily those of a sexually active age, i.e. younger adults. When these people die, not only are the main producers in the economy removed but the children are abandoned to the ageing grandparents, should they still be alive. These old-timers were raised in the belief that they would be cared for by their children, and, indeed, the entire community, when they grew old, as had happened since time immemorial. Thus in poor countries having many children is not just status and free labour, but also a form of social planning. Now their children have died and the old people cannot work and have no food. They have become orphans themselves. Ancient orphans. The little ones find themselves having to provide for their grandparents as well as themselves. And I mean children as young as four or five!

The witch children band together on the street and others are afraid of them. They are shunned but can bribe people for food under the threat of spells or cursing. Sometimes they may be lynched. Some find shelter elsewhere, where they are protected. Others fall readily into the hands of charlatan preachers who can exploit them for their own ends by gaining power within the local community or taking money from worried parents.

What is happening, however, despite its perhaps exotic appearance, seems to be the final act of suicide of a society in terminal decline, one that has decided to commit self-immolation. In an act of auto-cannibalism it has decided to deny its future by consuming its own children. Almost as if things are so unspeakably horrific, as if there is no point in this society continuing to exist. Almost as if they feel they don't deserve to exist.

The parents in this place love their children. They explain how their children had been given a piece of bread or some other food or drink by a neighbour with ill intent and thus had imbibed the sorcery. They relate how they have seen them kill other people. Usually, upon further investigation, this turns out to be a disease such as TB or another otherwise explicable illness.

Again in Africa, should someone suddenly acquire great wealth or power, or fall ill, it is considered reasonable to believe that this was done through the use of spiritual power. Often deeply unpleasant, spiritual power. The witch children can be seen as an expression of this idea. However, the parents or children probably don't know this or don't care. Nothing in Africa occurs without a reason and this is the most likely explanation for these unremittingly awful things that are happening to them and all around them.

The children are cured by prayer. This involves endless singing, walking around in circles, readings from the Bible (at full volume) and non-stop praying, the kids apparently earnest with eyes screwed shut and hands piously clamped over them. Except for the little ones: they always peep out through one eye.

Does it work? Is the Pope a Catholic? Course it does. Eventually. They know they are cured when they vomit copiously on the ground to great and general approbation. It seems to be particularly effective when they throw up material objects. There are wild claims of Bibles being vomited across the yard and other bits and pieces being spewed around the place. But the most tragic, the most symbolic and the most applauded is the puking up of a yellow diamond.

It is no accident that this stone is the source of the violence here in the vast, remote, densely forested north Congo. And how sad is it that in these children it has become the very emblem of the devil himself?

This isn't a game for these people, or for the children. Part of me believes that they revel in their exceptionalism. That in the mundane world of everyday horrors they stand out. Even standing out in a negative manner is better than the non-existence of rejection and the street. Here at least they are cared for. They get fed and clothed. They have friends here. They have a floor to sleep on and a blanket. They have a sort of education and it is almost certainly a lot better than wherever it is they have come from. Whatever it is they call home.

Besides, they like being witches. They're only getting cured cos their mums and dads insist or else because of all the above. But, hey, who wouldn't like it? Plump thigh of newborn-European baby anyone? Yum. Oh no, it must be off. I feel sick. Whoops.

Wow. A yellow diamond!

A STORY FROM THE CRAZY COUNTRY NEWSPAPER COLUMN
Pig thieves to be lynched

Mukono – Residents of Kilangira village in Nama sub country have resolved to lynch any person who will be found to have stolen a pig . . .

Rubber

It was violence that first opened up this previously impenetrable jungle. Leopold II's men cut their way through this forest over a hundred years ago in search of a prized commodity and cheap – preferably free – labour to harvest it for them.

Where people resisted, entire villages were massacred. To collect the bounty offered for the deaths of those who refused to submit, the hands of dead victims were severed and preserved so that Leopold's henchmen could prove to their master how successfully they'd done their job.

Before these men arrived, the population of the Congo was estimated at twenty million. By the time news of what was happening here leaked out, only eight and a half million remained.

The element that made all this effort worthwhile was – rubber.

Then Dunlop and the motor car came into the picture and rubber became a serious and brutally sought-after commodity. The demand and rewards were such that Leopold's administrators killed, tortured and mutilated in pursuit of the sticky white gold.

Ironically, it was another invention of the modern world that depended on rubber that finally exposed Leopold's brutal slave state for what it was – George Eastman's development of the Kodak camera.

One day, a man called Edmund Morel took a photograph of a man called Nsala sitting on a missionary's porch. In the photograph Nsala stares down at a small hand and foot, all that remains of his five-year-old daughter. She, along with his wife and son, had been dismembered, cooked and eaten by Leopold's henchmen. This was just part of 'the horror'.

When the world saw Nsala and his despair, the game was up. But not for the Congolese. And it still isn't.

Bouj

Bouj had flint-grey desert eyes. Did they deflect the glare like organic Ray-Bans? The lean, lined, fine-structured face was ageless, the face that perhaps only someone living in the exfoliating desert winds could have. He laughed a lot while in company. This was unusual. The others seemed to maintain a friendly silence nurtured over the years of travelling in single file alongside the camel trains or else reflecting the vast silences of this total emptiness.

Only in the Landcruiser was Bouj silent. He was too busy staring intently at the huge nothingness, this absolute topographical zero, this perfect nought of nature. Bouj was a desert guide.

I saw only endless sand, the odd scrub, an interestingly shaped dune, occasionally leavened by a passing camel train carrying salt south from Taodenni to Timbuktu. The Tuareg guiding the train and the caravanniers barely acknowledged our passing. Intent on his work, Bouj would nod and some indigo-turbaned head would turn to look back at us as we screamed past. This I took to be a welcome of some extravagance in this waterless world where, if Bouj were not with us, we would die within hours. To him it was home. As familiar to him as navigating the London Underground might be to us. Were the positions reversed, we would both flounder.

How did he know where he was going? From time to time he'd bark something at the driver but more often he held his hand out between the driver and himself, just below the rear-view mirror, and waved his hand left or right. We didn't stop once and in these trackless wastes he guided us 300 kilometres north of Timbuktu towards a buried town called Arouane.

Stopping in the desert is weird. There's no point in selecting a site. You just stop. It's all the same for miles. So we stopped and set up camp. There's no wood so we brought it with us. We cooked, ate, washed with sand, went behind another dune for toilety things, buried it with a flick of sand and got into sleeping bags.

I invented desert golf. You find a desiccated branch from a low scrub bush, collect your camel-dung pellets, place camel shit on top of desert thorn (vicious, nasty, everywhere) and let rip down the sandy fairway. Bouj and I played for about twenty minutes till I got bored. He got the guards to play with him. Why hadn't they invented it before, I wondered. Too busy looking at the stars. Too busy inside their own heads, the only place bigger than the space they walked upon or looked up at, I suppose. It's hardly any wonder that our great religions come out of the desert.

Left alone and insignificantly crushed between, under and upon the two vast eternities of ground and sky most people would probably come up with some mad psychedelic imaginings of a god. If they had only played desert golf perhaps we could have been spared all the grief.

Bouj led us straight into downtown Arouane. How? You can't see it until you are in it or, more accurately, on it. Arouane has been buried by the desert. Sand banks against the walls and doors and reaches up over the roofs. The few people who remain burrow daily in and out of their adobe homes. Arouane is the Venice of the desert, only not so beautiful; it's almost gone and whatever the difficulties of holding back the Adriatic may be, there is no way you will stop the vast seas of the Sahara, an ocean the size of the United States. Indeed, the very word Sahara means 'ocean' and the moving dunes are described as tides, 'ergs'. And the ergs were in full flood when they washed through Arouane.

This was Bouj's hometown. As we watched the night sky doing its nocturnal desert light show of piercing constellations, shooting stars and pretty arcing satellites he told me about himself.

'Arouane had many people when I was a child, I cannot tell you how big but the bush people lived near the town and there was a lot of trade here, caravans that came each day, people who brought millet, cows and sheep to the town. So, for everyone, Arouane was a hub. But then the sand came and the people moved far away. At first they did not want to leave for another place, fearing that if they did so their identities would cease to exist. The great Marabout was here and so people came from everywhere to study the Koran and many sons stayed if they found something to do. Back then we used camels to carry people, food, salt, everything. This was a great oasis. People came here to find something to eat; the camels rested and watered here.

Arouane was a sort of desert truck stop between the now dried-up river port of Timbuktu and the salt mines of Taodenni. People would stay for a brief time then continue on their way.

'There are people who go down to Gawa in Bemba or Alere just next to Nonon or go to the mines. The people of Arouane still walk the 250 kilometres to Taodenni in the winter to earn money in the mines.'

The salt is a dried-up sea from the days when the Sahara was a lush, green, fertile landmass. The weather began changing five thousand years ago and now the dried sea is still mined by slaves, criminals and the men from Arouane. In the summer the heat is unbearable so the free people of this town return here. Nothing grows at all in Arouane. Fuel for fires is the rabbit-dropping-sized camel dung for which the children search daily, endlessly. There is one well.

'By day it is too hot to walk to and carry the heavy jars or containers home. It is the children's job and so they wait for the cool of the evening. Each child is assigned a star. As they wait by the well and the sky darkens, so they watch the sky, singing and looking for their star. When it appears it is time for them to collect their water and go home. They are called the Children of the Stars.'

Bouj was quiet for a while. I asked him why they stayed here. Because it is home, he said simply. Because it is beautiful. And I looked out at the endlessness and the fabulous show overhead. I could have wept with the beauty of it all.

We were both silent. I offered him gin. He took a beer. Islam, like Christianity, can be practised whatever way works best for you. Bouj was Tuareg. You do not fuck with the Lords of the Desert. They are so proud it is said that when Islam first appeared in the desert the Tuareg refused it because they would not bow before anyone, including God.

'We are nomads,' Bouj says. 'This is our country. We walk it and know it. We keep our identity. Everyone should remain here so we can all keep our identity. The most beautiful thing in the desert is someone who has a lot of camels and who is far from home. The camels find good pasture, so in his heart he is well. He knows he will increase his camels to see him through the year.'

Bouj was afraid that the nomadic way of life is coming to an end and he is right to be fearful, for it is. Gradually the Tuareg are being pushed out of the desert again. The Sahara is growing even hotter and their way of life between the crushing stones of politics and environment is making them move again. Except this time there's nowhere for them to go save into the towns where they perch reluctantly on the edge of 'civilisation' in their tents and huts, one foot in the sand, the other on the paving.

'It is only the Tuareg who work in the desert; they have learned to adapt and since then they have known nothing but the desert. Tuareg still live in the bush on camels with sheep; that's how it is. But now over the years since the drought the people have been losing their strength in the desert; they have found other jobs. They are changing mentally.'

Like nomads everywhere, they have no concept of the common public space. In the desert you just dump stuff and move on. It gets swallowed up or blown away into the emptiness. It gets left behind. The Sahel towns of Africa are smothered in rubbish. Plastic bags are snared on the precious shade-giving trees. You feel as if you are walking through forests of polythene. Bits of rotting, ageing junk lie everywhere. 'Sahel' means shore and, again, just like the sea the Sahara ocean flings up its flotsam and jetsam all over these dull, dusty towns. The abandoned detritus of the nomadic lifestyle. Bouj prefers it out here in the cool, pristine cleanness of the open desert.

While we drove at full speed, slaloming sideways down one dune and rushing up the front of the next to gain height, I grew afraid. Was Bouj ever afraid out here in this place so inimical to life, so apparently hostile to humans? Wasn't he a bit like a sailor who understands the massive power of the sea and fears it?

'I fear that, if my camel has no strength, I will not find the well, so I become afraid. If the camel gets tired I will not be able to walk. I will not be able to move.' He would be adrift, rudderless without a sail to carry him on.

There is more silence. Silence is natural. Talking sullies the night, rips through the silence. I start when Bouj speaks.

'My father was a guide. He taught me everything. I travelled with him through my childhood. I learned the routes. I learned the sand, the dunes. I saw the stars. I looked at where there were pastures and wells. I learned all this from my father.'

There was another long silence. He sipped his beer. I had another gin. But how did he take people to some place that he himself had never seen or been to. He looked at me as if I was stupid.

'I ask,' he replied. 'I ask the old people for information. They tell me there will be dunes, what they will be like and after the dunes there will be markouba, a dense bush, after that there will be pasture, so it is all explained to me and I take heed of everything they say and I keep it all in my head and then I start. I look all around. If there are tracks I begin to follow them; if not I remember what I have been told in my head.'

Another silence. Suddenly from behind us, smothered in the sand, someone laughed. There was no light in the buried town save the stars. People went to bed when it was dark and slept, then woke and dug and swept away the sand blown in by the night. We sat on the dune and looked out over the stillness. Everything is biblical. It is quite true that there is in this minimal nothingness, in this unnoisy, uncluttered, clarity a palpable sense of the sacred. One's insignificance in the Grand Plan is apparent, humbling and liberating. The ego diminishes in direct proportion to the enormity of the cosmos. A great freedom flows from the insignificance of You.

'My father was blind,' Bouj casually dropped into the huge silence of the universe. I considered this. How was that possible? How could he take vast herds of camels and people across a featureless void?

'He smelt the wind. He tasted the sand.' Was he joking? Was this some stunt by the Saharan Tourist Board or something? Impress Whitey with the Wisdom of the Ancients stuff? Get him just as he falls into that romantic cosmos reverie thing.

'One time he took people 400 kilometres across the desert to a small village in Mauritania where he had never been before.' How?

'He asked people the way.' Ah, yes; the Wisdom of the Ancients!

'He asked them which direction the wind blew from. Where the wind passed through on its way so that he could smell it and knew the direction of the sand and dunes and he could feel them. He asked people the position of the stars each night. There is nothing to see here anyway; he did not lose anything by being blind and in his mind he knew where he was. Where he needed to go. He could feel it. He was a guide.'

He tasted the sand? Does sand taste? 'Oh, yes. He could taste the minerals and the salt and the different roots or bush. He had asked the old people what he could expect to find on his route and they had told him and so he looked for that taste!'

'One night the caravan had stopped. My father was asking the men the position of the stars. They knew he would next pick up some sand to taste. But they had played a joke. They had carried some sand from the last place they had camped and silently scattered the old sand around my father's feet so that he would bend down and pick up the old sand from the other place. When my father tasted it, he paused, stooped again, tasted again. Then he said. "We have just spent a long time going nowhere, gentlemen. Let us continue in the same direction." Everybody laughed. They could not fool my father. He was a great guide.'

Bouj laughed at the memory, the sound filling the silent, empty, glowing night. The flint-grey eyes stared out at the nothingness that for him was filled to the brim with everything.

The Man From Arouane

A Desert Doggerel
(with many apologies to Robert Service and
the Great McGonagall)

I met a man from Arouane
Who'd been through Timbuktu
His eyes, rimmed red, were filled with dread
But for the rest, he dressed in blue

He said:

I've blown south with the desert wind
To bring the awful news
That what once happened to Arouane
Has happened now to Timbuktu

The winds blew up, a storm arose
For days we couldn't see
And when at last that storm had passed
With horror we perceived

A city where three kings once lived
A desert seat of learning
Was now a rolling wave of dunes
O'er which the sun was burning

He took a drink and he closed his eyes
But his word hung in that room
Thus was told in Bamako
The death of Timbuktu

We stared at the floor, then we heard the door
Softly close behind him
He'd blown out and in with the desert wind
And the burning sun that blinds him

And as he rode hard south, from his sand-clogged mouth
Came the story no one doubted
For this was the man from Arouane
And death hung heavy 'bout him

Now there's many a tale of the desert told
And many who don't believe them
Of men who lust, driven mad with thirst
And the visions that deceive them

Of ghostly caravans by night
Carrying salt more precious than gold
That disappear as you draw near
Leaving nothing to behold

Or the shimmering shape of silvery streams
Green palms and waters cool
Of beautiful girls like desert pearls
Bathing in blue pools

But there's nothing there, just the desert bare
No water, colours, nor pearls, son,
Just endless sand in a barren land
And the desert men in turbans

But I'll never forget that Tuareg lord
The desert still on his shoes
There were no lies in those wild wide eyes
When he spoke of Timbuktu

He had told his tale and he took one drink
He begged no money nor room
Then he left as quick as he had come
Pale under the desert moon

I'm older now and my nights are short
But in my dreams I'm drowning in sand
And the last I'll see 'ere it buries me
Is the man from Arouane

The last I'll see 'ere it covers me
Is the man from Arouane
I wake with a scream from my awful dream
And see the man from Arouane.

Sisyphus in the Desert

There are 350 different types of black beetle in the desert. The Tuareg never kill them. They, like the Tuareg, are viewed as survivors and masters of this environment. But it goes further than that. They are not exactly revered as holy but there are superstitions attached to them. Kill one and you too will die.

The desert guides will tell you that, when lost, follow the beetle and he will take you someplace near water. I can't see it myself. They are everywhere and there is no water for miles. I assume they take whatever moisture they need from the night air. Little antennae waving at the stars, sucking at the dark. They emerge out of the sand, their humped shiny black backs flaring in the sun. Then they scurry around. But I could never see what for. Or they surf the shifting sand down a dune, legs splayed and delicately adjusting to the speed and movement of the individual sand grains their spindles rest upon. And then they zip under the sand again.

There is one type which, in extremis, has developed an extraordinary mechanism for survival. It is a sort of Sisyphean beetle. When there is no water and excruciating thirst overwhelms, this little fellow gathers a ball of sand or camel dung beneath itself and then begins to roll it up a dune. Like Sisyphus it never gets to the top. But unlike the Greek avatar of pointless activity, he allows the ball to roll down a bit and then begins his uphill struggle again. It begins to sweat. Beetles sweating? I know, don't ask . . . When it has perspired enough it rolls itself into a ball and rocks on its back till the sweat gathers in the curl of its stomach. Then it arches its head forward and sips at its own sweat . . . and life continues.

So cute! Fantastic!

The Night Commuters

The sound of the night is suddenly punctured by Ebola Mike and Bobbi Wine. It's 1a.m. In the morning I discover it's actually not Ebola Mike or Bobbi Wine at all because they didn't show up. It's some other scratch band from this remote area of northern Uganda and not the hip-hop stars they'd been expecting from the capital.

Truth is, nobody was really expecting them to pitch up. The big posters everywhere were really only a sort of wish list that one aspired to when one bought the ticket for the gig. The ticket price was based on the expectation and not the reality. They charged you for Mike and Bobbi but you got Joe Blow or whoever with no refund. No one seemed to mind. Oh the patience and fatalism of Africa.

Here was the night, shredded till dawn by the big boom beats of Kitgum. At 3 a.m. there was loud gunfire around the edge of town. Possibly about three clicks away. It was probably the Lord's Resistance Army who were in the area again. The bass drum easily blocked the crackle of guns.

Further down the red clay road from the Bomah Hotel, where the big stage had been erected in the garden underneath my window in the centre of town, there was hushed conversation, giggles or sleep sighs, night shouts from peaceful dreamers or nightmare-disturbed children.

Crowded and cradled into each other on the cracked pavements, under corrugated awnings, were the night commuters of Kitgum.

Tiny, ragged, shoeless and asleep.

They spilled out on to the mud road. They crowded the old hospital grounds. They were strewn about the WFP (World Food Programme) compounds and the stony playing field. Their bodies accommodated the pitch and roll of the uneven park and moulded themselves round the rocks and potholes of the main street. Around them lay the detritus of their nightly pilgrimage. For the luckier ones a torn blanket; for the others a ragged woollen jumper or single shoe. Touchingly, tragically, some even change into what were once pyjamas or nighties so as not to ruin the rags they wear at daylight. A string vest that was not supposed to be string but could no longer recall its old solidity. You want to scoop them all up and cuddle them. Take them home. Look after them. Protect them. And kill their tormentors. And I would. I really would.

Little scraps of humanity alone in this night of big beats and bangs. Three-year-olds being taken care of by their five-year-old siblings. Wonderfully, tenderly, beautifully, lovingly, dutifully being cared for. Snuggled up. Hands held. Eyes wide, hungry, till sleep arrives as it will, blessedly quickly, for toddlers who have just force-marched eight miles to escape their hunters. Their killers. Their abductors, torturers and rapists.

And then the older ones, gathered under the fizzy modern blue glare of the single pavement-illuminating fluorescent light, begin to do their homework ready for the dawn journey home where the stern teachers brooking no nonsense insist that they must still have their work done in time for school.

For eight years every night has been like this. Every night the parents pack the sacks (if they have anything to pack) in a thousand huts in a hundred villages and send the children hurrying up the small tracks before the dark falls. Grim with fear, with the terror that along the way they may be too late and never see their children again, they hurry the little ones along. Some walk part of the way with them holding their hands and then, where the track meets the road, they wave goodbye as the children become absorbed into the immense flow of this refugee tide of boys and girls. The kids skip off to meet the friends they see every night at this time. They feel safe in these numbers and I suppose, if the Lord's Resistance Army of lunatics wanted to, they could just attack this human convoy and grab what they needed. But they never have, so the kids chatter, play games and feel falsely safe for the first four miles and then lapse into the silence of the disciplined march.

When you encounter the fleeing children in your headlights it is like coming upon an army of wraiths. They appear out of the utter dark gradually until the car is engulfed with a steady flow of tiny humanity, some of whom are too small to reach up to your side window. Many carry huge burlap bundles on their heads containing the stuff the children of an entire village may need. Once they have understood that you are not a threat, that headlights might not mean immediate death or capture after all, they cavort and stare about you. The boys get cocky and brave and chatty, making Kung Fu motions in the headlight glare. The girls stare, giggle and point, noses streaming in the night heat. They show you their school books. They ask for pencils (always pencils!). They practise English. I wept. I called Jeanne and I cried.

You see, you always think you've seen it all. I have seen things no human should ever, or ever have to, see. I didn't mean to. I didn't even want to; it just turned out that way. I had never become inured to it. I remained frustrated by the misery and policy and politics of it. Couldn't stand it, in fact. But that such things should happen to children and people at the beginning of the twenty-first century makes me sick and enraged.

Jeanne was at a party in London. I stood on a clay road in north Uganda under a starless night. She stood in the salons of Mayfair surrounded by fabulous people, who smelt wonderful, and listened to the children of Aicholi province running to their sleeping spots on the stony streets of Kitgum. She listened to them and to me crying.

Then she went home, sadly unable to stay at the party.

Unable to sleep, we tiptoed through the pavements and roads blocked with the sleeping little ones. It was like being at a rock festival for under-fives. Junior Woodstock. Inside a bare concrete hangar they lay under the neon glares huddled and as still as massacre victims. The hangar was new. It had cost nothing to build. A few bucks. Outside, proudly displayed on a huge sign fixed to the wall, were the names of the wildly generous benefactors who had coughed up the pittance required to build this inhospitable shack. The European Union was predominant. That vastly rich conglomerate of nations, the richest aggregate entity on the planet, allied with some of the more famous names in the aid business, had built this large, latrine-like structure it proclaimed for these children. It made me sick. More money and thought had been spent on the stupid, meaningless, boastful, beautifully painted and constructed billboard than on anything that might benefit the children themselves. What wretched, wretched people are behind these futile, sickening displays?

We could still hear the concert as we wearily wandered through the night commuters sprawled about us. Those still awake we told to go to sleep. We were stern proxy parents. We told them they had to get up in the morning and walk home to school. They stared but did as they were told. Adults, like children, remain the same everywhere. There's a universal 'parent tone' that seems to make children everywhere do things they don't want to. Some we gave water. They clutched the bottles to keep. Or to show off to their friends tomorrow. An unexpected trophy of the night. We trod softly for we would have been treading on their dreams.

I don't know if the gunfire woke them. I don't know if they were frightened. I hope not. Somewhere out there in all that shooting children were being dragged out of their villages, dazed by sleep, uncomprehending, roped together or carried off to the bush screaming. Parents were being killed. All for a lunatic called Kony who, his followers believe, can see the future and them wherever they may be. I have met them and they believe this. So do the parents and the children who were sleeping through the distant snap, crackle and pop of distant, muffled gunfire.

I would like Kony dead. Why does someone not rid us of this monster who makes babies kill their parents, who distributes children as 'wives' to his 'soldiers', who beats them, who makes them eat the brains of their mates should they escape and be caught, who makes them bite their friends to death in punishment? Would this not be a good thing? I would do it. I really would. No probs. Bang, bang, you scum.

The children would go home. Grow up with their communities. Go to uninterrupted school. Sit in class unexhausted for once.

Things are complex. They always are. Unbelievably many people in this area have some support for Kony and the LRA. If he achieves some political power they will benefit as it is their province. Besides, their own children have been abducted and make up 80 per cent of his forces and, understandably, they do not want them killed in battle. So the parents will not tell the government troops where Kony is operating for fear of their own children's lives and, of course, reprisals. Their own children may be forced by Kony to kill them! When the 'army' has raided another village often the child soldiers will return to their own villages bringing the spoils of their 'victory' with them. Everyone benefits. So, yes, it is more complicated than it might seem. But on the other hand it isn't. The uncomplicated way to stop him is to find him and kill him.

I didn't sleep. In fact, the unbearable noise of the wildly inappropriate concert continued beneath my window until 7 a.m. It didn't matter. In a way it sort of helped. How could what I had just seen allow anyone to sleep? Ever again? I stayed up and waited for the morning to rush up on us, fully formed in the African sky.

Getting ready to leave I saw that the hotel staff were pulling down the concert equipment of the night but also digging holes in the driveway and inserting metal posts that would support a candy-striped awning under which grand tables were being set. Local big shots kept coming to check on progress until the first flag-flying cars pulled up to the hotel gates.

The European Union representatives and their cohorts had arrived, coming to look at their magnificent and indeed amazingly munificent work among the night commuters of Kitgum. That disgraceful breezeblock barn of emptiness in which lay huddled these tiny things of war.

The conference was to last two days. I asked the manager how much the whole thing cost. He told me willingly, impressed by the size of the budget out of which he would hopefully take a large chunk. The cars, flags, awnings, signs and bullshit cost twenty times what it had cost to build the shack of which they were so proud. What absolute stupid twats.

On the way to the field where the plane waited we passed through town again. The dust swirled off the football pitch and over the sidewalks where old men now sat out of the sun. The children had gone, melted away with the morning back to their villages. They will return tonight as you are reading this. They will return every night until someone ends this awfulness. How debased we have become.

On the plane I was humming Bob Marley's 'Hard ground was my bed last night and rocks were my pillow too'. It had stuck in my head from last night. The band had played it at some point as the patient crowd hung around hoping that maybe, if they waited long enough, Ebola Mike and Bobbi Wine would eventually show. Of course, they didn't. By morning the crowd had dribbled away.

You see, the only things in Kitgum you can count on showing up every night are the babies of war.

Agnes and Her Baby Escape

'Listen. I stayed for six years.

'I was eleven years old when I was abducted in the morning; they had gone to attack Namukora Centre. Forty of us were abducted, but the others were released in the end.

'They went with five of us, all children.

'We were young kids: four of us girls and one boy.

'In the bush they kill people.

'We were taken in the morning, then we went to the rebels' position. The army came and shot at us. Then the rebels separated us into small groups.

'Listen. They are atrocious.

'The boy was tied. The girls were unbound. We travelled like that.

'We were beaten.

'We moved constantly. The girls had to do the cooking and fetching water. We travel, when we reach a position, we start cooking.

'The boys fight.

'The soldiers are atrocious.

'They beat us.

'When we reached Sudan, the girls were distributed to the soldiers.

'I was twelve years old. I was scared. I did not know anything about men.

'The men were told to select us. We were given to them. He already had one wife. We started together well, and then I began loving him. He was kind to me. He thinks about me. He is not happy. But he beat me because I refused to go and sleep with him. I was pregnant and life was unbearable. I could not escape because the man kept a tight watch on me and if I escaped and was caught I would be killed. Then one night, at Omot in Pader, there was not battle. He was asleep and I was able to escape.

'I will go back home.

'He might come looking for me to see his baby, I don't know. He knows where my home is and I am scared. I do not love him.

'I don't want to go to another town, I want to go home. The people there will decide where they want to take me. I just arrived here yesterday. I sent information to my village. I am excited about seeing my family.'

Little Killers

It's not that weird that there are child soldiers. You can make children do anything. They're afraid of you. Especially if you've just forced them to kill their parents.

They get used to killing once they've got nothing to live for. Their morals have still not formed and 'they know not what they do'. After a while it just gets to be a scorecard. Except for the nightmares.

Children don't need to be paid and they don't need to eat much. They're cruel, and they're doglike, clinging to authority and trying to please it. The more they're beaten the more they try to please. They're nimble and quick, and though they don't yet have the muscles to stay constantly on the move they can be trained through fear never to falter.

Children are, of course, small, but weapons these days are also so small and light, they are capable of being carried by eight-year-olds. Nor do you need to be accurate. You just spray in a general direction and something is going to get hit.

An AK47 has a 7.62mm bullet that will penetrate brick walls three layers thick, spraying razor shards of brick and still-moving bullets around a room. It fires six hundred rounds a minute. In Hollywood movies people duck behind cars. Don't. The rounds from a high-velocity machine gun will slice through a traffic jam of vehicles hardly losing power. Children throughout the African wars charge towards each other in huge numbers, eyes closed, squeezing their triggers, spraying wildly, guns jumping in their little hands until one side or the other runs away or is killed. Weird. Armies of ten-year-olds lunging at each other controlled by their eighteen-year-old commanders.

Girls are good soldiers. Usually the girls are taken from their villages, terrorised and then made to be porters, carrying stuff, and servants for the commanders. They gather wood and forage for food. They cook and move on. At around the age of twelve they are given to commanders as 'wives'. They have children in the bush. Sometimes they hate their captor and sometimes, understandably, a bizarre affection grows between the 'husband' and 'wife'. To escape the fate of foraging and cooking – but not of being bush wives – the girls will become fighting soldiers. The boys are emphatic that the girls are treated 'exactly, in every way' the same as the boys. A soldier is a soldier is a soldier it appears. The girls are also more fierce and more cruel.

The status of a soldier is much higher than a servant and so the girls need to be tougher in the field to prove their value. The braver and more brutal they are the more their status rises. They gain respect. They stop being beaten. They stop being raped. They can speak again without lowering their tiny heads or whispering. You forget they are ten. I have talked to them. They are sullen. Quiet. Only when confronted do they know something wrong has happened. As soon as you leave you can see them playing games in a field. Little killers playing tag in skirts and shorts.

The armies know where each kid is from. If a girl or boy tries to run they will send a group to their village and kill everyone and torch the buildings, whether they are recaptured or not. If they are recaptured they will be beaten to death. When a village is raided and the children taken, there is an almost prescribed ritual. They will be tied loosely and led to the bush. Maybe sometimes they will have had to kill someone first. A parent, both parents, a friend . . . They will walk for a couple of hours then rest for the night. They will be told if they try to escape they will be killed. A guard is posted. The eight-year-olds realise the bonds are loose and inevitably one leaves. They were waiting. She was immediately caught and returned to camp where she was placed in a circle of her gathered friends; her friends, with whom she had been playing ball a mere four hours earlier, were instructed to bite her to death. If they did not or they did not bite savagely enough and rise from her flesh with skin in their mouth, then they too would suffer the same fate.

If they know where they have gone, some parents follow to plead for their children's lives or offer their own in exchange, or bring goats, the entire family wealth, to trade for their children. It never works. Some kids volunteer. Once, some 'Rwandans' in Congo took a small ten-year-old boy and his father and made them show the soldiers a certain village. Because the boys' uncle was in that village the father took them somewhere else. They shot him on the spot, and in front of the son, who immediately signed up with another force fighting the Rwandans. The bizarre thing is that he was accepted. He is older now and had been nine years in the 'army'. He has been demobbed but will still kill Rwandans if he encounters them.

Some only have the army. The family is gone. Or they have been thrown out because there are too many children. Or there is a remarriage, and the second wife refuses to take care of the children of the first marriage and then children of all ages are put on the street to be scooped up by the passing warring parties. Or AIDS has got the family and left orphans. Or simply because 50 per cent of the entire population of Africa is under fifteen! By definition you will not only have more children in an army and everything else, you will also have more children dying in general. Or it could just be that, like in Congo, after years of plunder and murder a society has just begun to eat itself. Consuming its own future almost as if it believes itself to be so decadent, so beyond repair it does not deserve to live and is committing national suicide.

Sometimes the kids are drunk or stoned. It helps the fear and the nightmares. Usually the nightmares don't come until the soldiers have been demobbed. By that I mean suddenly told to go away. There they are now on the anarchic streets of the ruined towns, their commanders now unpaid 'policemen'. They sleep in doorways, on the street. The girls are hookers. The boys feral thugs begging, robbing, desperate and hungry. Some go home if home is still there. Some go home and pray they're not rejected. Some can't go home because of what they've done.

In some places they have a ritual of cleansing, welcome and redemption. A profound adult understanding that these events beyond horror were outside the control of a child. That what was done was innocence perverted by power and fear. Two weeks after the family ritual all the greater family and villagers embrace the returnee in welcome.

One blank-eyed boy, still just nineteen and a veteran of eleven years, had done unspeakable things. He had risen to 'commander'. He had inspired fear and respect. Now he was silent and shunned. The others in the shed stayed away from him. His bush children had found their father again and they played with him. Children were all he could play with. Children were making him whole. Human again. Children were saving him. Alone he was silent and gaunt. A terrible emptiness surrounded him. An awful hollowness of the eye. One leg had been amputated above the knee. He said, 'I have done terrible things. Will they forgive me? Will they forgive me?' And they will, they really will.

But like the street thugs who know no moral parameters, who live a life without frontiers, for those abandoned 'Schengen' children, as they are called on the streets of Kinshasa after the borderless rules of Europe, there is to be no understanding of what has happened to a mind bludgeoned to an amoral empty nowhereland of brutality.

For our one-legged commander with his bush children, yes, there will be forgiveness and the village will embrace. But what stops the nightmares? What stops the memory? What stops the horror repeating like vomit night after night? What will ever stop the madness?

A STORY FROM THE CRAZY
COUNTRY NEWSPAPER COLUMN
Hubby loses genitals to former wife

Nairobi – A woman ran amok in Nyahururu town on Monday and chopped off her husband's private parts after a domestic feud. The woman, 28, divorced the hubby two months ago over claims that he was not giving his best shot in bed and had become unfaithful...

War

Three months before the genocide in Rwanda in 1994 a soldier made contact with the commander of the force of United Nations troops stationed in the country's capital, Kigali. He was offering secret intelligence. The informant – a former member of the personal security staff of the Rwandan President who was currently a trainer of the Interhamwe militia in the city – revealed that his men were being schooled in how to kill a thousand people in twenty minutes. Moreover, he had, he said, been asked to compile a list of all the Tutsis in Kigali, which he thought was 'for their extermination'. Weapons were being imported, including automatic rifles and vast quantities of machetes that could not be justified for farming purposes. He offered to turn over caches of weapons that were being kept for the coming massacres.

The UN commanding officer, the Canadian General Romeo Dallaire, passed the information on to UN headquarters in New York in an urgent fax. In it he also passed on information that plans were afoot to assassinate members of parliament upon entry or exit from the parliament building and also to target Belgian troops in the UN mission to 'guarantee Belgian withdrawal' from the country. In the fax he announced his intention to raid the arms caches and requested that the UN find asylum for the informant. But General Dallaire was refused permission to act. Furthermore,

UN headquarters did not share this fax with members of the Security Council.

It was not an isolated incident. There were many indicators that genocide was imminent. General Dallaire's force, the United Nations Assistance Mission for Rwanda (UNAMIR), had been set up just months earlier by the UN Security Council to implement the 1993 Arusha peace accords for the country. From the outset it picked up significant early warning signs. Against the country's background of a long and bloody history of massacres and other serious human rights violations, the radio station Radio Mille Collines, owned and operated by persons high in the government, was broadcasting propaganda which demonised the Tutsi minority. Government ministers publicly advocated mass killings. UN human rights investigators reported rumours of a network of senior officials devoted to killing Tutsis.

The accumulation of such clues ought to have aroused serious anxiety at UN headquarters at the impending violence. In the event the ominous warnings of the General's fax were borne out with uncanny accuracy. At the start, a group of Belgian peacekeepers were murdered and the Belgian government withdrew its peacekeepers, just as those bent on genocide had planned. Within three months some 800,000 people had been killed – From an unpublished report written by Paul Vallely for the Commission for Africa.

Ancient rivalries persist in Africa, and for good reason. Twenty years ago when I was in Darfur there were skirmishes going on between nomadic herders and settled farmers in disputes over land. The conflict was given added bite by the fact that the nomads were Arab and the farmers were black Nilotic peoples. Today the same groups are fighting.

It is not politically correct to say so but at root many of these conflicts are ethnic or tribal. Modern political scientists and development experts don't like to talk about such things. They prefer to see all conflicts as economic. Talking about tribalism makes Africans sound backward.

Things will not improve in Africa until people face up to the fact that much of the conflict in Africa is, still, between tribes and even within them. Competition for land (or, increasingly, for water) may be a problem, and one made worse by climate change and by the resettlement policies of various governments. But across the continent tribal rivalries are the often unarticulated problems in rows about migration and national identity, in clashes between political parties, in rivalries between governments and oppositions and in localised violence which can often spill across borders and lead to larger conflicts.

In the south-west border of Sudan and Ethiopia the Nuer people have been forced by conflict in Sudan into the old lands of the Anuak on the Ethiopian side of the border. The two are old rivals and cattle-raid each other's herds. They now live cheek by jowl. Add to this the resettlement of Amhara people from the highlands of Ethiopia and their victorious enemy the Tigrayan in the Ethiopian civil war who have also moved there and you have a recipe for governmental, ethnic, tribal and political conflict. It has already happened with genocidal accusations being made.

The Toposi in south Sudan are armed with modern weaponry by the SPLA Christian separatists fighting the northern Islamic government. The Turkana on the Kenyan side are in turn armed by the Kenyan government. Cattle raiding has now become a lethal, bloody battle as opposed to an occasionally murderous activity. When the Kenyans tried to disarm the Turkana, a pitched battle broke out in the streets of Lokichoggio which lasted an entire day. The Turkana kept their weapons.

Tribal is global.

Two modern phenomena make this worse. The first is the huge availability of modern weaponry which, since the Cold War ended, is flowing unchecked across Africa. Weapons are not a cause of violence, but they are a stimulant of it. When tension turns to conflict, and conflict to violence, it is the availability of small arms which makes disputes much more lethal. When AK47s rather than spears and arrows become the instruments of war the death toll inevitably soars.

The other problem is that often these ancient feuds are now manipulated by modern political or religious elites, which is what has happened in Darfur, where the jinjaweed militia – the word means nothing more than 'nomads' – are being backed by a government motivated by religious fundamentalism and Arab nationalism. This is how old conflicts can take on geo-political meaning, and can escalate to genocidal proportions with international repercussions.

Today in Africa violence causes as many deaths as disease. In recent decades Africa has had a worse record of conflict than any other continent. And where do the arms come from? To quote from the actual report of the Commission for Africa: 'Many of the largest manufacturers, exporters and brokers of arms to Africa are to be found in G8 and EU countries.' Those of us who take the smug view that everything is the fault of quarrelsome Africans need to reflect that one answer to the problem lies uncomfortably close to home.

Neet Deet

I'm too old for this shit. Too many years in rock'n'roll. I want a nice hotel.

The smell of piss seeping through everywhere. The squatting hole. The individually rationed wiping paper. Watching it fall on to someone else's in the carefully calculated hole. If you get the aim right. The cracked concrete floor with a steady stream of unknown insects calmly chewing through the abdomen of a gently thrashing overturned cockroach.

The single naked bulb glows unpromisingly underpowered. It goes out, then feebly, haltingly reignites. No point in trying to read.

I stink of Deet 50, my clothes of Deet 100 – Neet Deet. Don't get it on your skin. It melts it. It melted my camera. My fingers stuck to it. It's the only thing that kills the fucking mosquitoes. And the other things battering the dull bulb like bloated bees at a bursting pear in summer. Get me the fuck out of here.

I've taken off my clothes. Too hot. The sheet's nylon. It's always nylon. Just so you can stick to it. Just so you can glide on it in your sleep. Just so your sweat doesn't stain. But it does. The outline of heads and bodies. Like antimacassars on a Victorian armchair, like the Turin Shroud, like the permanent shadows of the evaporated at Hiroshima. My mind sees bits of hair, skin flakes, the stains. Maybe they're really there, I don't know, I'm not going to look. Lay the Deet-impregnated mosquito net on the bed. I begin to itch. Maybe there's no reason to itch, but my skin thinks there is. I scratch.

I've killed the mosquito I saw. They're easy to get when you see 'em, it's when the lights are out and you're almost gone . . . They die indifferently. I feed one to the things inside the belly of the still-pedalling cockroach. They ignore it. Indeed, they push it aside and some clone manhandles it away from the main body of workers who diligently pick at the eyes and innards of the winged black thing they are slowly dragging down into the darkness of the crack slanting diagonally underneath my bed. Underneath my bed a world of horror. Silent insect screaming.

I forgot the bottled water. Fuck. I chew an Airwave gum. Mint taste. Floss it through my teeth. Build up spittle in my mouth so I can take my Malarone. Try to swallow the pill with just the spit. It sticks and the spit's gone. Fuuucck. I'm going to get malaria. Cerebral fucking malaria. Twenty-four hours and you're gone. It's beginning to disintegrate in my mouth. It tastes horrible. It's beginning to burn my throat. Cough it up and push it into the chewing gum. Swallow the lot. It's gone. Begin to panic. Will the chewing gum melt in my stomach and release the tablet? Or is it rubber? What the fuck is chewing gum anyway? Fuuuck. I'm going to be bitten. Going to get malaria. I'm going to shit out a solid lump of gum with a fucking Malarone in it. If it doesn't stick in my gullet and I die anyway.

Above the bed new mosquitoes lunge expectantly in the thin bulb glare. My arms itch from last night's bites. My face burns from today's sun. The stretched skin of ankles, wrists and feet lies taut, blood deliciously at the surface for the nightly feast of flies. Lights out. The heat-shimmering night croaks and fizzes. I'm in Africa again.

The Names of Things

God is everywhere here. It is true of Africa's traditional religions, and of the imported varieties too. God is present not just in the spiritual or imaginary realm where you might ordinarily expect him to hang, nor just in the natural world which he clearly had a hand in constructing, in that old pantheistic way of his – but in the sober, everyday, almost unseen ubiquity. To the religious, God has always hidden in plain sight, but here he manifests himself clearly and visibly to everyone in everything, every day.

Here he is on the buses and in taxis, riding the waves with the fishing boats and enticing customers into shops. He speaks from baskets carried on heads, his name echoes inside plastic buckets, and it is he who will advise you on the latest hair styles in the Jesus Guide Me Beauty Salon, or recommend the Take This and Eat roadside food joint to you.

Everything is devoted and dedicated to an ever-present reminder that all things come from, and are of, God. There is nothing odd about this. In the past, Africans transformed everything they touched into carved, moulded, drawn, rendered, painted or hewn fetish animals or anthropomorphic representations. Nothing was, or is, inanimate. Within everything there is a spiritual force that may be used as an intermediary to a God or an ancestor, or to a representation of a God, or as a dedication, or perhaps as some symbolic sacrifice akin to a Catholic's wine/bread/body/blood ritual.

Look at the pregnant or priapic totemic figures of every people throughout Africa - throughout the world, I suppose – for food, children, strength. The abstract masks to ward off illness or evil, to signify power or clan, or simply as the visual metaphor for the various divinities in each theology. Look at the exquisite granary doors of the Dogon, with their female breasts protruding from the rough-hewn wood and often surrounded by representations of protective spirits. It is obvious that the granary holds food and life and requires protection. All of this is above simple craft or folkloric traditions. Because these objects are manifestations of the importance of the everyday, of belief and practicality, they have been invested with urgency and sincerity, reality and spirituality, need and desire. And of course they unknowingly aspire to art, as every collector, auction house and interior design magazine will unhesitatingly confirm. There is an intuitive understanding here that it is only through the creative that man aspires to the divine. Art as the intermediary to God.

The African past, which Westerners collect so avidly, has now transformed itself into the modern. When African languages were largely unwritten, visual representation stood in their place to communicate intent or memory – the doors, fetishes, etc. Story-telling, metaphor (masks, dance, theatre) take on greater import than they have in those societies whose myths and beliefs exist in book form. But now, with writing, God can be seen to be in everything, and to protect and to provide everything. The heavy wooden bucket or calabash of yesterday needed to be carved with care, the inscribed symbols conveying meaning. Whereas today the light, plastic equivalent which can be elegantly carried further balanced solidly on the head can have daubed across its multi-coloured front the proud proclamation: Take This and Drink It.

SHOP NAMES IN GHANA
Amazing Grace Fashions
Redeemer Cold Store
God Cares Vision Enterprises
God Says Yes Who Can Say No
Beauty Salon
Jesus is Mine coca cola
God is my Refuge plumbing
Trust God Agro Chemical
Saviours Drug Store
In Jesus Name Photos
Goodness and Mercy Grocery Store
Sweet Jesus Sweet Shop
He is Alive Fashion Centre
No King but God shoes
Seek Ye First Hair Styles
The Holy Innocent Refrigerator
and Air Con

The Latest President

The picture of the latest president gazed down from the wall. It was positioned in such a way that one could feel protected under such a benevolent gaze. A gaze that could not only see the shining path to the future if you would just trust its owner to lead you there, but also one of munificent benevolence which was able to see you everywhere, and all dangers that might harm you; would you but give him your loyalty he would protect you.

His huge girth imparted well-being and future health for a thin country of stick people. His creased epauletted shirt and khaki button-down breast pocket, while non-military, was smart enough. In this country of ragged-clothed individuals here was a man not to be trifled with and by extension all those whom he protected.

No one knows who distributes these photographs or who ordains they be displayed but everyone puts them up in the most prominent parts of their shop or home. Just in case.

Obviously, the larger the photograph the greater the loyalty and gratitude to the Great Protector. A poster-size framed glossy can only indicate the sheer love the displayer must feel towards his president. It's just that the big ones are so expensive.

Under his rule, the business, the city, the whole country would prosper and thrive. The state would finally and justifiably take its rightful place among the family of nations. Which didn't happen with that loser, the last president. No, the latest president would see to that. One could rest assured about that. Oh, the glory of it all. And it was up to us, together, to join the latest president in his great and noble endeavour, his life's work.

By contrast then, the smaller photograph tucked somewhere off to the side between a cut-out photograph of the Alps or a lake or the Holy Trinity or David Beckham could be viewed somewhat suspiciously. Queries as to the exact amount of enthusiasm and conviction one was showing towards the latest president, and therefore, frankly, the country and its administration, might awkwardly arise. Insufficient ardour towards his magnificent revolutionary achievement could perhaps be mistakenly implied, with all the unfortunate consequences that may, erroneously and through no fault of anyone, follow.

'Are you not the man whose cousin was macheted after watching his wife being raped to death and his children slaughtered and then eaten? That's all over now. C'mon, let's let bygones be bygones and pull together as one. Under the latest president we have all experienced a great catharsis. A national closure, so to speak. We have to strive now, all of us, to move on, as the latest president has. He alone is taking us forward.

'Yes, it was a horrible time, but something needed to be done about the last president and the latest president did what was necessary. We shouldn't be sad, we should be grateful. That last president was ruining the country. Raping it, for goodness' sake. Between you and me, and I was in a position to know, he had gone mad. You can see that, can't you? Agreed, the horror was unfortunate but, honestly, what was the latest president supposed to do?

'And besides – and I'm saying this as a friend – your cousin, let's face it, being a big supporter of the last president, we just felt he'd infected his whole family with the virus of mistaken enthusiasm for a very bad man. We know this. It was reported. There was not just one, but three, three mind you, quite large pictures of the last president in his office and his house, for goodness' sake . . .

'And now you with your small photograph of the latest president . . . What on earth are we supposed to take from that? Eh? I ask you. Put yourself in my shoes, my friend. It is not just small, it is a snap. A snap. We can see the mark of your photograph of the last president on your wall, so let us just put your portrait of the latest president within the lines of the last president's photo and what do we find? Eh? You can see now, can't you, how it is much, much smaller? Much smaller. Are you trying to hurt the latest president? Is that the game? No, of course not. We are all grown-ups here, eh? So . . . could you not find a better place, a more suitable situation for your photograph . . . and I think perhaps a bigger one. Yes, a bigger photograph in a better place so everyone can see your love for our latest president.

'Yes, bigger and bolder! It will enhance not only your room but your business and your standing as well! Let us come back in two weeks and see how we're getting on. See if I'm not right, eh? The latest president is doing his best for you too, you know. He is working every hour, day and night, for us all. He would know about people like your cousin and it would sadden him. Not just your cousin's unfortunate attitude but also what happened to him. Yes, he would be saddened, for he is a just and kind man.

'Do you know he has already met the American president? Did you know that? Does that not make you so proud of our country. And do you know what the American president said to him? He said, "I know what your country has been through and I need to tell you that all Americans feel your pain." Did you hear that? The American president felt our pain. The American president felt your cousin's pain. And that is exactly what our latest president does. He feels your pain too.

'The loss of a cousin is a dreadful pain to bear for any man. But how much worse to lose your own daughter or son or wife, eh? And yet . . . sometimes even that must also happen, and I can assure you the latest president would feel that pain too. Grieviously, sorrowfully, no matter how necessary the extreme measures required. The latest president knows who the enemies of this country are, and for us to be great again they must be surgically and eternally removed!

'Now, even a man like yourself can see that. We really can't afford any ambivalence towards the latest president's reforms, can we? No. This is the way forward for all of us. All pulling together under large portraits of our leader. That's right, the larger the better. In every home, office and school; and hospital . . . when we build them. Which will be very soon now. Yes, all of us pushing together, urging on the latest president to ever greater, radical progressive action. The latest president looking fondly upon us all in his great work. This great father of our country and we, his grateful children, working harder to achieve the goals set out by him for our benefit under his dynamic and enlightened leadership.

'Your picture is too small for the great task ahead. The latest president deserves better. Please do not continue to insult him or the nation. I will return in two weeks.'

Language

There are estimated to be two thousand separate languages on the African continent. Most Africans can speak four or five languages, sometimes more.

They use their own local, group or ethnic one primarily, often Swahili, perhaps as an African lingua franca, and then one of the colonial languages such as English, French or Portuguese as a common tongue between the different peoples and, finally, a handful of disparate dialects or completely different tongues of nearby tribes or countries. These can be spoken by millions of people like, say, the Mande group of languages in West Africa spoken by nine million people.

Africans speak in metaphors, proverbs and parables. This can be very beautiful when it is translated into English but sometimes it seems the speakers are getting into a metaphor competition with each other and it can go on forever. I haven't a clue what they're on about. And a lot of the time neither have they.

In one translation I have in front of me I had been in conversation with some old boys under a tree, where everyone meets, and one of them who had been talking a while said, 'There is a saying which goes; a man who seeks his own advice is like a man who carries his belongings on a goat.'

In the translation it says '[pause]', a sort of stage direction which means that there was a silence while even the speaker tried to work out exactly what he meant. I remember there was a lot of sage nodding of heads by the other elders as if they understood perfectly well what the other guy was on about. Then one of them piped up, 'What does that mean?'

My personal favourite is: 'Never slap a fly while he is resting on your scrotum'! When does a fly REST on your bollocks? And if it did, why would you SLAP it? Wouldn't you shoo it away?

Language is so flowery, so highly developed, because the Africans never bothered with writing. As a result all knowledge was passed on through the spoken word and obviously people best remember knowledge when it is relayed in a memorable way. That's why the Gospels and the teachings of Jesus and other spiritual masters were probably correctly transliterated into the sacred texts when they were eventually written down. The Good Samaritan etc.; the stories of this, that and the other.

Ireland, too, was for historical reasons an oral society and the Irish developed the art of talking. Blarney. The sport of articulation. And when it came to be translated into English a different voice came through. Different ideas and stories. And when it came to be written it rocked the literary world.

The same is true of Africa and its thousands of tongues. People gather in the heat of the day or at nightfall around a fire under the tree to hear their histories related or to hear the storytellers speak, recite the poetry or tales, entertain the village. This is how and where the community arrive at an understanding of who they are. And all of it reminds me so much of old Ireland, where the storytellers and the bards were huge stars. The same is true throughout Africa. History is in the head and learned through the word. There is a great emphasis put on accuracy. Just as when you read a bedtime story to your kids and deviate even slightly from the text or plot and they force you to go back and repeat the whole thing, so too the storyteller who is respected for his dramatic abilities under those trees across a continent.

But because it was deemed unnecessary to write things down it appeared to Europeans that these communities had no histories. They could see no evidence of this. Where were the records, the tax rolls, the decrees, constitutions and laws? Nor could they hear anything, for they made little effort to understand what was being said to them in the hundreds of dialects they were bombarded with. And none with a Latin root. They therefore leapt to the conclusion that these people were primitives without structure or governance. Without kingdoms and empires, without legends or myths or theologies.

Of course this was stupid and wrong but it suited the colonialists. It allowed them to pretend that if no countries or states, as we would recognise them, existed we could, for their benefit, you understand, impose such things upon them. It meant that, as their religions were clearly pagan without any apparent or discernible theology, we should 'save' these poor unenlightened wretches and bring them the unassailable boon of civilisation. Our version of it anyway.

Whenever there was evidence of something remotely sophisticated we dismissed it out of hand or claimed that some earlier white people had got there first. The castles of Gondar in Ethiopia, the stone city of Zimbabwe, the staggering art of the Benin, bronzes, the empires of the Ashanti, Dahomey or Malians ... The list is endless.

In the 1980s I wrote about being in the north of Niger. The provincial governor was showing me the areas of famine in his territory. It had been as devastating there as anywhere. Everywhere was abandonment. Empty houses. Dead animals. Huddled, skeletal people. Parched, cracked earth. The governor sat heavily on a bleached white log on the ground. He reached down and picked up a handful of the dead earth. He allowed it to run like sand through his fingers and then slapped his palms together, dusting them and wiping them clean. He looked around in silence at the devastation of his country. It was an awful, weighted silence.

Harar, Ethiopia

Uganda

Congo

Ghana

Uganda

Car load of cash, money market, Hargeysa, Somaliland

Sanga, Dogon Country

One of my guards

A mosque is a space with a roof on it. The desert brought inside

Jinka, Ethiopia

Harar, Ethiopia

The High Priestess, plus acolyte, Ouidah, Benin

Turkana

TV repair shop, Timbuktu

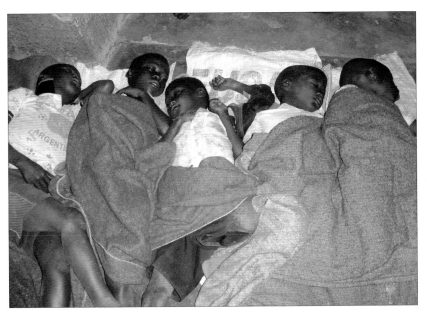

Night Children, Kitgum, escaping kidnap

Amateur miners, Likasi

Bar Girl, Kisangani

Almost home. The four-mile walk from school

Husband and wife cocoa plantation workers, Ghana

Yasser, that's my baby, North Africa, 1991

MAKE POVERTY HISTORY

Nelson's column, Trafalgar Square 2005

And then he said, 'There were three hundred languages spoken here. Three hundred. All different. Now they are gone. Nothing. Rien.'

I wrote then and I rewrite now. I never heard those languages, but I miss them. In these ways the lights of human genius wink out.

Guns

Guns. After a while you don't notice them casually pointed in your direction or accidentally poking you in the ribs on a crowded bus. The fourteen-year-old kid vacantly staring off into nothing, his chin resting on the upturned barrel of his cocked Kalashnikov ceases to surprise. Maybe you should but you don't think he's going to blow his head off any second now. There's an assurance and confidence about the insignificance of a child carrying one of the most lethal weapons ever invented. Partly, I suppose, because they've been carrying and handling these things since they were four or five and they do it so effortlessly. Like it's an extension of the body. Like they seem, as they feel, undressed without them. And maybe they're stoned but they seem so quiet, so peaceful, as if nothing could disturb their equanimity, nothing could provoke them to a sudden fury and flurry of gunshots. But it could. It's just that you forget.

Yeah, everybody's packing. But they always have. They used to carry knives, spears and swords, and now they carry knives, spears, swords and guns. It's partly a boy thing, partly a practical thing – hunting, fishing, working wood – partly a status thing, but mostly it's a security/war thing.

When they go to the bars and discos at the weekend they hand their spears and stuff into the hat-check girl.

You can pick up an AK47 for $6.

Ferengi

I don't like being in the picture. I am outlandish in this landscape. Why do I keep having to put my stupid face into every frame? What do I possibly add that is not better without me? Does no one say, 'Yeah, good show, but it would've been better if Geldof hadn't been in every shot'? And it would be. I'm not meant to get in the way. But I do. I am supposed to be there to root the audience in the moment. But the moment is horribly false. I really do want to meet the people we see, but the unalterable, unavoidable central fact and condition of myself in Africa is that I am white. White puts all sorts of notions into the locals' heads and makes me feel embarrassed and alien. Not apologetic, unwelcome or guilty, just out of place.

I remember reading a book about Africa that said white people were 'half-finished'. God didn't see much value in them so He didn't bother 'fully cooking' them. Which is funny. The thing is, you begin to think about it because everyone notices you. I suppose, for example, my clothes are ridiculous to them. They are, no matter how hard I try, preposterous to the circumstances I am in, but were I to wear their wholly suitable, airy, light, man-made costumes, I would be an even greater object of hilarity, and frankly farcical to both myself and the viewers.

My skin is raw with the sun. My pores leak. I squint, but wearing glasses against the glare distances myself still further from my desire to be accepted. They also seem to make you assume inappropriate airs of superiority and unfriendliness. The hat I have to wear against the sun was bought at a boot fair in Germany for five euros but was made in Comanche, Texas. It's a proper Stetson and is wide-brimmed to protect my neck and face and tall to circulate cool, shaded air around my baking brain. But it looks like a joke hat. Like a 1920s Hollywood cowboy. Tom Mix or someone.

We wander through the market. I am repelled by the liquid filth I squelch through and which covers the stupid groovy denim slip-ons I got for the summer holidays in Majorca. Shit jets between my toes and under my heel. I watch the basket people pass unconcernedly through the ooze of pissing goats, shitting sheep and trampled khat that rises to their ankles. They laugh at my foppish attempts to find a piece of solid ground, and when I skittishly leap from one island of solidity to another, I inevitably slip and miss and sink again into the mire, covering afresh my feet in disgusting slime inside the feeble slip-ons. I am covered in shit and shame as the market appears to erupt in pointed laughter, and crowds of cruel, grinning children shout 'ferengi', which translates directly as foreigner but indirectly to me as 'wanker'. Just one word needed to sum up any explanation needed. 'Foreigner'. Say no more.

And I am. Of course I am. No matter how long I stayed here I would always be 'ferengi'. Don't get me wrong. I don't want to be them or pretend I am one of them, I just want to disappear into them. To see what they are. To listen and hear what they are. But I cannot. I am as marked out here as they would be in my world. Forever white, forever black.

Being Irish in Britain has never really posed a problem for me and if it ever did it would only come about when I opened my mouth and my accent was heard. Being black you carry your accent on your face, your hands. Your accent is visible. In the hierarchy of difference and fear of the stranger, of mistaken and inverted superiority, it is of course possible to pass unnoticed if one has the same skin colour as the next person. But speak and you are revealed. And what is true to a minute degree in the social hierarchies of Britain and Ireland is equalled here where dress, dialect, colour and accent readily reveal your tribal affinities.

Like a black man in the snow, I am a white man in the coalfield. Standing out bizarrely. Heightened and delineated by my backdrop. A visitor welcomed but always, disappointingly, the object of quite justified hilarity and curiosity.

'Just step into frame, Bob.' Don't want to. 'When you're ready, please.'

TOLEKA

Because of the war there has been no petrol in Kisangani for years. Bike taxis (tolekas) are personalised and made attractive by individualising the back carriers to attract the most delicate bottoms by their spongy crocheted seats that guarantee comfort on the pot-holed roads. Tolekaness! 'Get out of the way!'

Going Home

Africa starts early. It starts before the sun does. You get whatever needs to be done quickly in the balance hours that join the night to the day. That time when the night feels the tickle of heat that will send its delicious dark cool scurrying to the shades of more hospitable worlds.

The gathering of goods and wood. The feeding of the animals. The water collecting. The setting off on the road to market. And on the levelled ground of the thousand tiny airstrips that dot the continent, the pushing out and revving up of aeroplane engines before the thin night disperses and the heavy heat makes life harder for the old engines as they lumber up into the sluggish air.

And at the chaotic airports the extraordinary exhausting pre-boarding rituals conducted in that classically African time-forgetting slowness, which ignores the sleep-shattered passengers forced to rise at 3.30 or 4 a.m. to make the mandatory two-hour check-in. Indeed, it is preferable to stay at the airport for the night rather than go to bed at all. For if you arrive at twelve or one, it will take you at least an hour simply to get through the roadblocks, militia, army, police guards, unofficial baggage handlers, official baggage handlers, just to finally and exhaustedly gain entrance to the terminal where the real chaos begins.

It's always worth checking the actual flight time last thing the day before your trip. Schedules in Africa are relative. They respond to the elasticity of Afrotime. Often the planes simply don't come. And why worry so long as you ultimately get where you're going? The meeting/reunion/whatever can only take place when you arrive anyway. Everyone knows that, so it's up to you to know when the plane leaves. And the plane leaves whenever it's ready to leave, so if you're just kind of there when it's the right time, then the journey can begin. No one is actually 'waiting', they're just kind of hanging around preparing. Patience or impatience is redundant and inappropriate, the trip will begin when it begins.

Unlike in Europe, planes are rarely delayed; rather they are brought forward even earlier than the pre-dawn optimum. No one really knows why this should be. Probably because if there are enough people to fill the plane it may as well leave there and then. Perhaps because the older, more befuddled tribal country peoples returning from their big city visit need time to understand the process and rituals of modern travel. Time for the security scans that require them to remove endless belts, jewellery, bits of kitchen equipment, a rifle, sword or the odd forgotten bullet at the bottom of the basket carrying the chickens, which they don't understand because no one tells them that the pinging gate they suspiciously and slowly walk through detects metal. And so they go round over and over again, sometimes three or four together. Peremptory, exasperated comments bewilder them further. The necessity of putting every twine-tied cardboard box, every double-bagged plastic receptacle on steel rollers and pushing them through the all-round X-ray machine is alarming. These are precious goods. What is happening to them? Even when it is explained to them or they are shown the X-ray image, there is no concept of what they are looking at.

Young daughters try to shepherd their bewildered parents through the interminable demand for tickets, passes, boarding cards and travel tax, only equipped with the curiosity and dauntlessness of youth. They are as unfamiliar with this world as their elders. They are, however, neither frightened nor dazzled by it but like us confused and irritated by it.

Having found their various and varied baggage pieces, they shuffle off to the next encounter with a world they have little need of, or desire for. Its usefulness to them confined to the durability and prettiness of plastic shoes and basins or from the endless stuff of modernity, the few carefully selected things that are pertinent to their pared-down, uncluttered, less precious and much harder lives.

Seating is unassigned. You have a ticket, you have a seat, what does it matter where it is? There is no rush to the front or desire to be first. There is no congestion in the aisles, save for packages and parcels which are placed anywhere until after take-off. Only children are accommodated. People move for the children. Those universally laconic announcements of aeroplane-speak sound even more measured, unhurried and indifferent on African planes. The only imperative seems to be to get up into the cool sky before the sun does. But the plane, delayed by the inevitable mechanical problem, is slow off the ground. It beats and claws at the thickening air as if drawing its way through a material substance. Twenty minutes earlier and it would have lifted easily into the cooling breath of night; now it thrashes at the ether, wheezing and bumping through the folds of enveloping and circulating heat, jolting and thumping with effort and being pushed and jostled by the glaring bully who cannot countenance a denial of its power.

It takes time, but finally we break free of the sun's fiery grip and skim along the margins of the sky where atmospheres collide and man outside his miniature, artificial world cannot survive above or below for more than a few minutes. Above us infinity, below the great Burntlands, still, barren, naked under the aggression of the sun and, for those staring longingly out of the windows with their turbans, togas, knives, swords, rifles, baskets and parcels stacked about them on their knees and in the aisles, home.

The Smell of Africa

No one writes about Africa's smell. They don't do olfactory. They write about the heat. They write about the bugs. They write about the strange diseases. They write about the cruel terrain. They write about the dangers of exotic wild beasts. But no one writes about the smell.

It is the odours and scents which are some of the most potent assaults on the senses of the stranger in Africa. There is the smell of the rainforest, earth after rain, a moist greenness so heavy you feel you can cut it. Deep, sticky, pulsing, panting, luxuriant and many-layered as the vegetation; broad-leaved, bushed, vined, creepered, insistent, insidious and invading not just the nostrils but creeping into the fibre of your body. It is a smell of new growth and of festering decay. It is a smell that conquers and unnerves.

The smell of the thick, milky, opaline sea. Briny and marine, froth and spume after it has picked up the dust and animal scent on its way to you. There is the smell of the market. Of cinnamon spice, heady cloves and fresh green cardamom. Of drying fish, pungent onion, putrid meat, mealy breadfruit and dusty sorghum. The faint, petrolly smell of tomatoes, the yellow-green rawness of banana and yam, the sweet perfume of mangoes and the sour whiff of mouth-puckering guavas. Mix into that the scents of unknown pastes and powders and the hot sharp smell of the human body. And against it all the undertow of fetid putrefaction that mixes rotting vegetables and other human discards.

Above all, there is the smell of the refugee camp. Of dust and woodsmoke, of sweat and urine and human faeces, of the bare earth baked and rebaked in the blistering sun. It is a scent impregnated with human misery. It is a smell of vinegary sweetness, of concentred food-aid milk, of babies' possetted vomit and of the sweet sickly odour of death.

The smells of Africa. They are smells that never leave you, smells that haunt the nostrils forever, inhaled deep into the core of imagination.

The Winds of Change

Here's an oddity. Visit experts on Africa – which I did at great length while working on the report for Tony Blair's Commission for Africa – and you find one common denominator. I found it among the development economists and other specialists in places like the London School of Economics. I found it among the professional Africa watchers all across Europe. I found it among the scholars and policymakers who came to the seminars I ran throughout G8 countries to discover some new thinking on Africa. In fact, I found it everywhere in our rich world.

It is a kind of despair. The problems Africa faces are intractable. Drought, famine, hunger, disease, ignorance, witchcraft, corruption, bad government, bureaucracy, war, AIDS, death. Yadda, yadda, yadda. Afro-pessimism, they call it. Africa is fucked, is what they actually mean.

It's easy to think that, looking from afar. Africans who, years ago, left their homelands and now live comfortably in the West often indulge in it, too. So do many of those who claim they love Africa and have its interests at heart. But they are weary, drawn, jaded and cynical. And cynicism is the greatest enemy.

Revealingly, what you encounter in Africa is the opposite of all that. Among the people of this shimmering continent there is no despair. Rather, there is a sense of flux and of opportunity. There is dynamism in the air, and change. Africa today is very different from the place I first visited twenty years ago at the time of Live Aid. Sure, there are many of the same problems. But the context has changed. Utterly.

The end of apartheid shattered a psychological barrier. It gave Africans a sense of ownership of their continent. The end of the Cold War might not have brought the end of history but it has brought a moment when political blocs are giving way to trading blocs. September 11 may have brought great uncertainty but it has also generated a sense that 'development is a security issue' – and that the voices of those who are disempowered and disaffected must now be listened to in a different way.

Over the past five or so years the first signs of change have swept like a tide across the continent. When I first went there two decades ago there were about twenty wars being fought across the continent; as I write there are just four. Then, half of all African countries were dictatorships; today more than two-thirds of the countries in sub-Saharan Africa have had free-ish and fair-ish multiparty elections. Some have even produced changes of government – though creeps like Mugabe hang on and even one-time good guys like Museveni in Uganda are outstaying their welcome. But elsewhere there are signs that a new generation of political leaders is emerging, many of whom show a new commitment to the social ideas of the common good of their people. They are setting up new institutions – like the African Union – which might just work if they stay serious and mature. Almost half of all African countries had economic growth of more than 5 per cent in 2003 – far better than most Western countries achieved, and, yes, admittedly from a very low base start. But y'know…twenty years ago, that was impossible. A new entrepreneurship is in evidence. In several countries there is a growing middle class. The flow of cash back home to Africa from relatives abroad has increased dramatically.

Everywhere there are the first signs of what could be a real momentum for change. A new optimism is abroad. It is tempered with African realism, but it is joined with African hope and driven by African joy.

A Continent Moves

Africa's landscape is as diverse as its people but in its different environments and cultures there is one common factor: survival is a constant struggle against disease, drought, predators and heat.

People here evolved into hundreds of different cultures, all of which found their niche somewhere within the different landscapes. They adapted in ways that made sense in their context: small, mobile groups of nomads, fishing communities, farmers and so on. In a few places where food was plentiful great civilisations arose but, because human beings emerged from and evolved in Africa, their parasites and diseases were uniquely prevalent too.

Disease spreads rapidly among people congregating in large numbers and consequently has been a constant constraint on the establishment of large urban centres on the continent.

In 1945 there were only forty-nine cities in the entire African continent with populations of more than only 100,000 people and most of these were in North or South Africa. In fact, twenty-five of these cities could be found in Arab North Africa and eleven in white-ruled South Africa. The bulk of the continent – the big bit in between these two other worlds – still lived in small village communities. Between the Sahara Desert and the Limpopo River in the south only thirteen had reached the size of these small 100,000-population-sized towns and four of those were in Nigeria. Even in the 1960s fewer than 20 per cent of the population lived in urban centres compared to 60 per cent in Europe and North America.

When the Europeans got together to take a slice of what the Belgian King Leopold described as Africa's *Gâteau Magnifique* they permanently disrupted the ancient systems of survival and development which had developed from the particular African conditions of landscape, climate and environment. Large groups of people suddenly found themselves trapped behind invisible borders – populations so large the land could not support them. Crossing these borders in search of pasture, water or food incited war, commencing an endless cycle of violence and disruption. African societies that had worked successfully for centuries were torn apart forever.

Today Africa is on the move again although the population still remains for the moment largely rural. About 68 per cent of the continent still live in their villages. That is why any growth or development in Africa must be based on agriculture, not just simply for food but, equally importantly, for economic development.

However, because 50 per cent of the population are under fifteen – unschooled, unemployed, hungry and ambitious – there has been a vast exodus from the countryside to the ever-burgeoning cities. Young men looking for work crowd the shantytowns clinging to the edge of the bursting metropolises, which overflow with people, untreated sewage, bad water and crime. Within thirty years the bulk of the African continent will live in cities.

This will be a vast and unprecedented reversal, a huge upheaval, which even now the cities are struggling to deal with. The countryside, with its still viable and essential social network, will have disappeared into the mayhem and anarchy of the twenty-first-century African city.

A Parallel Africa: Some Thoughts on the UN, etc.

There is another Africa we often see but rarely register. It is an alternative Africa that functions in a manner that we would understand and approve of. A parallel, floating world of functionality that lives alongside but removed from the norm of organisational chaos that pertains.

This other world's structures are wholly democratic. Meritocratic even. Women are treated as equals and are the leaders within it. It has a relatively incorrupt bureaucracy and by and large it works.

This is the parallel Africa of the UN and its many arms, NGOs and the other great international institutions of the wealthy world, the IMF and the World Bank.

All of these provide the extensive alternative bureaucracies to the African states themselves, which they either ignore, save to pay cursory lip service to, or, more generally, condemn or criticise.

This hurts and annoys the Africans and they deeply resent it. They are excluded from the decision-making boards of the bigger institutions, they have no voice in the election process of such boards and yet they are by and large subject to their economic strictures while simultaneously needing and resenting the presence of their policing.

It makes one uneasy to see traffic jams in cities made up of UN cars with their inviolability-giving CD plates, with the honking horns of the various aid agencies from everywhere in the world blaring insistently behind them. These same NGOs resent government restrictions on their obviously necessary and laudable activities but I have witnessed shocking displays of arrogance possibly borne of frustration but, equally possibly, deriving from an ingrained, unacknowledged and profoundly unattractive sense of, if not exactly superiority, certainly arrogance.

I have witnessed ministers of sovereign states kowtowing to the well-paid international bureaucrats of the multilateral groups. I have seen them panic if they are held up by the traffic jams of the cars from the very institutions they must report to or consult with on a daily basis. That fear of being late for the boss. What price independence?

Is this not just a different form of colonisation? I know that sounds pathetically bien pensant, gauche caviare, champagne socialist or whatever, but what is it if not that? And how humiliating must it be.

Still, I suppose those that are helped feel only relief, sometimes possibly gratitude. The humiliation and resentment they should direct towards their own woeful governmental incompetence. But then again, many African governments are not inadequate or incompetent. They're simply poor.

Nine-tenths of the African economy is informal. That is, it is unregulated. As a result the state cannot collect taxes. Indeed, the cost of setting up a tax-collecting structure is often greater than the amount of tax you could possibly collect anyway. This conundrum exists in many African countries. The result of this is that the state would not be able to afford its programmes of health and education and general benefit to the tax payer, even if it had the programmes in the first place.

And even if it had the programmes how would they be implemented? There is no effective bureaucracy because there isn't money to pay for one. So the smart people emigrate for a better life.

Often to the UN or an NGO.

Today, 70 per cent of African intellectuals live outside Africa. Consequently their institutions are weakened. No economy, no tax. No tax, no policies. No policies, no loyalty to the state. No state loyalty, so loyalty to the strong man or tribe or supra-national identity, like Islam or Christianity, where you at least find structure and benefit.

What a mess. And someone's got to keep the show on the road.

In the fieriest of their Redemptionist preachings the Evangelical churches will often refer to the Book of Revelation and John's frightening visions of the Endtimes. And the Four Horsemen of the Apocalypse: War, Death, Famine and Plague.

For the Africans, and particularly up here on the Kenyan/Sudanese border where I write, this is not some nightmarish, futuristic vision. It happens daily. It is happening just outside their church door. It's what they live.

Congo, Uganda, Zimbabwe, Rwanda, Sierra Leone, Côte d'Ivoire, Liberia, Sudan. Take your pick. The armies of children and their disturbed, de-mobbed, feral street children. The disease-stricken societies too remote or poor to handle the plagues of HIV, polio, malaria (the great killer) and TB and, having no medicines, resorting to the ancient rites of traditional belief for comfort if not cure. The endless endemic droughts as the desert heats up again and marches south. The wars that leave people without food so that tonight, like every night, most African children will go to sleep hungry again. And all, at its extreme, leading to premature death.

All of this is a result of one condition – poverty. All of this is because Africa is poor. If you are wealthy you can afford medicines and food. War isn't worth fighting; it's only going to make you poor again.

In the meantime the UN – the will of the international community – tries to hold the fort. Without the UN vast numbers of people would be extremely vulnerable, at the mercy of St John's rampaging Horsemen. But will the UN be here forever? Will we continue to pay for this vast base of troops and planes? Will they still keep their thousands of soldiers in Africa? Will the locals still support them or, as in the Congo, refer to them derisively as 'Butterflies'? Pretty to look at but useless for anything else. What are the political implications of their permanent presence? Have they in reality pushed aside the sovereignty of the state and created a sort of protectorate governed by individuals inside a skyscraper in New York? Haven't they and their NGO satellites in truth become new twenty-first century colonialists?

And if they are not to stay, what happens to these people?

You Say Potato...

One of the great disconnects in Africa is that between politicians and people. There is a widespread cynicism about politicians. That is because many of them are corrupt, incompetent or both.

But disillusionment is also fed by the way rich countries have told African countries that if they want loans they will have to change their economic policies to favour imports from the West. What that means is that an African politician often stands for office on a manifesto the voters applaud. But, once elected, he then has to abandon it at the insistence of the IMF – the international financial policeman through which rich nations can impose their will on Africa.

Small wonder that voters become pissed off. Turnout in elections is in decline all across Africa, and even where Africans do vote the ordinary voter is often cowed by the local apparatchik of the state into voting for the 'correct' candidate. To secure this they use various forms of sticks and carrots. Food aid for votes. A good thrashing for opponents of the government.

The result is often a parody of a Western form of democracy, which locals see as lacking political legitimacy. This is why, in the Wolof language of Senegal, the word politig has come to mean lying or deception. And in the Lingala language co-op, a word derived from cooperation and a term much used by international donors, has come to mean 'a bargain of dubious morality'.

Everywhere there is a palpable disconnect between the political elite and everybody else. Where politics and nationalism are seen to have failed something is moving into the vacuum. That something else is religion. Contrary to twentieth-century predictions that religion was in irreversible decline worldwide, people in Africa are converting in large numbers to Christianity and Islam. There is also here a big revival of Africa's traditional secret initiation societies.

The importance of religion in Africa is nothing new. Most people on the continent engage in some form of religious practice from time to time. Many Africans voluntarily associate themselves with religious networks, which they use for a variety of purposes – social, economic and even political – that go beyond the strictly religious aspect. But the role of religion in Africa has grown in recent years.

Today Africa is experiencing one of the most active periods of Christian expansion anywhere in the world – in Catholic and Protestant churches, most particularly of the evangelical pentecostalist brand. Although definitive statistics for Africa are difficult to come by, estimates suggest Christianity is growing at around 2.5 per cent annually. Of Africa's seven hundred million people some 382 million are Christians. And there are now more than seven thousand Christian indigenous churches.

Muslims are not far behind. There are some 380 million of them and Islam is growing too, most particularly in the puritan Wahhabi sect (converting both Muslims and non-Muslims), thanks to money from Saudi Arabia and missionaries from the Indian subcontinent. Even the smallest towns I came across in African countries with sizeable Muslim populations are having impressive concrete mosques built among the mud huts with money which has come from the other side of the Red Sea.

Religion is making an impact in many ways. In the Congo, the Catholic Church is the only reasonably coherent nationwide infrastructure and therefore acts as the only working post office.

People will go to a Catholic church in a part of the Congo and leave a message; sometime later it will be transmitted to somebody else in another part of the country.

For many, religion also embodies the language of hope and aspiration. In northern Nigeria many women like sharia law – contrary to the popular Western perception that Islam is anti-women – because they can use it to get divorces that deeply misogynist traditional and state courts refuse. In Senegal the Mouride brotherhood has expanded to cover almost a third of the population with a singular mixture of Sufi Islam, entrepreneurial enthusiasm and committed members overseas who remit significant amounts of money.

Religion, particularly Islam, offers a way to plug into globalisation. Saudi Arabia and Persian Gulf countries have become part of an African trading network as well as places that offer jobs to African migrant workers. African cultural and political systems are also being affected by the growth of Islamic fundamentalist movements sponsored by these foreign states.

Religion can also be a partner in development. Churches and mosques have traditionally played a key role in healthcare provision, social care and other welfare services. And religious leaders and witchdoctors (who are responsible for 80 per cent of healthcare in Africa) have great influence on shaping social attitudes, community relationships, personal responsibility and sexual morals. In Kenya medical workers are already using shamans to transmit primary healthcare. Clerics, traditional religious leaders and Islamic imams are increasingly prominent in the fight against AIDS.

Religions can, of course, be a force for bad as well as good. They can produce great passivity and fatalism in their adherents. Some religious beliefs further the spread of HIV/AIDS. We are not just talking about the Catholic Church's ban on condoms here. Cultural practices such as initiation rites, scar-tattooing, blood-brother practices, traditional means of breaking the umbilical cord, polygamy, cultural requirements for widows to sleep with their dead husband's brothers, and traditional healing practices – all these are big factors.

Traditional religion can also be malign – as when a farmer who has good crops may be accused of using the spirits to prosper at the expense of his neighbours – leading to a 'we're all poor together, so let's pull down the successful' culture. Religion can also be a vehicle for fraudsters, conmen and criminals. Its followers can be responsible for appalling human rights abuses. And religious extremism can play a part in global terrorism with weak African states becoming havens for terrorists and other criminals; al-Qaeda had bases in Africa long before September 11.

To an old atheist like me this is a perplexing business. Yet what is clear from all this is that religion can be a force for good or bad in Africa but it must certainly not be ignored.

A STORY FROM THE CRAZY
COUNTRY NEWSPAPER COLUMN
Juju arrests vanilla thief

Mukono – Mayhem broke out when Joseph Ssekando, 75, a vanilla farmer in Lweeza village, opted for witchcraft to protect his vanilla . . . 'I was desperate to get rid of thieves from my shamba and did just everything he (witch doctor) told me to do' . . .

Africa Calling

Africa is wired. Or, to be more precise, wire-less. One of the most extraordinary developments over the twenty years I have been visiting Africa came in a little village so small and inconsequential I can't even remember its name. It was your typical African village. Huts with walls of sticks and mud. A thatched straw roof emerging from the giant fronds of banana trees. Kids playing with old hoops. Women pounding corn on stones. Men sitting in the shade of a giant thorn tree. A place of subsistence, for eking out an existence on the bare edge of survival. A roadside coffee shop constructed from bent poles with a tattered old cloth stretched between them for walls. Tea and coffee brewing on a battered tin stove.

And there, in the midst of it all, stood a vast, gleaming satellite dish, pointing – this being the tropics, straight up into the inexorably blue sky. There was no electricity. Only a satellite dish. We passed on through, on the way to somewhere more important, so I never learned whether it was a dish for a battery-powered telephone system or a TV powered by a generator. It didn't matter. It stood for both – both of which I was to come across everywhere in my travels across a continent which is still, in the popular imagination in the West at any rate, a place of backwardness. Except for those with eyes to see.

Africa has skipped the age of wires that afforded the telecommunications technology to the rest of the world. It has leapfrogged straight into the wireless era. In dusty little towns, without hospitals or any real shops to speak of, you can virtually guarantee to come across thriving internet shops and cafés. The hand-painted signs on the shop fronts may look crude and amateurish but there is nothing of that about the technology these little buildings house. The dishes perch everywhere, like totems of globalisation.

There are plenty of people to communicate with, too. There has been a massive brain drain of skill and expertise and talent from Africa in recent years. The continent loses an average of seventy thousand skilled personnel a year to developed countries. Zambia has lost all but four hundred of its 1,600 doctors in the last decade. And 70 per cent of all Africa's intellectuals now live outside the shores of the continent. But unlike previous diasporas – the Jewish, Italian or Irish – the African diaspora is the first for whom technology has made return easy for the very generation who earlier quit their homeland. They can return by remote, via easy international telephone connections and the internet. In the past when Africa picked up the phone there was no one on the other end who wanted to hear what the continent had to say. Now on the other end are Africa's own people.

And they are coming back physically too, to build houses and businesses. The diaspora's loyalty and affection for the homeland has always seen them send money to their relatives back home. But the amounts of cash have risen dramatically in the past decade. These remittances are now worth more to many African economies than all the aid from the Western world.

It's not just money. Individuals are returning too. Within the space of a week I met a civil engineer who had come back to Ethiopia from London confident that the legal and banking structures, and property rights, were now sufficiently in place to ensure his savings were safe. In the Puntland region of northern Somalia I met the owner of a printing firm who had returned from Montreal to make a

$200,000 investment because the area had been free from fighting for almost ten years. Again in Ethiopia I met a young, thoroughly Westernised internet entrepreneur who had returned from Seattle, to which he had been taken when he was only two, because the dead hand of a Communist state had been removed from private enterprise. They are more than returnees. They are citizens of a globalised world who know they can keep some money abroad while bringing some home, and who intend to school their children in Africa but then send them back to the West for university. The diaspora has become an engine of change.

Such people bring back with them new practices and technologies which are quickly being taken up by the emerging middle class which has begun burgeoning in many parts of Africa over the past five to ten years. And from the middle classes they spread outwards. Perhaps the most obvious symbol of this is the mobile phone, which is changing life throughout the continent. The use of mobiles in Africa is increasing much faster than anywhere else in the world. Some 75 per cent of all telephones in Africa are mobile. Africans who never experienced the cultural leap of connectedness through fixed lines are undergoing a new experience with the cell phone. It is happening even among the poor, who will share a single phone between an entire community if necessary. Where there is no rural electricity they are charged on car batteries or by other means. In South Africa mobile servers on motorbikes are now providing telephone connections in rural areas.

All this is transforming lives in most unexpected ways. The driving force in the spread of mobiles has been the great African need for people to keep in touch with family news. Births, marriages and deaths are still the cement of many African societies, in a way our fragmented Western world finds it hard to take on board. Mobile phones now link rural communities to urban ones where men have left the fields and migrated to the towns in search of work, leaving their families behind them in the countryside. Cell phones are also used to help poor people in remote areas find employment and business opportunities without travelling long distances.

But the new technology is bringing many other spins-offs. In farming communities in Tanzania butchers cannot stock large amounts of meat because they have no electricity or cannot afford a refrigerator. In the past shops often ran out of meat. Nowadays customers use mobiles to place orders ahead of collection, enabling butchers to buy the right quantity to satisfy their customers' needs, thus developing the entire supply chain.

And the continent is ahead of much of the world in the use of pre-paid phone cards as a form of electronic currency. Africans in the developed world are buying pre-paid cards and sending them, via cell phone text messages, to their relatives back home who can then sell the cards to others. Thus the cards have become a form of currency by which money can be sent from the rich world to Africa without incurring the commission charged by banks and other financial organisations to transfer money in more conventional ways.

There is more. Using cell phones to collect data on healthcare delivery has the potential to increase efficiency dramatically within health budgets; pilot schemes in Uganda are already showing savings of as much as 40 per cent. The mobile phone is creating virtual infrastructures and raising the possibility of dramatic transformations in African culture, infrastructure and politics. One study has shown that when 20 per cent of a population has the ability to exchange news and ideas through access to cell phones and text messaging, dictatorial or totalitarian regimes find it hard to retain power.

Changes such as these should alert us all to the possibility of developments which it is difficult, if not impossible, to foresee. Just as the cell phone has, as it were, allowed rural peasants to 'leapfrog' the technology of refrigeration – finding a way around what they do not have or cannot afford – so it is possible that technology might undermine some of the traditional assumptions in our thinking about development. In the way that a developed country like Ireland leapfrogged from an agricultural to an information economy, without old-style, heavy manufacturing industry in between, so it may be that some unthought-of changes are possible in Africa too. In Africa we must learn to expect the unexpected.

Down at the Bar

I could no longer bear the airless heat of the hotel bedroom. Its ineffectual fan and failing light induced a depressing claustrophobia and only added to my natural twilight melancholy. I left the room, remembering to padlock the door, and went to the bar to find another face other than my own to look at. I was looking for companionship to ease my way down into the night. And though I wasn't hungry, possibly to join me for the dinner I would eat simply in order to give some purpose to an otherwise featureless evening.

A slight breeze stirred the tasteful awning that covered the walkway to the hotel bar, but that small relief ended once inside. I was too early. The place was empty. No one, it seemed, had got quite as bored or desperate as me so early. I ordered a double gin. It wasn't so much a drink that I wanted; in reality, I wanted something – anything – that would take me out of the awful emptiness that was gripping me.

It was an unfriendly place. It made a virtue of its lack of comfort. Discomfort seems to lend loneliness a purpose. It gives the condition a tangible pain more tolerable than the psychic unease. And, really, loneliness becomes a tragic farce when you are thrown into the false bonhomie of the barroom friendship.

When the drink arrived I made a half-joking play with the barman that, after five days there, he should know I didn't take ice in my gin.

He didn't acknowledge my enthusiastically arch 'it's-okay-I'm-only-joshing' grin but kept his eyes fixed firmly on the plywood bar top. Then he scooped the three unwanted cubes from the glass with an unwashed tea strainer, the sullen indifference of the African etched on every pore of his glowering black face.

Sexy Jungle

There is a sense that in these deep, dense, hot forests nature has wantonly and joyously run amok. There's a riotously exuberant growing going on. A berserk, almost pornographic, abundance of birth, growth, decay, corruption, death and rebirth happening everywhere all the time, immediately, now, forever. It smells so . . . green! So earthy, musky, mushroomishly fungal, so fertile. So dirty. Like every experiment nature can think of will happen here. And it has happened. And is happening. God knows how many plants, fruits, insects, trees, parasites, viruses and bacteria have been tried out in here and failed. Or succeeded and still hide, locked away inside this dense, sexy hothouse of mad, wild, verdant fertility and abandon. I wish I had a girl here. I want to do it too. Now.

Selling Stuff

The bloke in charge of the docks at Bosasso was pleased to meet us. Yahye Abdulla Mohammed had trained in Grimsby. When I say that, compared to Grimsby, Bosasso is a shithole, you will know all you need to know about the place.

But it was busy. Yahye showed us round the bustling quayside of the small port in the north-east of Somalia. There were dhows from India, from which teams of sweating stevedores were manhandling sacks of flour, cases of tomato paste and huge bundles of clothing in the mid-morning heat. There were tramp ships from Dubai, from which ancient cranes were winching television sets and fridges. There were dusty bulk-carriers from Oman carrying cement and other construction materials. There was a tanker with diesel oil from Iran. There was even a ship carrying sugar from Brazil. Elsewhere on the dockside were stacked huge piles of other imported goods: rice, palm oil, ginger, garlic.

'So, what do you export from here,' I asked the man from Grimsby Technical College.

'Goats,' Yahye said. Then he considered, and augmented his one-word answer. 'And frankincense. To Saudi and the Emirates.'

There in that one little port is the story of Africa's problems with trade. It imports . . . everything. And exports . . . fuck all.

Why is Africa poor? Because it does not trade enough. Look at the history of the world over the last century and you'll see that it is trade that usually drives economic growth. It happened in Europe and America, then Japan, then Singapore and the other East Asian tiger economies, and more recently India and now China. Trade is what has transformed other countries that were once classed as underdeveloped. Two decades ago 70 per cent of the goods exported from developing countries, particularly in Asia, were raw materials. Today 80 per cent of exports from those countries are in manufactured goods.

But not in Africa. The last twenty years, by contrast, have seen Africa's share of world trade fall from around 6 to just 2 per cent. Africa has been left behind. And the task of catching up gets harder every day.

Back in the sixties, as the world's former colonies began to become independent, the place everyone worried about was Asia. It had a huge population and big problems. The people of Africa were poor, too, but they had vast riches in the form of gold, diamonds, copper and ground so fertile that plants seemed to grow overnight wherever you dropped a seed the day before. Africans earned double what Asians did. Africa would be all right.

Forty years on and things are decidedly not all right. Today Africa is the poorest region in the world. Half of the population live on less than one dollar a day. Life expectancy is actually falling. The average life expectation is just forty-six years. In India and Bangladesh, by contrast, that figure is now a staggering seventeen years more.

Why has Africa fallen so far behind? Partly because the infrastructure the colonial powers put in place in Africa was primarily designed to extract raw materials rather than to aid a general economic development.

Set a map of African railways alongside those of India and you'll see what I mean. India's railways link the subcontinent; Africa's merely join the mines and plantations to the ports. On the Indian subcontinent an effective colonial administrative system was established. But Africa emerged from the colonial era with far weaker infrastructure and admin systems than other ex-colonies.

There was another problem. Africa's blessings proved also to be a curse. The countries with the most oil, diamonds and other mineral wealth are those that have experienced the most war and armed conflict.

The madcap economic experiments of the post-independence African leaders didn't help either. On top of all that, in the seventies, Africa became the battleground on which the American and Russian superpowers fought out their proxy battles during the Cold War. Both sides backed corrupt dictators who were less interested in developing their countries than in thieving money for their private Swiss bank accounts. South Asia was busy expanding, building roads, railways, ports and irrigation systems, educating its workforce and building up manufacturing industry. But Africa stuck to exporting minerals and crops on which world prices are four times more volatile than everything else the world trades . . . And individually pocketing the results.

Until Africa builds its ability to produce more goods and better infrastructure to cut the cost of trading, it will remain in an economic ditch. The report of the Commission for Africa shows how it can change all that – and how rich nations can help the process by targeting their aid better. They must also must stop hindering Africa's economic development by slapping import tariffs on African goods as they enter rich countries' markets – and they must abolish the outrageous and unnecessary subsidies to European and American farmers, subsidies which in 2002 totalled more than the entire income of all the people of Africa put together.

Without that Africa will continue to rely on crops like cocoa, the price of which has fallen by 71 per cent in the past two decades. Or coffee, which is down 64 per cent. Or cotton, down 47 per cent. And it will import sugar, a crop it ought to produce itself, from places like Brazil because it cannot compete against Brazilian methods of production on a world market in which the price of sugar has fallen by 77 per cent in the past twenty years.

And ports like Bosasso will continue to have a list of imports as long as your arms. And a list of exports that can be written on the back of a postage stamp.

And if that imbalance continues, with all the poverty and hardship that implies, we should not be surprised one day to see not just Yahye Abdulla Mohammed but his entire people turning up in Grimsby. Dump or no dump.

The Parade of Dying

She was a prostitute who had unprotected sex with her clients. Why? Because the men almost all refused to use condoms. But what if she got AIDS?

Her reply was devastating.

'If I get AIDS it will take me five years to die. But without the money to buy food my baby will not survive five months. Where is my choice?'

Such is the terrible logic of poverty. For her, having unprotected sex for money was the rational thing to do. It was the only way of keeping her baby alive.

AIDS is killing more people in Africa than anywhere else in the world. The scale of the pandemic is chilling. In Africa, twenty-five million people – half the population of the UK – have died from AIDS. Two million more people will die this year. And twenty-five million more are infected with HIV. In many parts of Africa life expectancy has fallen back to what it was in the 1950s. Of Africa's forty-three million orphans more than a quarter have lost their parents from AIDS – and that figure is set to grow for at least another decade. In Zambia, by 2010 every third child will be an orphan.

Why? The answer is nothing to do with medicine, or morality. It is to do with poverty. And it is to do with culture.

Outsiders look at Africa and so often jump to the wrong

conclusions. AIDS would be sorted if only we could get the anti-retrovirals and other medical treatment to Africa. Wrong. AIDS would be sorted if only enough condoms were available. Wrong. AIDS would be sorted if only Africans were less promiscuous or followed a stricter moral code. Wrong. Wrong. Wrong.

So many of our Western assumptions are wrong here. Our medicines interact with social processes we don't properly understand. Our morality is underpinned by the assumption that autonomous individuals make informed choices based on proper understanding of the facts. Our economics are based on the assumption that many people in Africa have alternative commodities, other than sex, that they can sell for food, school fees, exam results, employment or survival itself.

It is no coincidence that Africa is the worst place for AIDS anywhere in the world. Some 62 per cent of the world's fifteen- to twenty-four-year-olds who live with HIV are to be found here. In some places nearly 40 per cent of the population are infected.

The human, social and economic implications of all this are not, even now, fully clear. The disease does not just devastate a single generation. It attacks three generations: the individual living with HIV or AIDS, and also the children born with the HIV virus and grandparents who are pressed into levels of childcare and food production for which their advancing years ill fit them. Evidence presented to the Commission for Africa, for which I spent most of the past year working, shows that AIDS has an especially destructive impact upon the economy since it primarily attacks those of working age. In addition to the terrifying human cost this means that Africa's already struggling nations will be harder hit. Teachers in Zambia are dying faster than they can be trained.

AIDS will not be checked until poverty is tackled. One large-scale AIDS testing scheme among pregnant women found that only 30 per cent of them returned after the birth of their child to get the results.

The medics running the scheme were mystified. Then someone pointed out to them that the women knew there was no point in coming back for the results because they could not afford any treatment anyway. It was not ignorance but knowledge that lay behind their thinking.

Nor will AIDS be checked without a better understanding of African cultural attitudes. An understanding of African cultures is crucial here. Much in reducing the transmission of HIV/AIDS turns on attitudes about what it is to be a man. Manliness, for many African men, is demonstrated in fathering as many children as possible. They see condoms as an insult to their virility. Others see them as a dulling of sexual pleasure: 'you don't eat a sweet with the wrapper on' is as common an African saying as 'you don't have a bath with your socks on' is here.

Likewise there are questions about whether a woman is a 'real woman' until she is a mother. Tied into that are cultural factors about the earlier onset of sexual activity for girls, the lower status of women and women's powerlessness to insist on the use of condoms even where they have been educated to want them. Ways to combat the diseases which do not address local culture fail.

The outsiders who ran a workshop on AIDS in Angola recently learned that. They came to pass on their knowledge about transmission and prevention. They wanted the locals to spend their time discussing virginity, condom use, monogamy and the like. When they left, their eyes had been opened to the cultural practices that were so much a part of people's lives.

Only then did they come to understand why all their well-meaning education programmes had not resulted in higher use of condoms or lowered rates of infection. They had not known enough about local cultural norms and values on sexuality, let alone about gender relations and power hierarchies or about African cultural fatalism.

Africans frequently remark on the linguistic similarity between

'AIDS' and 'aid'. This is more than a not-very-good joke. It reflects a widespread suspicion that AIDS is something that has been foisted on them by Western scientists. Dismissing this notion as barmy might work in the Western world but in Africa it resonates with the profound ambiguity that Africans have about the nature of the power that emanates from the West. Unless we deepen our understanding about African culture the scourge of AIDS will continue its deadly parade.

A STORY FROM THE CRAZY COUNTRY NEWSPAPER COLUMN
A drunken man beaten, gets a running stomach

A drunken man, who was caught red-handed trying to defecate at the doorway of a pit latrine in Banda, was thoroughly beaten till he soiled his pants. An eyewitness says the middle-aged man, who was heavily staggering, branched at the toilet that serves a nearby drinking joint in Banda and found a padlock fastened. Instead of looking out for the key, the man later identified as Maraka, took advantage of the semi-lit place to defecate there . . .

Your Darkness or Mine?

Out in the trees there's still Kurtz. There's always Kurtz. Conrad didn't write about Africa, he wrote about us. Africa wasn't dark to the African. It was a land suffused with light and life. Then Stanley opened up the great snaky, sluggish river and out poured darkness and death. Ours. Bringing trade and commerce and misery in equal measure to its marshy banks.

Thousands of books written by white people have the adjective 'dark' in their titles. Why? Are they not describing our psychologies? Our fears of the black man? The impenetrable mind of the African, the unknowable places of their land, the fear of their religions, the unwillingness to examine their cultures or histories, the wild animal in us, the forgotten savage? Is it not our fears, misunderstandings and ignorance we project on to an entire continent?

There have been and still are many darknesses here. The Belgians and their beheadings, whippings, amputations on children and cannibalism. Mobutu's massacres and slavery and lootings; the uranium used in the first atomic bombs that came from the soil of this place; the AIDS that sneaked out of its forests; the armies of amoral children; the genocides; the warlords; and, finally, the lunatic self-appointed 'generals' and 'commander' militia paid for by outside interests and nations to rape, torture, brutalise, mutilate and kill. Out there in the trees. In the exact same place where Kurtz lived. They're still there.

Conrad based his monster on a Belgian called Captain Rom. Rom lined his gardens with the skulls of his victims. He lived at the top of the river near Stanleyville, today's Kisangani. Now there are new Roms out there. Let's take one of them. His name is Commander Jérôme.

He's an ex-traffic warden. He refuses to come in from the cold. He controls his fiefdom through raw terror and he pays for it with slave labourers working the diamond and gold mines and terror raids on other villages. He is tall, thin, has a stupid moustache. When not wearing candy-coloured, striped T-shirts he wears green army fatigues with bright red epaulettes and a gleaming silver pistol tucked into the middle of the belt around his waist which I hope accidentally discharges some day. His victims are buried under the football pitch and in his garden in the town of Aru, where he can be found daily, slouched outside one of Aru's three dingy cafés. Drinking Fanta orange.

His 'army' beat and stab people to death. They punish them publicly by impaling them on sharp poles inserted in their rectums. They are left in the main street to die in this manner. He flogs his soldiers, some as young as ten, almost to death. His favourites he offers sex slaves and the specially favoured get to play with his pet baby chimpanzee.

Sixty thousand people have died since 1999 in the Ituri region where Jérôme operates. Not all of the victims are his but enough are. Meanwhile, at the West's urging and in an attempt to try and bring the mercenaries into the plans for new government, the President of the DRC has offered real generalships in the national army, such as it is, to these brutes.

Last week there were more outrages. The UN have finally begun to respond but what about the past? Is that simply to be forgotten in the name of expediency?

Meanwhile, Floribert Kisembo, Bosco Taganda, Germain Katanga and our own favourite Kurtz-of-the-Month, Commander Jérôme

Kakwavu, are under house arrest in the capital, Kinshasa. House arrest involves sitting in the bar of the Grand Hotel sipping gins and tonic while Jérôme slugs his habitual Fanta and discussing their generalships while ordering new brutalities on the terrorised and impoverished country people under their control. All from the bedside telephones of their generals' luxury five-star suites. You tell me. Your darkness or mine?

...I Say Puhtahto

What does Africa need? Development. So that's all right then.

But ask the bigger question, 'What is development for?' and you get different answers according to who you ask and where they're from.

In the West development is about increasing choice; in Africa it is more about increasing human dignity. And there's something else. In the West we see it as about choice for individuals; in Africa living a good life is something wider – to do with wellbeing, happiness and membership of a community.

It is hard for those of us steeped in a culture of materialistic individualism to understand fully what Africa is all about. But there is a word that goes some way to explaining it. It is a word from the Nguni language family, which comprises Zulu, Xhosa and other Bantu tongues. The word is *ubuntu*.

African philosophers define it in this way: 'A human being is a human being through the otherness of other human beings.' Which sounds a bit poncy. Bono has a neater way of expressing it. He sums it up as: 'I am because we are.' *Ubuntu* is about interdependence. How we need each other and have a stake in each other. How one part of the community can't thrive truly while the other part of the community is in the dirt. In tending to them, we will be better off ourselves. It's that simple. *Ubuntu*.

But there is one other key thing. The 'me and them' implicit in this idea is not just a relationship between the individual and society. In Africa, as well as 'me and them' there is an 'us' which refers to family and wider ties of kinship. An African has duties to family members that are not expected of a Westerner.

Digging around in African history it's easy enough to see where this came from. In pre-colonial Africa, clans – groups of people who claim the same ancestor, either through birth or kinship – were the central units of administration. One thing that was common to many of these family clans was that they developed a way of making decisions, which relied on consensus rather than on the judgement of an individual leader. The business of living in a hostile environment taught them that they survived best when they worked together.

This mutual accountability crossed boundaries between those who were well off and those who were poor. The wealthy were never allowed to lose sight of their obligations – and the poor were never slow in claiming their due from their better-off relatives. It was a recognition that, whatever the personal merits or strengths of the individual, success in life always relied to some extent on membership of the group. There was no room for rampant or impersonal individualism.

Many of these strong kinship ties persist in Africa today. Not least in the 'big man' culture which requires a successful member of the clan to offer patronage to other members. Patron–client relations should not be dismissed as temptations to nepotism and corruption; they reveal something about African senses of community. It is hard for outsiders to understand this. But unless we do we will never go beyond some of the stereotypes we have inherited about Africa.

Cultural difference cannot be an excuse for the blatant levels of corruption that bedevil many parts of Africa. Corruption is one of Africa's key problems. African societies are riddled with it – from kleptocratic leaders at the top, salting money away in Western bank accounts, to soldiers at roadblocks demanding bribes to let you through, to clerks in government bureaucracies charging to hand out official forms. But we in the rich world do not have clean hands here. Corruption is fed by big Western companies that routinely offer bribes to African leaders. As one of the biggest thieves in the history of Africa – the former Zairean dictator President Mobutu Sese Seko – once said: 'It takes two to corrupt – the corrupted and the corrupter.' And he should know.

We are talking ginormous sums here. The amounts now lurking in Western bank accounts run into billions of dollars. One particularly bad area is in official government purchases of goods and services. The Africa Commission report shows that wide-scale corruption adds at least 25 per cent to the costs of government projects, and often results in inferior quality construction and unnecessary purchases. Abuse of this system takes many forms. When public sector contracts are put out to sealed tender, bribes can be requested or offered. Quotations can be doctored to build in false costs. It is not only the politicians and public officials who create the problem: it is also the bankers, lawyers, accountants and engineers working on public contracts.

Flying on one internal African flight recently I met an Asian oil executive. He compared Africa with his own continent. 'Our politicians are pretty corrupt but they only take 80 per cent.' I thought he was joking. But he had examples of countries in Africa whereby – after the governor of the central bank, a couple of generals and the president had taken their cut – the 'signature bonuses', as he called them, reached 90 per cent of the investment. And then, when work finally began, some other official came along to remind the oilmen that they had forgotten his 10 per cent.

There are lots of ways of fighting corruption. It requires a clampdown from willing African leaders. It requires Western multinational companies to refuse to pay bribes and Africans to report those companies which offer them. It needs governments in the West to require their banks to send the looted money in the private accounts of corrupt Africans back where it belongs, which would be easy using existing laws on money laundering for drugs and terrorism. All of which we set out in the Africa Commission report.

But it also requires a better understanding of African culture. It means asking, for example, if there is a point at which nepotism is not corruption to an African in a way in which it would be to an American? Should we reject nepotism completely, or should we simply draw the line only where a political leader's relatives actually can't do the job as well as someone else would? And should the West accept that it's hard to control a large-scale organisation like a government in multi-ethnic societies like Africa's, where attempts to discipline bring charges of favouritism?

If these questions seem straightforward, the answers to them are certainly not.

MUMBO JUMBO

Language or ritual that appears meaningless to the listener.

Origin uncertain, but probably derives from the Mande speakers of West Africa.

Mande is a group of 20 languages spoken by around nine million people.

Applied to a masked figure worshipped by the Mande.

Mama Djumbo

Mama = ancestor

Djumbo = pom-pom wearer

Death Highway

It's a small town. A truck-stop town. The shotgun shacks line the broad, wide roads that break out on to tarmac ten miles on. Behind the breezeblock bars or the wattle and daub single-room huts are the yards and then the bush and then the rainforest and, behind all that, the jungle.

The huge road cruisers are parked up. They tilt sideways down the slope in the road, their wheels resting in the drainage gully. Most of them have curtains drawn inside the roomy cabs where the drivers are sleeping. It's just before dawn. Nothing's moving save a couple of pigs snuffling between the tyres; a few scrawny chickens are softly clucking and a goat or two gently nibble the pair of drying trousers hanging on the back of the big trailer bound for Zanzibar.

A low fog hangs on the tree canopy and a light drizzle floats down on to the all-weather surface making it glisten in the early half-light.

From one of the huts a man emerges pulling on a faded, patched plaid shirt that he leaves unbuttoned. He stands in the doorframe scratching his chest and yawning, then begins to urinate on to the road. He walks down the road to the red Mac and turns the key. The engine coughs, belches black smoke from the chrome exhaust stack and the first of the day's cargoes is underway.

By six the noise of engines shatters the dawn. The girls have already begun lining the doorways and lounging in the bars and hotels with the modest blanket doorways. The drivers do their teeth bent over into the ditch, scrubbing them with a green twig, naked to the waist. Women gingerly teeter down from the cabs and walk home. Some make a fire near the truck in which they have spent the night and make breakfast with food supplied to them by the driver. They cook for one.

By 7.30a.m. the road is a shuddering stretch of smoke-belching, petrol-fumed highway. Trucks roar past in both directions. To cross now requires nerve and skill. These things won't stop for anything now except one thing. Quick, roadside sex from the women hanging round all over town. They aren't dressed provocatively. They are in normal day attire, they don't wear extravagant make-up, if at all, and their hair and shoes are the same as you see on every other woman all over the area. But this is Death Highway and these girls are hookers and besides the cargo the men are carrying in their trucks, they carry in their body that other product of this place. AIDS.

Why does modernity bring so many tears to this continent? There are hardly any roads in Africa. When the first cars arrived here there was not only nowhere for them to go, there was no way of getting there. Most people still walk on this continent and they walk on single-lane pathways. In the conditions of climate and environment that exist here it makes sense. Cutting more than what is in front of you in the bush would be a waste of energy in this heat. Walking anything other than single file uses energy. You don't talk, you don't have to cut for two bodies instead of one. Trample the path down with feet.

But Africa desperately needs roads and until recently there was nowhere to connect to. There were few cities on this vast continent and the colonialists only built those roads that would take goods from the capitals to the ports. A lot of national roads end hundreds of miles before the internal borders of Africa for old imperial security reasons. Sudan, a vast country five times the size of France, has a grand total of only 1,200 miles of paved roads!

But there is this one big modern road. Death Highway. This ribbon of asphalt many thousands of kilometres in length was built specifically to link all the countries of the centre, from Rwanda to the Democratic Republic of Congo in the west and to the Kenyan port of Mombasa in the east. Most of the trade of central Africa will pound up and down this all-weather road. It joins the cities and towns and the truck stops and it carries vast amounts of trade along its route. Since sometime in the early 1970s it has also begun to carry death. And gradually it brought it all the way across the continent to the coast and from there to the world.

This is too much for Africans. They feel they are being blamed unfairly for this horror that is devastating their own continent. It is bad enough, they feel, that we in the developed world always view Africa through the prism of Hunger, Poverty, War, Corruption, and yet now the final insult – the bringers of death through sex to the planet. Many of them have rejected this out of hand. And it is not simply the common man who has done this; it is intellectuals and politicians also. They will not have this laid at their door. It is all too humiliating.

It is ridiculous, of course. No one blames Spain for the Spanish flu. Or China for the avian variety. Or the Middle East for the plague, etc. But they feel it. They feel ashamed. And they shouldn't. AIDS is neither a source of shame nor pride. It is simply another medical condition, one that in our world we have learned to hold at bay with medicines. Medicines that we can afford but which most Africans cannot. That is the real shame. That is the source of the scandal. And that emphatically is our shame not theirs.

It is nonetheless almost certain that HIV broke out of the Congolese jungles sometime in 1931. Nearly all victims today can be traced back to a common ancestor of that year. It is probably likely that a monkey equivalent of HIV crossed into humans in the dense forests where monkey hunting and eating is still fairly common. The earliest well-documented blood sample containing HIV-1 was taken from a man in Kinshasa, the capital of the Congo, in 1959. What helped HIV to become epidemic was the extensive expansion and use of hypodermic needles and syringes in the middle of the twentieth century during periods of mass vaccination and injecting antibiotic use.

When man emerged from Africa most of the bacteria and viruses that fed on him emerged and developed too. In the developed world we found solutions, cures, to many of those illnesses, but when we attempted to spread the benefits of that control we had obtained over polio, TB, malaria and other things still prevalent in Africa we brought with us the technology that may have allowed this killer to break out. Thus the very means by which the well-meaning world was trying to cure these ills was actually planting the seed for even greater disaster. The modern world bites Africa again.

Scientists believe that HIV has been around a lot longer than even 1931, but, like Ebola or Lassa fevers which kill within hours, it never got the opportunity to spread and died out or hid away in the forests until its time had come. It remained localised until the forests started to be felled. As the modern world arrived with its methods and medicines, and the new roads gave AIDS new opportunities, this dirty little killer was cleared for takeoff.

The truckers know all about AIDS. So do the hookers. Everyone does. They know how it's spread. But …

The girls sell themselves because they are dirt poor. They have families they are responsible for. They know about rubbers but for most of them that's simply another way to make more money. They can charge more if the man won't wear one. They are resigned. Fatalistic. They're going to die anyway. Makes no difference. Competition is fierce. Now there are women who don't charge more for not wearing one. So the others must follow. Their babies get the disease then. But …

The men are the same. They're going to die. They want sex. They want companionship. Yes, they know they give it to their wives and then their babies. But …

In some African countries 40 per cent of the population has AIDS. It is destroying the continent.

Searching for an explanation as to why all these events and miseries should happen to them many Africans, always happy to believe rumour and conspiracy theories, believe that HIV was made in a laboratory in the US and then planted in Africa after being tested on gay or drug-injecting prisoners in America. This is useful for removing Africa's 'blame' but unfortunately does not fit the scientific facts to hand.

Many people believe that AIDS was manufactured or distributed out of the medical faculty at Kisangani University. During the 1950s some Belgian and Congolese doctors were doing research on polio there. The files are still there. Mouldering boxes stuffed with glass sample slides spilling out on to the cracked terrazzo floor. Water drips down the wall and tropical fungus mould spreads over everything. Glass is smashed and roofs have caved in. Vines begin to choke the building. But still it's used. And still the boxes are there in a bleak, abandoned lab room that has an office furnished with three orange plastic chairs. The office belongs to the doctor who teaches and works there. He is the Guardian of the Slides.

It's a good story, but it's rubbish. There are no AIDS in those samples dating back to the forties, but it suits lots of people to believe there are. It suits us as a modern version of *Heart of Darkness*, located exactly where Conrad placed his fictional character Kurtz on the upper reaches of the Congo. It suits the Africans because it neatly conflated the theory of a 'white plot' to control and kill Africans further by cooking up a cocktail of fiendish diseases under the guise of aid, a concept, incidentally, widely viewed here with both resentment and suspicion, and the truth that the spread of the disease was probably due to unsafe needles.

Beside the awful tragedy of the illness a further tragedy has resulted. In many countries large sections of the inhabitants refuse to be vaccinated or inoculated for many other diseases. They fear either being infected through a needle, or that they are being injected with AIDS, or, as in the case of Islamic Nigeria, all of the above plus the fact that it's an American plot. As a consequence polio, which had all but been eradicated in Africa, is epidemic once again, as is TB, which has taken on an assistant role in the spread of HIV.

Out on the Ugandan border with Kenya it's getting dark. Some of the boys will roll all night but others will pull in. The girls swarm around the cabs. The truckers stare laconically down. Most of them won't bother to get down. The girls start climbing up. Others begin to light some fires and the men hand the food out of the window. It's all part of the package.

Later that night some of them will roar off into the dark, down Death Highway, their big beams picking out a startled beast or a woman in the pitch of the black forest crowding the roadside. That same jungle from which the Beast escaped, that same road that carries it now through the African night, stopping a little while in the shanties of Congo, Burundi, Rwanda, Uganda, Tanzania and Kenya before meeting us some evening perhaps in a smart bar in Madison Avenue, the Champs-Elysées or the West End.

A Passing Thought

We find it very hard to imagine other people's lives. And, perhaps because of that, we imagine they must want lives like our own as that is the only life we know. We find it difficult to accept how anyone could want a life different from ours or why they would choose to live the life we see them leading. Life, it turns out, is a cultural construct.

Wealth created the philosophical landscape of our modernity. Irony and post-modernism have removed our culture from the actual business of living. Life is something to be viewed from a distance and preferably through a sceptical lens. Life is only experienced in the context of 'making a living'. We have constructed this purely abstract view of staying alive which largely involves undertaking meaningless tasks, to a lesser or greater degree, in order to gain a notional value of 'income', 'wages' or 'salary'.

In order to purchase food the actual stuff of life has now been subsumed into the category of entertainment through time-filling exercises in restaurants and supermarkets. It is ironic that one pays the most where one receives the least. And that, in the giant superstore of modernity, bread and water have become the most valued and most expensive of foods, with their bottled varieties and their focaccias, ciabattas, baguettes etc. Food is sport and status. Life just happens behind a desk.

Here, however, life is still about staying alive. Every second, every single carrot or tomato, demands attention, care and labour. There's no abstraction here. No fun. No irony. Just struggle. This in its postmodern idiom is literally 'the real thing'. It's life undistanced from itself.

A STORY FROM THE CRAZY COUNTRY NEWSPAPER COLUMN
He can't keep bum appetite

Drama unfolded when a boda man decided to let his hands stray to the bums of a lady passerby. The lady turned and slapped the man heavily across his face, asking angrily whether she was his wife. The man, unable to answer but still attracted to the well-shaped bum, simply trembled. His eyes remained fixed on the bums, while his lips failed to utter a word.

Suhra

The planet Venus is named after the Goddess of Beauty. We always say 'she' or 'her' when we refer to her. For some it is the Evening Star, the first out at night, the prettiest, the brightest. For others it is the Morning Star, the last to leave, the one that heralds the new day in the lightening sky. The Somalis call her Suhra. They will tell you that when doomsday comes all the stars will fall from the sky except Suhra the Beautiful, the Evening Star. For she is too beautiful even for God to wish to destroy.

A Different World

It's hard to type here. I spend too much time swatting the flies. It's a tin hut with a concrete floor and files that say Endalek, Abiyu, Kassa and Worku.

This is the Save the Children office in a place called Sekota. I have to type fast because the power comes and goes. And it might go again soon.

Outside, children wearing togas drive the cattle or goats down from the hills into their houses to sleep beside them to keep them warm. It's nearly dusk and it's beginning to grow cold up here in the high mountains.

Mothers are calling out for their children still up on the ridges. They ululate – a weird, high-pitched warbling that each child recognises as his mum's distinctive sound and answers her back with the family call.

The smoke drifts up through the dusty evening sky. The scorching day cools rapidly and some young yobbos lounge around the single street lights marking the entrance to 'town'.

Today I watched more hungry people face down approaching death. Today I saw some travelling players act out death by AIDS – what this killer is, how you get it, how to try to prevent it. The already weak loved the show. Twenty per cent of the appreciative audience will already be HIV-positive but probably will not know it. Being weak from hunger because of the lack of food, because they could not grow anything, because the rains didn't come they will probably contract AIDS and they won't know it and will pass it on to their wives who will pass it on to their babies whose immune systems weaken from hunger and disease and then get TB or malaria from the lethal mosquitoes or . . . And then everyone dies. And I see it.

I traipse around with my stupid hat and anger and shame and then I say things on television that I shouldn't and then . . . that's all I can do.

But the people who don't send the food we have in surplus abundance, the politicians who stop these people having cheap or free medicines or even making their own, who will not let them send us whatever products they do heroically manage to produce but insist they open their markets to us, the banks who insist that these people who have nothing, NOTHING, pay us back some pathetic amount we don't notice or need are wiping out the farmers, herders, teachers, thinkers, doctors, nurses, artists, builders, fathers, mothers and endless waves of quiet wide-eyed frightened children who don't want to die and don't understand that they are.

And do you know something. Neither do I.

Tomorrow, I will walk again through the uncountable misery of the poorest, most wretched people of our world and again I won't know what I'm doing there. I should be at home for Father's Day. But that's a different world. One I should, but cannot, let myself consider today.

One as utterly unimaginable to these friendly, warm, brave people as the latest sci-fi movie is to us.

What am I doing here? I don't know, I really don't know.

Somewhere in a gilded room in a fancy mansion somewhere in the beautiful French Alps, eight men are gathering around a polished table as you read this.

I'm walking empty fields and bare hills of a ruined land amongst a ruined people.

Over pastries the very important world leaders ruminate and consider our world and their pathetic plans for it.

The people I am with in Ethiopia will not be in those plans. The leaders will break for their coffee and the children here will wait for their handful of grain.

The leaders will resume their very, very important talks and these children will resume dying.

I'll walk on and you will finish reading this and turn the page.

Somewhere along the line all of us got things very, very wrong.

Bob Geldof introduces
The President of the World

This is the year. This must be the year. And if it is not this year . . . then when? I am tired of the politics of being nice. I want the politics of responsibility. I am sick of standing in squares and linking arms in foreign cities, of tear gas and pop concerts and records.

This year. This is the year. This year we will go to the mountaintop of world politics. And we will get there. And we will get there together.

And when the leaders of the rich world, our lucky world, come to the UK they must not have the isolation of Gleneagles to deliberate that which has already been decided. Rather they must be persuaded to do that for which they are paid. They must lead. They must understand it is not simply their job to manage the world in which they live, but rather to enable the world we wish to create.

And so I say again, a living cliché, Feed the World. Feed the World. Yes. Still. For we starve for justice. We hunger for dignity. We thirst for an end to degradation and hurt. Feed the World, for we are empty of hope and too full of despair and have nothing to nourish our dreams.

There is one man, however, whose very presence nourishes dreams into waking reality. Whose entire life is emblematic of dignified resistance in the name of justice. Who tore down the last tyranny of the twentieth century by the quiet sacrifice of his life and who will resound in history because of the humility and grace he showed his tormentors in his hour of victory. The President of the World, Nelson Mandela.

Trafalgar Square, March 2005

Endpiece

At the end of the trip, having travelled for weeks, I was too tired and too dirty to be able to marshal the kind of neat and compact thoughts that television demands for the end of its programmes. But still, for me, Ethiopia with its vast landmasses and many people remained a paradigm country of the rest of Africa.

Its almost insurmountable problems of climate, geography and politics remain, but, in the twenty years since the world first took notice of this beautiful country and its terrible plight, things may look the same but in fact have vastly improved. Yes, there is endemic hunger for far too many, but far, far fewer than before.

And politically Addis has become the diplomatic centre for a new, different kind of Africa, spawning a large, educated and increasingly influential middle class. Farmers have begun sending their children to school and the ancient, magnificent, traditional peoples who want to come in from the past, understand that the interface with modernity must be education.

And we, for our part, must alter our political and economic behaviour to assist them. Africa is not a poor continent; it is vastly wealthy, with its natural resources and creativity. And it will be this that will create its own wealth and development. And with that wealth Africa will be able to afford its own health and education, which in turn will allow it to produce and compete equally on the world stage. That is where a continent as romantic and timeless and beautiful as Africa deserves to be. And it is where we need it to be.

Declaration of the Commission for Africa

The Commission for Africa finds the condition of the lives of the majority of Africans to be intolerable and an affront to the dignity of all mankind. We insist upon an alteration of these conditions through a change of policy in favour of the weak.

Having analysed and costed how this may be achieved, we call for our conclusions to be implemented forthwith in the cause of right and justice and in the name of our shared humanity.

On the edge of this new century, in an age of unprecedented wealth and economic progress by all continents, it is unacceptable that Africa drifts further from the rest of the world, unseen in its misery and ignored in its pain.

The Commission, its members acting in their capacity as individuals, has assimilated the analysis of years and all extant reports into our findings. These clearly show how things may have been otherwise.

However we exist in contemporary realities. The world is vastly different to that of 20 years ago when we forcefully acknowledged the pity of the Great Famine of 1984–85. The world, then locked into its Cold War political stasis, remained rigid in its competitive ideologies. The breaking of this deadlock, and the increase in global trade that followed, allied to new technologies and cultural shifts, have created a more fluid, less predictive yet more interdependent world.

This world in flux has brought great opportunities along with confusion, change and anxiety. But such change poses great possibilities for us all and especially for Africa, that great giant finally beginning to stir itself from its enforced slumber. We need, then, to seek to understand these newer forces in play about us, attempt to define them and in so doing set the framework for policies that favour the poor.

The great nations of the world, in alliance with their African neighbours, must now move together, in our common interest. How they may proceed will be determined by each nation's needs and desires. But all must immediately begin the journey that leads us to the ultimate common destination of a more equitable world.

Our task was the first step. It is done.

11 March 2005

Tony Blair (Chair)
Fola Adeola
K.Y. Amoako
Nancy Baker
Hilary Benn
Gordon Brown
Michel Camdessus
Bob Geldof
Ralph Goodale

Ji Peiding
William S. Kalema
Trevor Manuel
Benjamin Mkapa
Linah Mohohlo
Tidjane Thiam
Anna Tibaijuka
Meles Zenawi

Live 8

Three days ago, in the late bright afternoon, I wandered across the scissor-mown lawns at Gleneagles. I found a little clearing among some trees and hunched down. Overhead, the hummingbird helicopters clattered and thumped in the evening air as the world's most powerful people left what the Secretary General of the United Nations called the most successful and important G8 Summit for Africa there has ever been.

They couldn't see or hear me and I didn't really understand it but I began to sob. I felt weird, empty. I don't know… It was over. It was over.

Because of this thing – this concert, event, lobby, protest, gathering, moment. Because of you. And the bands. And the crews and technicians and thousands of people who made this thing that was Live 8. Because of all this, the men in those helicopters had just written a cheque to double aid to $50 billion for the poor of Africa over the next few years. Unbelievable.

I thought, 'Now we have to make sure they cash it', and we will. We will get them to spend the money, we will name the corrupt who try and take one cent of it and we will try to speed up the 100 per cent debt cancellation for the poorest countries that was also confirmed at Gleneagles.

I think I cried because I was never sure it was going to work. That billions of us could force the process to move. I was worried that they would remain for ever remote, unreachable in the isolated vacuum of their national power. But it did work. In the end there were just too many of us.

In other places in this book you will see what it was all about and what it means for the future of the poorest and weakest people on our world. You already know how we roared on behalf of those who were mute, how we moved power for the powerless, how we walked that long walk for many who cannot even crawl and how billions of us stood up for the beaten-down and put-upon.

We were led there by our bands, by musicians who articulate us better than we can ourselves. They talk a global language of understanding understood by all humanity, and they have led us on this long twenty-year journey from Live Aid. In their music is the sum of our longing for a universal decency. They communicate dismay and disgust at the daily carnival of dying that parades across our television screens. In the nightly pornography of poverty vast hundreds of thousands die annually simply because they are too poor to stay alive.

What a glorious, magnificent day. What a rejection of the defeat of cynicism, I thought as I watched the TV monitor side stage showing me four continents, nine countries and their greatest artists, nine cities and their greatest sites, millions physically present and thousands of millions spiritually there as they watched this one concert, one moment, one idea winding itself around what was truly one world that afternoon. And then I got a bizarre tickling sensation, thinking just maybe this is going to work.

Three days ago, crouched down among the chopper-beaten trees of Gleneagles I was shocked that 'the plan' had indeed worked. The Commission for Africa on which I worked was no longer just a theory for the reconstruction of a continent's economic life and, as a result, a better life for its blameless inhabitants, it was now a paid-up reality.

The Long Walk. Over. The Summit. Over. The concert?

The concert plays out daily in my head. The magnificent bands. The brilliant young Turks and the ageless greats. I know them, they are not like what you read. They are not the mean-spirited midgets those tiny thorns of tabloid spite would have you believe. I know them as they appeared to you on that stage. They are great. And they are good.

As are you. At home. In the parks or streets or stadia or squares of the world on 2nd July 2005. This was the day we pulled it off. This was the day the powerful were powerless. When they bent in the force of our noisy gale. When we drowned out their endless No's by our boundless Yes. Where the promise of twenty years ago was cashed. Everything that rock'n'roll had ever been about to me, or seemed to suggest or vaguely promised was made real on that beautiful day.

We should never need another event like it. But if we do, new generations know what must be done and they will not fail. The power of this wild music to call us to gather 'bout the electronic hearth of the TV or PC screen will continue. But will it, can it ever be expressed with such power, such elegance, passion and joy as on that summer's day last week?

My phone rang. I'd had it on 'loudspeaker' for weeks because it was constantly in use and I feared imminent brain cancer, ear rot, overheated temples or whatever. Now with the helicopter noise I couldn't hear. I put it on 'normal' and tried to listen. I had to go. I wiped my eyes and stopped myself being shaky. Didn't want to look silly.

That's it for me, I thought, as I clambered into our minivan. On the ground the riot police and machine-gunned army waved us past the great security fences. Overhead, the choppers thundered through the glens carrying the men you had made listen.

I will never forget that day. Neither will you. Neither must you. Tell your children you were there. That you watched. That you changed the world. You and your mates. All 3.8 billion of them. And when they say why? tell them that you couldn't stand it. It wasn't fair. It wasn't right. A great injustice was being done. Tell them you were not powerless. Tell them that the bands played and you danced and sang and laughed and in so doing you allowed others you would never see or meet to do the same some day in the future.

We played our hearts out. 'And we played real good for free.'

Thanks for everything.

Bob Geldof, July 2005

The Road Taken

Michael Buerk

'Dawn, and as the sun breaks through the piercing chill of night on the plain outside Korem it lights up a biblical famine, now, in the Twentieth Century.'

Those words opened Michael Buerk's first report on the Ethiopian famine for the 6 o'clock news on October 24th 1984. His reports sent shock waves round the world. The Live Aid concert, a direct consequence of Bob Geldof watching that broadcast, was watched by half the planet.

Michael Buerk has reported on some of the biggest stories in our lifetime: the Flixborough chemical plant fire, the Birmingham pub bombing, Lockerbie. He was in Buenos Aires at the start of the Falklands War; he reported the death throes of apartheid in South Africa.

He was the face of the BBC flagship evening news for many years and has fronted everything from the popular BBC1 series 999 to the erudite Radio 4 programme *The Moral Maze*. He has won every major award and is universally admired and respected for his intelligent and honest journalism. Here, he also reveals the private Michael Buerk, his bigamist father, his long and happy marriage to Christine and his delight at fatherhood.

'An exceedingly good book'
Michael Parkinson

arrow books

Samira and Samir

Siba Shakib

From the bestselling author of *Afghanistan, Where God Only Comes to Weep*, the extraordinary tale of a young Afghan girl following her heart in a man's world

When Samira is born, her father is devastated. He needs a son to succeed him, so ashamed and feeling he has failed as a man, he decides to bring Samira up as a boy. Samira becomes Samir.

Yet, as she approaches adulthood, Samira become increasingly troubled by her false identity. And, when she falls passionately in love, she is faced with a heartbreaking choice: she wants to live as Bashir's wife, but to do so she must betray her family, reveal her female identity, and in doing so, give up her freedom . . .

Samira follows her heart but she hates wearing the veil. Eventually the torment is too great and Samira realises there has to be a third way for her – the way of a self-confident woman who bravely takes charge of her own life.

arrow books

Skeletons on the Zahara

Dean King

In the tradition of *In the Heart of the Sea* and *A Perfect Storm*, a gripping story of survival in the 19th century Sahara

The western Sahara is a baking hot and desolate place, home only to nomads and their camels, and to locusts, snails and thorny scrub. On 28 August 1815 the US brig *Commerce* was dashed against Mauritania's Cape Bojador and lost, although through bravery and quick thinking the ship's captain, James Riley, managed to lead all of his crew to safety.

What followed was an extraordinary and desperate battle for survival in the face of human hostility, hunger, dehydration and despair, as the crew were captured, robbed and enslaved. They were reduced to drinking urine (their own and the camels'), flayed by the sun, crippled by walking miles across burning stones and sand. And over time James Riley and Sidi Hamet, slave and captor, came to recognize in each other men worthy of respect and the ransom not only of Riley himself but also of a handful of his crew suddenly seemed possible. But Sidi Hamet had enemies of his own, and to reach safety the sailors had to overcome not only the desert but also the greed and anger of those who would keep them in captivity.

'Genuinely gripping, full of twists and turns of fate . . .
mesmerising'
Daily Mail

arrow books

Shake Hands With The Devil

Lieutenant-General Roméo Dallaire

The number one International Bestseller, winner of the Shaughnessy Cohen Prize and the Governor General's Award

When Lt. General Roméo Dallaire received the call to serve as force commander of the UN mission to Rwanda, he thought he was heading off to Africa to help two warring parties achieve a peace both sides wanted. Instead, he and members of his small international force were caught up in a vortex of civil war and genocide. Dallaire left Rwanda a broken man, disillusioned, suicidal, and determined to tell his story.

The result is an unforgettable contribution to the literature of war and a remarkable tale of courage, it is also a stinging indictment of the petty bureaucrats who refused to give Dallaire the men and the operational freedom he needed to stop the killing.

'Indisputably the best account of the whole terrible Rwandan genocide'
RW Johnson, *Sunday Times*

'*Shake Hands With The Devil* is one of the saddest books I have ever read and one of the most heart-breaking eyewitness accounts. A kind of naive and painfully honest confession of the failure of an organisation, a meticulous description of one of the worst betrayals in the history of humanity'
Guardian

'Read Roméo Dallaire's profoundly sad and moving book.'
Madeleine Albright, *Washington Post*

arrow books

The Frank Family That Survived

Gordon F. Sander

This is the inspiring story of a German-Jewish family named Frank which, like Anne Frank's family and 25,000 Dutch and other 'stateless' Jews, 'dived under' in Nazi-occupied Holland in 1942 — but miraculously survived.

Told by the grandson of the head of the family, this is the gripping odyssey of the other Frank family: from childhood in an assimilated German-Jewish family at Breitenheim, through the deceptively good life of Berlin in the 1920s, to the rise of Hitler and their flight to apparently safe Holland, the nightmarish ordeal of their thousand-day-long 'submersion' in a small apartment in The Hague, and the joy and pain of liberation and their final journey to America, the same route Anne Frank might have taken had she not been betrayed.

Based on personal testaments, records and family interviews, the book describes their life behind closed curtains in constant fear of discovery. In 1945, after many adventures and appalling vicissitudes, they finally emerged to face the uncertainties of postwar Holland and the promise of the New World.

'A remarkable wartime story' *Mail on Sunday*

'An extraordinary tale of survival, part-family memoir, part-history, in which the author's passion and judgment are finely balanced . . .'
Christopher Sylvester, *Sunday Express*

arrow books

The Flamboya Tree

Clara Kelly

Memories of a Family's Wartime Courage

When the Japanese invaded the beautiful Indonesian island of Java during the Second World War Clara Kelly was four years old. Her family was separated, her father sent to work on the Burma railway, and she together with her mother and her two brothers, one a six-week-old baby, was sent to a 'women's camp'. They were interned there until the end of the war.

Clara's descriptions of the appalling deprivations and impersonal brutality of the camp – standing in the baking heat for hours of 'Tenko' role-call, living on one cup of rice a day – are countered by the courage and resilience shown by all the internees, most poignantly her own mother.

'Kelly's survival and her book is, in effect, the most moving tribute to her remarkable mother, whose courage and indomitable spirit kept the family alive'
Daily Mail

'A wrenching memoir . . . These stories clearly demonstrate that terrible atrocities are committed – justified even – in the name of war'
Seattle Times

'A moving, immediate account of a relatively unknown wartime drama . . . Unforgettable'
Booklist

'Fascinating'
People Magazine

arrow books

**Order further Arrow titles
from your local bookshop, or have them delivered
direct to your door by Bookpost**

☐	**The Road Taken** Michael Buerk	0099461374	£7.99
☐	**Samira and Samir** Siba Shakib	0099466449	£6.99
☐	**Skeletons on the Zahara** Dean King	0099435926	£7.99
☐	**Shake Hands with the Devil** Romeo Dallaire	0099478935	£8.99
☐	**The Frank Family That Survived** Gordon F. Sander	0099443295	£7.99
☐	**The Flamboya Tree** Clara Olink Kelly	0099445530	£7.99

Free post and packing
Overseas customers allow £2 per paperback

Phone: 01624 677237

Post: Random House Books
c/o Bookpost, PO Box 29, Douglas, Isle of Man IM99 1BQ

Fax: 01624 670923

email: bookshop@enterprise.net

Cheques (payable to Bookpost) and credit cards accepted

Prices and availability subject to change without notice.
Allow 28 days for delivery.
When placing your order, please state if you do not wish to receive any
additional information.

www.randomhouse.co.uk/arrowbooks

arrow books